More Than Singing

THE INTERPRETATION
OF SONGS

by

Lotte Lehmann

TRANSLATED BY FRANCES HOLDEN

DOVER PUBLICATIONS, INC.
NEW YORK

This Dover edition, first published in 1985, is an unabridged and unaltered republication of the work first published by Boosey & Hawkes, Inc., New York, in 1945.

Manufactured in the United States of America
Dover Publications, Inc., 31 East 2nd Street, Mineola, N.Y. 11501

Library of Congress Cataloging in Publication Data

Lehmann, Lotte.
  More than singing.

  Reprint. Originally published: New York : Boosey & Hawkes, 1945.
  1. Singing—Interpretation (Phrasing, dynamics, etc.) I. Holden, Frances.
II. Title.
MT892.L46M7 1985 784.9'34 84-21064
ISBN 0-486-24831-3

To my brother

Fritz Lehmann

Whose understanding has always
been a source of inspiration to me.

TABLE OF CONTENTS

DEAR LOTTE!

Do you know the fable of the eagle and the wren? How the wren won the wager that he could fly higher, by letting himself be carried to the heights, hidden in the feathers of the eagle, and then flying a little above him? You enact this fable in your book, in that your knowledge looks down from above on the accomplishments of your talent and in a kind of pilot's logbook describes your flights in the stratosphere of art.

I gladly write this foreword for which the publisher has asked me, even if it be only to add my voice to the chorus of your friends who will welcome a book on Lieder singing from your hand with great delight. Who could better speak of the Lied than you who have such a deep understanding of its nature and the demands of its style? Who can give wiser advice to the younger generation of singers? But are you really so wise and knowing or is it not rather that your art is distinguished through the depth of your intuition and the force of your feeling? I believe, dear Lotte, that you are just so wise and knowing as the true artist should be, for your knowledge has been the student of your talent. For you it has always been a question of first singing and then considering. You may teach because you, yourself, learn from intuition.

You love animals, so you will not be offended if I again revert to the zoological motive with which I began my foreword, and attribute to you the cat's eyes of talent, with which you see clearly along the darkest ways of art. For you only need the light of wisdom in order later to confirm your vision and with its help, correct details.

This is the only legitimate method for any artistic interpretation. Your art belongs to its noblest manifestations and your book will teach rightly because the prime factor—intuition, is its foundation. So continue, dear Lotte, to teach with your word, to delight with your singing.

In friendship,

Bruno Walter

FOREWORD

I think that it may be understood, why the greater part of this book has been devoted to German Lieder. I am best known as a representative of the German Lied, and I have tried through these years of German dissolution under the Nazi regime to hold fast and help to preserve that which once so beautified and ennobled the land of my birth: Music. . . Music which outlives world shaking catastrophies, because it exists in a world entirely apart from political misconceptions. Music which shows that beauty cannot be destroyed, that what has to-day been trampled down through brutal power, must rise again. . . Music which speaks an international language which is understood by all — the language of the heart, the language of the soul, the language of eternal and indestructible beauty. . . America, that wonderful country to which I now feel that I belong, has, during this bitter time of war, never forgotten that this German art stands above the confusion of the present time. . . This is a sign of such great understanding, such great generosity of spirit, that I bow before it, filled with gratitude and humility. . .

I believe that one expects of me, above all, this immortal German music — and for this reason I have devoted to it the greater part of this book.

I had hoped to make a brief survey of the songs of other countries, but the limits of this book have only made possible the inclusion of a few French, Old English, Italian and Russian songs which have become classics and which I have used in my own repertoire.

If a concert is successful, one gives encores. If I have written the German section of the book, so that it has pleased you—then take the second part as my encore—as a token of my gratitude for your understanding.

Santa Barbara, Calif. Summer 1945.

INTRODUCTION

Interpretation means: individual understanding and reproduction. How then is it possible to teach interpretation? It seems almost paradoxical to emphasize the necessity for individuality in interpretation and at the same time want to explain my own conceptions of singing. . . First and foremost I want to say that this book will fail in its purpose, if the young singers, for whom I am writing it, should consider my conceptions as something final and try to imitate them instead of developing their own interpretations which should spring with originality and vitality from their own minds and souls.

For imitation is, and can only be the enemy of artistry. Everything which breathes the breath of life is changeable: a momentary feeling often makes me alter an interpretation. . . Do not build up your songs as if they were encased in stone walls — no, they must soar from the warm, pulsing beat of your own heart, blessed by the inspiration of the moment. Only from life itself may life be born.

What I want to try to explain here is not any final interpretation, but an approach which may be an aid toward the development of your individual conceptions. I want to open a way which might lead from the lack of understanding of those singers, who seem to consider only voice quality and smooth technique — to the boundless world of expression. And it will be seen that there is not just *one*, — but a variegated pattern of ways, which lead to this goal. Only he who seeks it with his whole heart, will find his own approach to interpretation.

I have listened to many young singers, and have found with ever increasing astonishment that they consider their preparation finished when they have developed a lovely voice, a serviceable technique and musical accuracy. At this point they consider themselves ready to appear before the public. Certainly no one can question that technique is the all important foundation, — the a b c of singing. It goes without saying that no one can carefully enough master the technique of voice production. Complete mastery of the voice as an instrument is an ideal toward which every singer must work assiduously... But realize that technique must be mastered to the point of being *unconscious,* before you can really become an interpreter.

That fine God given instrument—the voice—must be capable of responding with the greatest subtlety to every shade of each emotion. But it must be subordinate, it must only be the foundation, the soil from which flowers true art.

It is only with the greatest hesitation that I dare to put into words my ideas regarding the interpretation of Lieder. For is it not dangerous to give definite expression to something which must essentially be born from inspiration and be above all things, vitally alive? Yet I have so often been urged by experienced musicians to help the younger generation with such a book as this, that I have decided to put down my ideas in spite of my hesitation. But I should like to place as a kind of motto over everything I write—Goethe's words from Faust: "Grau, teurer Freund, ist alle Theorie—und grün des Lebens gold'-ner Baum." (Gray, dear friend, is all theory and green the golden tree of life.) So may you, young aspiring singers, for whom I write this book, take the fullness of my experience, of my studies, of my development and discoveries as the simile of the golden tree, but it is for you to pluck the fresh, living fruit from off its branches. . . It is for you to infuse with your own soul, that which comes to you as advice, as suggestion. When you have a deep inner conviction about a song— the words as well as the music, — then be sure that your conception is a right one. Even though it may deviate from what is traditional.

For what is tradition?

The mother earth, from which springs everything which may grow and flower. The creator's conception of an idea, a deed, a work of art, which has been handed down from generation to generation, which has been cherished and developed until it spreads before us as a network of definitely determined paths which are to be followed without questioning. Strict tradition dictates that not a single step may be taken from these paths. . .

But you are young and the youth of every generation is eager and should be eager for new ways. You have a different viewpoint from that of your parents and teachers. . . You don't care for the old, recommended, well travelled roads. You want to romp over new, alluring fields, to lose yourselves in the mysterious depths of the forests. I know that I am committing a frightful sin against the holy tradition when I say: Excellent! Seek your own way! Do not become paralyzed and enchained by the set patterns which have been woven of old. No, build from your own youthful feeling, your own groping thought and your own flowering perception — and help to further that beauty which has grown from the roots of tradition. . . Do not misunderstand me: naturally I do not mean that you should despise the aspirations and the knowledge of earlier generations. Far from my thought is any such revolutionary idea! I only mean to say: consider tradition not as an *end* but as a *beginning*. Do not lose yourself in its outspread pattern but let your own conceptions and expression be nourished from it as a flower blooms from the life forces provided by its roots, but let them bloom more richly in the light of your own soul. Certainly you will make mistakes, you will often take the wrong road before you find your true way, just as I have. I grew up in Germany, in the tradition of Lieder singing. I might much earlier have come to that holiest of all: — the Lied, had I not been so completely immersed in the theatre. I so to speak, lived in the opera house and took my few concerts as a side issue without much preparation. May Schubert, Schumann, Brahms and Wolf forgive me for the sins which I committed in their name!

As the reputation which I had won through my work in the opera became known through other countries, concerts became more frequent with the result that there dawned upon me a new and overpowering realization: the realization that as a Lieder singer, I was at the very dawn of an awakening. . .

This was the first step: the awareness of my ignorance. . .

My approach was a groping one and I often went astray. In the beginning I felt that it came more from the word than from the music. If I had not been born a singer, endowed with a touch of the golden quality of voice of my good mother, I would without doubt have become an actress. Actually throughout my whole life, I have envied those who are free to express without the limitation of opera singing. . . So in singing Lieder, the word, the poem became the main thing for me, until I—much later—found and captured the balanced interweaving of word and music.

In general I find that the word is entirely too much neglected. On the other hand I should like to protect you from this stage which I had to go through: of feeling first the *word* and then the *word* and only finally the *melody*. . . Learn to feel *as a whole* that which is a whole in complete harmony: poem and music. Neither can be more important than the other. First there was the poem. That gave the inspiration for the song. Like a frame, music encloses the word picture — and now comes your interpretation, breathing life into this work of art, welding word and tone with equal feeling into one whole, so that the poet sings and the composer becomes poet and two arts are born anew as one. . .

That is the Lied.

The fundamental basis of my conception is this: never approach a Lied just as a melody. Search for the ideas and feelings which underlie it and which will follow it. Out of what mood or situation was the poem born? What drama, what dream, what experience was the inspiration for its conception? I never begin to study a Lied without first considering what brought it to life. I must picture it so vividly that I feel it is my own soul, my own being, which is now creating it.

Complete harmony can only be attained in a Lied, when the singer has at the piano an accompanist whose mood and feeling are identical with her own. He must be a part of the singing and the singer must be a part of the accompaniment, the one fitting into the other as one feeling, one will. For *you* sing what the piano expresses, you in your heart are singing the prelude, the interlude, the postlude. . .

Not only your voice sings — no, you must sing with your whole being — from head to toe. . . Your eyes sing, your body, animated by the rhythm of the music, sings, your hands sing. How great is the power of expression conveyed by the eyes and the hands! I do not mean that you should ever make a gesture which would disturb the frame of concert singing . . . You should only be in harmony with the song and being in harmony means feeling the unity which is all embracing. Be careful that you do not cultivate the possibilities of expression with the body from the outside, so to speak, — I mean by artificial movements, — you should learn to *feel* what you are singing with every nerve. Not until you understand clearly what I mean, should you really begin to work out a song in this way. A young singer, who had the fault of most singers:— of staring fixedly at one point, while inwardly concentrating on vocal technique and perhaps upon her struggle for expression, was a striking proof to me, of how little my approach seems to be understood. I had said: "Don't always look so fixedly at one point." She asked very astonished, "Shall I always look around when I sing?" That means— "I will do what my teacher tells me but I don't understand why." . . . No, you must feel what you sing with your whole being, from head to toe, then your eyes *cannot* be cold and lifeless—they will also have to sing, as an essential part of one complete harmony. . . If I say occasionally in this book, for example: "Lift your head slowly," I say it not for the outward effect, I say it because with the mounting flow of the music, with the development of the poetic thought, you simply can't remain standing with bowed head or you will break the spell of harmony which must always be one's goal.

Not every young singer has the gift of imagination. All that is possible should be done to develop this capacity. Periods should be arranged in the daily plan of study which should be devoted entirely to developing imagination and expressing what is imagined. The students should be given assignments which they should work out for themselves. For example: they should take a book and try to act as they would feel if they were happy and were about to read a gay romance, as if they were absent minded, or sad, or as if it is a forbidden book. . . They should imagine writing or receiving a letter containing good or bad news, a threatening letter, a funny letter. If they can learn to observe themselves in this training, learning to feel how an emotion can be expressed without either word or song, it may perhaps be easier to transfer this new ability to their singing and they will discover that the possibilities of expression are by no means exhausted by the range between *forte* and *piano*. . . Dynamic shadowings are like sketches but the enchanting in between colors alone can give the tone picture a personal quality. . . There is a clear, silvery *pianissimo* which sounds light and ethereal, and there is the veiled *pianissimo* which trembles with passion and restrained desire. There is a bright *forte*—strong and forceful like a fanfare — and the darkly colored *forte,* which breaks out sombrely, in grief and pain. The "veiled" *piano* which I have mentioned, is a vibration of tone which holds no place in the realm of technique and yet, in my opinion, it cannot be neglected in inspired singing—in fact it is of the utmost importance. How much restrained passion can be conveyed by a veiled tone and how much floating purity in a clear flute like *pianissimo!*

One seldom hears a voice which is capable of altering its timbre. For me it goes absolutely against the grain to sing always with the same tone color. Dynamic gradations seem dead without the animating interplay of dark and light, clear and restrained.

It almost seems superfluous to say: never forget that a phrase must always have a main word and with it a musical highpoint. Yet it is incredible how often this elementary and selfevident fact is neglected... Again and again I am astonished anew by a lack of musical feeling for the essential nature of the phrase. Every phrase must be sung with a sweeping line, not just as a series of words which have equal weight and no grace. It is the floating sweep, not just a long breath, which makes the beautifully rounded phrase. . . The best help in learning to feel how a phrase should sound is to recite the poem. In speaking, you would never give equal emphasis to every syllable as you so often do in singing,— through eagerness to hold the tempo or to give each note its exact value — or above all to show that your singing is supported by excellent breath control. . . In my opinion, more important than all these factors, valuable as they are, is giving life to the phrase through emphasizing what is important and making subsidiary the words which have only connective value. It sometimes happens that the musical phrase is not in complete harmony with the text. That a pause, for example, interrupts a sentence which should continue without interruption. As an example of this let us take the phrase from "Die Lotosblume" by Schumann:

Here you must make a compromise between the words and the music by apparently connecting the word "ängstigt" to "sich vor der Sonne Pracht." Spin out the "gt" through the pause so as to connect the two words which belong together in thought. You should already be thinking "sich" while still singing "ängstigt" and through the force of suggestion you will retain the connection of the words without interfering with the intention of the composer.

On the other hand sometimes a musical phrase will continue and tie together sentences, which should really be separated. For example: In "Von ewiger Liebe" by Brahms the poem reads:

> *Nirgend noch Licht und nirgend noch Rauch,*
> *Ja, und die Lerche, sie schweiget nun auch.*

But Brahms wrote:

Here with great subtlety you must make a pause after "Rauch" and tie the "ja" to the next phrase without simply carrying it over. But the "ja" cannot be lifted out as something important. . . So sing it like a light sigh—your breath exhaled audibly (very subtly) separates the word from the first phrase and connects it with the next one, thus achieving the solution.

Singing should never be just a straight going ahead, it should have a sweeping flow, it should glide in soft rhythmical waves which follow one another harmoniously. (I want to draw your attention to the fact that I am referring here to the musical line of a *phrase* and not to sliding from syllable to syllable which generally has a sentimentalizing effect and should only be made use of most sparingly.) Each new sentence should have a new beginning, the new thought should live, should breathe, emerging from the previous sentence. Create each new thought as if it had just come to life in you — yourself. Let it arise from your own inner feeling. Do not sing just a melody, sing a poem. Music lifting the poem from the coldness of the spoken word has transfigured it with new beauty. But you, the singer, must make your listeners realize that the poem, far from losing its beauty through becoming music, has been ennobled, born anew in greater splendour and loveliness. Never forget: recite the poem when you sing — sing the music as you recite the words of the poem in the Lied. . . Only from the equal value of both creations can perfection arise.

I should like to touch here upon a question which often arises, as to whether a woman should sing Lieder, which according to the poem are written for a man. I say with emphasis: Yes!

Why should a singer be denied a vast number of wonderful songs, if she has the power to create an illusion which will make her audience believe in it? It would be a very sad indication of incapacity if one could not awaken in the listener suffient imagination to carry him with one into the realms of creative phantasy. If you sing of love and happiness, you must be a young person convincingly — and perhaps in reality you are neither young nor beautiful. . . The stage decrees limitations which simply don't exist on the concert platform: on the stage you *see* the person who is represented, your representation must in some measure correspond outwardly to the character which you portray. The imagination of the audience has its limits: it sees the figure before it clad in the frame of the role, surrounded by the characters of the story which is being unfolded. In a certain sense it is very much more difficult to retain the illusion of the portrayal when the limits are set by reality. On the other hand on the concert stage it is the unlimited power of your art which must change you into just that figure which you seek to bring to life. You are without any material aids, without any gestures, without the ramp which separates so wonderfully the world of the stage from the world of reality. You stand close to the audience — almost one with it, you take it, so to speak, by the hand and say: "Let us live this song together! Forget with me that I cannot have a thousand real forms, for I will make you believe in all these forms as I change my personality in every song. Let us together put aside reality, and let us, singing and hearing, soar away into the limitless realms of phantasy . . ." As Mignon says in Goethe's Wilhelm Meister —"und jene himmlischen Gestalten, sie fragen nicht nach Mann und Weib . . ." (And there each celestian presence shall question naught of man and maid . . .)—so the singer soars above all limitations, is young, is beautiful, is man or woman, longing and fulfillment, death and resurrection. . .

It is my hope that through this book I may open a door which may lead you to feeling what you understand — and understanding what you feel.

The Lieder, which I have tried to analyse and explain, are only examples. If you work through each new song which you add to your repertoire, in this way, you will have grasped my approach. If this may be helpful, I shall be very happy.

The road to the ever unattainable goal: Perfection, — is long and hazardous. No success with the public, no criticisms however wonderful, could ever make me believe that I have reached "Perfection." Everyone has his own limits and imperfections. Everyone is to a certain extent the victim of his nerves, his momentary mood and disposition. With justice I am reproached for breathing too often and so breaking phrases. This is one of my unconquerable nervous inadequacies. It is often not enough to *know* and to *feel* and to *recognize*. Human, all too human are the weaknesses under which all of us suffer, each in his own way. In a certain sense, it seems that perfect technique and interpretation which wells from the heart and soul can never go hand in hand and that this combination is an unattainable ideal. For the very emotion which enables the singer to carry her audience with her into the realm of artistic experience, is the worst enemy of a crystal clear technique. Perhaps, in this case, I am the well known fox for whom the grapes hang too high . . . May be! . . . But I have found again and again, that a singer who delights in technique (much as I may admire her virtuosity) still, in some way, leaves my heart cold... For heaven's sake do not misunderstand me: control of the voice is the soil from which interpretation springs — — — but do not despair over small imperfections, over mistakes which are difficult to eliminate . . . For if your soul can soar above technique and float in the lofty regions of creative art, you have fulfilled your mission as a singer. For what mission can be greater than that of giving to the world hours of exaltation in which it may forget the misery of the present, the cares of everyday life and lose itself in the eternally pure world of harmony. . .

FRANZ SCHUBERT

1797—1828

IM ABENDROT

C. Lappe   *Franz Schubert*

This Lied is for me one of the most beautiful treasures of our whole musical literature. The deep emotion which flows through it like a stream of warm gold, is overwhelming in its extreme simplicity. Sing it simply, sing it as you would a prayer. Sing it with folded hands.

Imagine that you are weary of life and wounded perhaps by a bitter disappointment. You are sitting by a window, your head buried in your hands. Looking up from out of a deep melancholy you suddenly see before you the beauty of the sunset and you awaken to its overwhelming loveliness.

This is the atmosphere of the prelude. As it begins raise your head which has been slightly bowed. Your eyes open. With an exquisite joy you realize that all your sorrows have been meaningless and insignificant. The glow of the setting sun is like a gateway opening upon heaven — and peace and eternal beauty flood your heart. You feel that God is very near you — so near, that you speak to Him, calling Him simply "Father". . .

Begin with a soft voice — in a lovely *legato* — breathe after "Vater." Make a warm *crescendo* at "wenn das Rot, das in der Wolke blinkt" and go back into the most subtle *pianissimo* "in mein stilles Fenster sinkt." The short interlude of two bars is your expression of prayerful gratitude.

Begin the second verse with a slightly quickened tempo — but without disturbing the never changing floating *legato*—: "Könnt' ich klagen". . . etc. The sorrows which had wounded you, the melancholy which had oppressed you, are now almost ununderstandable in the light of this mood of inner contentment. Sing *crescendo* "Könnt' ich zagen" and then again *piano* "irre sein an dir und mir." This *piano* is the expression of an hesitant and almost shameful confession: yes, I doubted — I complained — I was afraid—. But all that is now over. I am myself again — the child of God who gave so much beauty to this world in showing the image of His heaven in the golden sunset there before my eyes. . .

Sing now with a warm and soft ecstacy with a beautiful *crescendo* from "Nein, ich will" to "Himmel schon allhier." It is like an oath, like a holy confirmation which shall bind your earthbound soul to

Heaven: understanding the grace of God you take into your heart God's Heaven.

Sing "und dies Herz, eh' es zusammenbricht" with a warm *piano*. You are thinking: I shall fill my heart with heavenly beauty. May it be like a cup from which I may taste eternal glory. I shall drink the glow of its warmth — the clarity of its light. . .

Build up the beautiful words with love and care: make use of the consonants in "trinkt," "Glut," "schlürft" and "Licht." *Paint* this phrase with music and word. . . Your expression should remain ecstatically elated throughout the postlude.

GRETCHEN AM SPINNRAD

Goethe   *Schubert*

Begin this song looking downward, and without much expression. Here you have to build up very carefully. Imagine that you are sitting beside a spinning wheel which turns ceaselessly under your nervous feet. Again and again you have said to yourself—"Meine Ruh' ist hin, mein Herz ist schwer." Have you ever in your own life had the experience, when something tremendously important has gripped your thoughts, of finding yourself unconsciously repeating one sentence again and again, senselessly, torturingly, inescapably? It is in this way that Gretchen repeats over and over to herself — "Meine Ruh' ist hin, mein Herz ist schwer".

Raise your head and look up as you sing: "Wo ich ihn nicht hab'." Your body should sway backward slightly so that there is a possibility of coming forward at — "mein armer Kopf". *Imagine* that your hands grip your forehead with the palms pressed against your temples. If you can make this gesture real in your thoughts you will have the right expression.

Coming back to — "Meine Ruh' ist hin" your eyes are again cast downward. You are bent over the spinning wheel trying hard to concentrate, but it is in vain. Again his image floods your inner vision. You gaze sadly into the empty space before you — "Nach ihm nur schau' ich zum Fenster hinaus". Here you begin a slow *crescendo*. You completely forget yourself and in an enchantment from which you cannot escape, you surrender to your passionate love.

After "sein Kuss" you fall back exhausted. (I mean, of course, only in your imagination.) The next repetition of "Meine Ruh' ist hin" is no longer a subconscious thought. It is torturing reality. It should be sung with desperation.

When you start to sing "Mein Busen drängt sich nach ihm hin" begin *piano,* with a shy gesture, as if withdrawing into yourself, for

you are ashamed of this burning desire which is consuming you —
you — the pure, virginal maiden. You can scarcely understand how
it is possible for you to be possessed by such a passion. You have enjoyed the kisses of your beloved but they are not enough! You were
shy and restrained with him, even when he embraced you, but now
you want to forget and overcome this shyness and kiss him once with
all the passion which is searing your heart. Sing *piano* when you repeat
—"O könnt' ich ihn küssen". This is a very effective nuance but it also
gives an opportunity for resting your voice for a moment — your
voice is under great strain in this song. You will not spoil the effect
by this, on the contrary the necessity for being vocally restrained, becomes a virtue through actually increasing your expressiveness. Go
over in a *crescendo* from "an seinen Küssen" and sing the repeated
climax—"vergehen sollt'" with a glowing *forte.* Imagine that your
head falls forward, your body exhausted and trembling is bent over
the spinning wheel which continues with its monotonous melody as
your feet go on turning it mechanically.

Sing the last "Mein Ruh' ist hin" as if through tears and retain
to the end your expression of exhaustion.

DAS FISCHERMÄDCHEN

Heine   *Schubert*

A quietly floating line is most important in this song. Variations
are only very subtle, and in this particular song come much more from
the music than from the poem.

You should reflect the music of the prelude through your whole
body. If you *feel* the rhythm, you will give enough of the idea of
being one with it. Your gaze soars out over a vast expanse. Before
your inner vision is spread the ocean, with the little boat of the lovely
fisher maiden swaying near the shore.

The first phrases should be sung as if they were a friendly call.
Then after "setze dich nieder" sing with a very soft and seductive *piano.*
The music here is as if it were woven of something white and shimmering, each tone merges — but with clarity — into the next tone.
There must be a subtle and delicate differentiation between the first
call and the alluring melody of your caressing words. During the
interlude you are radiant, feeling again one with the rhythm of the
accompaniment.

"Leg' an mein Herz" is again like a call and the following phrases
— "und fürchte dich nicht so sehr" to the end of this verse should
be sung caressingly, as if you were talking to a frightened child.

Always be one with the feeling of the interlude. You are smiling, gay, sure of victory.

Give a lovely *crescendo* at "Sturm und Ebb' und Flut" and play with the consonants — S t u r m, F lu t and color the u darkly.

This word painting is very helpful. It is too often entirely neglected. It is of the greatest importance to vary the timbre of the voice. Everywhere about one is light and shade and light is always brighter when darkness deepens the contrast.

Now you have told the pretty fisher maiden that your heart is like the ocean, — this should be a well known element for her. Add with tenderness and a touch of shyness, which takes from your words any suggestion of self importance or boasting — "Und manche schöne Perle in seiner Tiefe ruht". Sing this with a noble expression as if you were saying — "Yours shall be the wide ocean of my heart, with all its storms and surging tides and with all the delicate feeling which is buried in the deep ground. It shall all be yours!"

Keep a soft and smiling expression until the end of the postlude.

DER DOPPELGÄNGER

Heine   *Schubert*

It is very important for you to visualize clearly the background of this sombre Lied, which has a balladlike quality. Feel the mystery of the still, moonlit night. Feel the silence all around you. See the ghostly shadows of the houses and the motionless trees. See yourself standing there as if transfixed, abysmally lonely, your pallid face raised toward the windows behind which your beloved once lived. . .

The first four measures of the prelude paint more adequately and more nobly than any words could: the amosphere of the night — so charged with mystery. There is brooding tragedy in the sombre *pianissimo* chords. I can never hear them without shivering to the marrow. Sing with the utmost *legato,* with a darkly colored timbre, *pianissimo* and without any sentimentality. Avoid any slurring (don't slide or scoop.) Change your timbre at "In diesem Hause wohnte mein Schatz". You tremble with the pain of your suppressed longing. Your voice is now a little more brightly colored, your face has an expression of grief. You see clearly before you the forsaken house as it stands out in the brilliant moonlight, its windows like black holes staring at you with empty eyes. . . Sing "Sie hat schon längst die Stadt verlassen" with bitterness and with a tormented expression. As if with inner amazement sing "doch steht noch das Haus". (Have you ever in your own experience lived through a sorrow so great that you simply couldn't realize that the outer world has gone on just as before?

When one loses a loved one forever, it is very hard to understand that everything goes on just as it has in the past and will continue to do so.) Your voice should convey this feeling of saddened amazement, when you sing "doch steht noch das Haus". . .

It is as if your mind were confused. Perhaps you see your reflection like a shadow on the moonlit window panes, — perhaps in your bewilderment you create a phantom image of yourself which stares at you from out of the darkness. You sing "da steht auch ein Mensch" in a veiled *pianissimo* as if paralyzed by your mounting horror. Develop the *crescendo* which leads up to a *forte fortissimo* ascending broadly to a climax. Sing "mir graust es" very distinctly but at the same time very *piano*, breathing audibly and with an inner trembling. The *crescendo* mounting to *fff* is still a further increase beyond that of the preceding phrase. If the power of your voice cannot be greater than *fff* you can still attain an increased effect of power through your expression. Sing with wild horror "eigene Gestalt". If I say that you should sing the following phrases *gaspingly*, I do not mean it to be realistic. Never forget that you must respect the limits imposed by the style of Lieder singing. . . Try to find out how you would say this if you were an actor. Recite it and then transfer this expression to the restricted frame of the song, — then you will find the right way. Sing with great bitterness, *crescendo*, mounting in both tempo and expression. Note exactly all dots, sing with sharp accentuation, with very distinct enunciation. Pause after the *ff* chord, do not overlook the quarter rest before you begin to sing broadly and forcefully and with dramatic power — "so manche Nacht". Sing a *subito pianissimo* — "in alter Zeit". It is as if you were saying to yourself: it is so long, so very long that I have suffered, I have forgotten that I was ever happy. I do not dare to think how long I have been so miserable. It shames me to feel the weakness which chains me to this scene of my grief. All these feelings flow together in the words "in alter Zeit" — flow in a stirring *pianissimo*, run like quiet tears over your face, which, disconsolate and without hope, looks up into the white moon. . .

Remain so until the end of the postlude dies away.

DIE FORELLE

Schubart   *Schubert*

The accompaniment of this charming song is the melody of a splashing forest stream. Feel its flowing rhythm which, while unvarying in its musical form, is capricious and sparkling like the water of the foaming stream, which leaping over sticks and stones as it plunges in its downward course carries all the freshness of lofty mountain springs through the shady woods.

Sing the beginning of the song without tying the syllables. I want to avoid saying — sing *staccato,* for this might lead you into an exaggeration which would disturb and break the graceful lines of the song. You should only reproduce with very discrete word and tone painting, the scurrying and flashing of the trout.

For some time you have been watching with delight the playful antics of the gay little fish. Sing "Ich stand an dem Gestade" with a lightly flowing *legato* as if in pleased contemplation.

The short interlude of five measures again reflects the play of rippling water in the first two measures. You are smiling, listening with delight. Suddenly a rumbling and murmuring sounds in the accompaniment and you see the fisherman with his menacing rod. You watch him, frowning. You are annoyed that such a discord should disturb the sunny peace about you. But don't forget that there is no question of tragedy in this song. Don't be too dramatic! On the contrary: a half smile should never leave your face. The catastrophe which the fish experiences is a tragedy in miniature, it doesn't grip your heart, it doesn't really make you sad. It just momentarily disturbs your complacency; so try to give a playful lightness to your interest, your compassion. (This applies to the interpretation of the whole song.) Sing "Ein Fischer mit der Rute" with visible displeasure. The fisherman is very unsympathetic to you. You see in him a being totally devoid of any imagination: he pays no attention to the graceful dancing play of the guileless little fish. He only thinks of how fast he can hook his victim. . . The lust for the hunt is in him, while in you is a warm love for anything which breathes and plays. . . You sing "So lang' dem Wasser Helle, so dacht' ich, nicht gebricht," as if with a sigh of relief. You think — "Oh how I hope he doesn't know of the bad tricks of fishermen, oh how I hope the sly little fish will escape him!" You are happy like a child and sing "so fängt er die Forelle mit seiner Angel nicht", — smiling and triumphant.

The interlude (again five measures) has in the first two measures the same playful, dancing, rippling melody, but then it changes to a threatening rumble —

Frowning, you watch the fisherman who seems to be more skillful than you had thought. With increasing concern, in a slightly quickened tempo, with distinct enunciation, you sing: "Doch endlich ward dem Diebe". The "und eh' ich es gedacht" is like a frightened cry (in miniature), accent the "eh". Hold the dotted notes at "*zu*ckte *se*ine Rute" very exactly, singing in a very sharp almost exaggerated rhythm: one must feel the sudden jerk of the fishing rod in the word painting through the distinct emphasis in this phrase. Sing "das Fischlein, das Fischlein zappelt' d'ran" with a *crescendo*—like a shock of sudden disillusionment. Then return to a lovely legato at "und ich mit regem Blute" and sing to the end with an expression of smiling compassion, such as one would have in listening to the complaint of a little child over a broken toy. Hold this expression until the end of the postlude.

ERLKÖNIG

Goethe   *Schubert*

Galloping hoofs, the blackness of the night, the uncanny sighing of the wind as it sweeps through barren trees and over the withered heather, are all conveyed in the prelude of the great ballad: "Erlkönig". Feel in the first measure the atmosphere of the stormy night. Your face has an expression of concentration: it is as if you were peering into the darkness of the night. Your whole being is tense. The first phrases should be sung quietly. In the first verse the accompaniment is the important thing: it describes the dark night, the galloping horse. Your voice quietly questioning and answering is heard through the wildly animated tone-painting of the accompaniment. It is warm and reassuring as if you were simply observing what is passing before you. In the first question of the father color your voice darkly. It is of the utmost importance that the three voices: father, child, Erlkönig, should have absolutely different tonal qualities. Alone from the standpoint of timbre, you must be capable of making the tragedy convincing.

The child sings with a light breathy voice, trembling with fear. The father's answer is dark, warm and comforting. The whispering, entreating voice of the Erlkönig is brightly colored and has a demonic restraint which is at once seductive and threatening. . . You will get this quality most successfully if you, so to speak, sing between your teeth. . . Let the vowels glide and draw in such a way as to suggest the illusion of wind. Have you ever heard wind sighing over a barren heath? This idea of the wind must be in your thought as you sing the part of the Erlkönig, the demonic seducer. Of course I don't mean that you should sacrifice the musical beauty of the phrases or through exaggeration produce anything approaching a caricature. This is an instance in which the inner idea cannot become reality but if you have within you the idea of the sighing wind, you will find the right tonal quality for the voice of the evil spirit.

The Erlkönig promises the child lovely games, gay flowers, a coat of gold, but even in these promises is something like a secret threat. The child senses the evil which lurks behind these flattering words — "Mein Vater, mein Vater" is a cry filled with fear. Go over into a frightened, whispered *piano* at: "was Erlenkönig mir leise verspricht".

The voice of the father — dark, soft, reassuring, full of love — comes like a mellow cello tone into the dramatic wail of the child. The Erlkönig whispers, urgent and vehement. The tempo is quickened. (Always *pianissimo*)

With horror, the child feels that the ghostly being, whom before he had only heard, is now taking form: from out of the drifting mist emerge forms—the pale faces of women dissolving like vapor, shine weirdly from out of the darkness of the night. The child is terrified. Sing with a piercing cry: "Mein Vater, mein Vater" and close again with a *decrescendo* going over into a frightened whisper.

The answering voice of the father, although remaining darkly colored, now loses its reassuring quality: the father now feels with horror that his child is near death. It is the raging fever which conjures up phantom forms in the poor feverish brain of his sick little child. Fear trembles in his voice. In vain he seeks to quiet the child.

The accompaniment bursts in upon his last words with a demonic frenzy. The Erlkönig, now weary of his seductive wooing, slowly reaches out with his strangling grasp, already the threat of death blazes in his eyes even though his words are still smooth and dissembling. . . But the Erlkönig is already victorious. Feel in yourself the triumph of destruction, stand very tall and erect. Your whisper is no longer seductive, it is now possessive. Your words are like greedy hands which close about the piteous prey. They are deadly and inescapable. . . Sing very distinctly, very accentuatedly — make use of the consonants, and the vowels. Your whisper mounts into a realistic *forte* at "und bist du nicht willig". The final phrase "so brauch' ich Gewalt" should be thrust out with the hardest accents, between your teeth, brutally, with murderous force. The voice of the child is a single wail of terror. Be careful not to force here, never forget that this is a song, not a stage scene and that too much realism would overstep the frame of Lieder singing. If you sing the last wail of the child with dramatic power, you will, though remaining within the style of the Lied, still have the proper dramatic effect.

The voices are silent now. . . With an elemental power the wild storm of the accompaniment breaks in upon the cry of the dying child.

In a breathless *accelerando* the ballad drives on to the end. The father's fear of death, the storming hoofbeats of the galloping horse, terror, horror, despair, rage in the *fortissimo* "er hält in den Armen das ächzende Kind"... Gasping, bending foward, — sing with strong accents — "erreicht den *Hof* mit *Müh* und *Not*". . . The emphasis on the individual words gives the illusion of gasping exhaustion. After "Not" straighten up with an audible indrawn breath as if a sudden shock has made you catch your breath. Sing "In seinen Armen das Kind" *pianissimo*, with an expression of pain, and end with a whisper lacking in any tone (but distinctly) "war tot".

If you can put yourself into this situation, feeling the terror, the shock, the grief of the father, you will find the right tone for the ending of this wonderful ballad.

ROBERT SCHUMANN

1810—1856

WIDMUNG

Rückert   *Schumann*

This Lied is a hymn of devotion, a happy confession of the deepest love. The first bar is like a burst of joy. Your whole being expresses blissful happiness. Start with a *mezzoforte* and develop a full
crescendo up to "Wonn". "O du mein Schmerz" is *decrescendo*. Sing
this phrase with warm feeling, softly and somewhat subdued. You
must give the impression that with a warm embrace you take the
whole being of your beloved straight to your heart.

The next phrase "du meine Welt" is like a new beginning. Soul,
heart, bliss and pain are all subjective things, they are in yourself, they
are *your own* love. On the other hand — "the world in which you
live, the Heaven in which you soar" are *outside* yourself. The new
idea should be started with a different expression. Your gaze sweeps
about you: "du meine Welt", give an accent to "du". Raise your head,
feel yourself soaring through the blue eternity of the sky when you
sing: "Mein Himmel du, darein ich schwebe".

Don't be sad when you sing "du mein Grab". Here the grave has
no mournful implication. The basic idea of this poetic conception is:
the grave receives the body of one who has *completed* life. This is the
final state, nothing can alter it, one can never arise from this grave
for one dissolves into the earth which receives the body. So — with
this eternal finality, you place all your pains, all your worries, all your
doubts, in the hands of your beloved. You know that he will take
your whole being into his own — with finality, in eternity. (When
one loves, one always plays with the idea of death. Nothing seems to
be enough, no surrender quite complete. One says with exultation:
"I want to die with you. . ." So the seemingly gloomy picture of the
grave is really very natural here.)

When you sing the phrase "o du mein Grab . . ." your hands should
convey a slight suggestion of a gesture of blessing.

Now imagine that all your sorrows have been put aside, you know
now a blissful peace. Change the expression of ecstatic devotion with
which you have been singing until now, into one of tender prayer. Sing
"du bist die Ruh'", *piano,* with deep devotion and make a *crescendo* at
"du bist vom Himmel mir beschieden."

"Dass du mich liebst" is a new idea. Sing it with increasing vivacity
and make a *crescendo* (if possible sing "dein Blick hat mich vor mir

verklärt" in *one* breath) going with accentuated *ritardando* over to the change of key.

dein Blick hat mich vor mir ver -

klärt, du hebst mich lie - bend ü - ber mich.

The *crescendo* lasts until this change, then sing a *subito piano* and *a tempo*. Give an accent to "über". The phrase "mein bess'res Ich" is the transition to the renewed *tempo primo*. The *ritardando* with which you make this transition is an expression of overflowing happiness and gratitude. Take up the repeated phrases with your whole being, free and proud, with increasing emotion. "Mein guter Geist" is *ritardando* and accentuated. Make an emphatic climax with the last words "mein bess'res Ich!"

Don't stop singing with your thought with these last words. Always keep in mind: the postlude is YOU. Your feeling and your thoughts must float on through the piano music. Your expression remains one of blissful happiness.

DIE LOTOSBLUME

Heine   *Schumann*

Imagine a deep, quiet pool, overshadowed by high ferns, with creeping vines and velvety moss upon the stones about it. And there in midst of the bluegreen water, surrounded by broad leaves, rests the lovely milk-white Lotos flower. The sun shines with a golden light through the swaying ferns, and a brilliant sunbeam caresses the beautiful flower. But look: it is closed, its glorious blossom has not yet opened to the sun . . . You look at the flower lovingly, dreamingly. The secret of this strange and wonderful flower resounds like a melody through your heart—like a poem—and you start to sing . . .

The chords of the accompaniment are subtle,—like drops of dew falling through the green silence. Sing the first phrases in a warm *piano* tone. Spin the word "ängstigt" in a suspended breath through the last half of the measure. (This phrase is not well balanced, the music is here the main thing. But by making a compromise you can bring to life as much harmony of word and tone as possible if in bridging the gap between "ängstigt" and "sich", you hold "ängstigt" as if it were not the end of a phrase but carry it over to "sich", just hold the last consonants *gt* with your breath and so guide it over into the next phrase. See Introduction.)

Your face should be soft and relaxed, your body with slightly bowed head should be in harmony with the poem: "und mit gesenktem Haupte".

"Der Mond" begins a new idea. Your face lights up, your gaze sweeps toward the sky where you picture the moon. Give your voice a light, silvery quality, slightly veiled by an audible breath—as if you were telling a beautiful secret.

"Er weckt sie mit seinem Licht"—hold "Licht," developing it as if the flower were slowly unfolding. The opening *crescendo* continues until "freundlich," then go back to a soft and vibrant *pianissimo* at "frommes Blumengesicht". You are moved by the purity and fairylike white beauty of this incredible flower and this must be revealed through your expression in these two words.

The phrase "Sie blüht und glüht . . ." is full of desire. Play with the consonants and with the vowels: bl*ü*ht, gl*ü*ht, st*u*mm! Always begin these short phrases *piano* and end them with a *crescendo*.

Sie blüht und glüht und leuch - tet, und
star - ret stumm in die Höh', ____

This brings into these phrases the necessary feeling of restlessness and longing. The tempo is quickened—but take your time at—"und zittert". Don't slide too much. Do "Vor Liebe" very subtly with just a very light combining breath.

The last phrase should be sung with the softest *pianissimo* and *ritardando*. Hold the last tone letting it fade away. There must be harmony between your face, your body and your hands until the last note dies away. Don't break the spell too quickly.

In this song there is the peacefulness of a hidden pool, a dreaming white flower . . .The sweetness of moonlight—ecstasy and trembling delight, but no tragedy, no passionate outpouring, no reality. Everything must be restrained, silvery and unreal. You must create the atmosphere of a fairy tale! You can only do this if your whole being is relaxed, soft, full of repose. Be like the Lotos flower itself—feel: *I am like it.* In the last phrase, the repetition of "Vor Liebe und Liebesweh" feel that it is your own heart which speaks: "Yes, I am like this flower dying of love and love's pain."

WER MACHTE DICH SO KRANK?

Kerner   *Schumann*

This and the following song should always be sung together. There is a close connection between them, the music being similar and the idea of the second being a continuation of that of the first. The first is a sorrowful questioning of fate—realization and a bitter answer . . . The second is a dreaming recollection—resignation and surrender . . . I have often sung "Alte Laute" as a single song, but I have come to feel that both constitute a whole which should not be sundered.

In the first song you are a victim of a gnawing illness. You lie upon your sickbed, weak and miserable, seeking again and again to discover what it was that made you ill. (A being very dear to me, stricken in the prime of his life by a fatal illness, continuously tortured himself with the question: "What have I done that I am sick? Have I not lived a healthy life? Did I not have enough strength to resist the dangers of life?") So you question yourself in this song: "What have I done, what have I neglected? What have I done which was wrong?"

With the first sustained chord, you raise your head, looking far into the distance, seeking with urgent questioning, as if the answer might come from beyond, as if fate itself might give you the answer. Sing in a veiled *piano,* with great delicacy. Make an almost unnoticeable *crescendo* and *decrescendo* in each individual phrase so that a swinging rhythm runs through the whole song. Putting it briefly—don't sing straight ahead, sing smoothly with a sustained flow.

At "Kein Schlummer und kein Träumen im Blütenbett des Tals" sing very *ritardando,* fading away softly. It is as if you sink back upon your pillows from which you have raised yourself. Now sing the next phrase "Dass ich trag' Todeswunden" with a much darker tone quality. Your sick heart is flooded with bitterness. You have suffered from severe disillusionment, you have known sombre realizations. These have burdened your heart and made you ill . . . So sing with a dark timbre (but *piano*). Your face again reflects bitter realization. Sing with distinct accentuation, but always with restraint. Sing "Natur liess mich gesunden" with a lovely broad *crescendo* as if you were emerging from suffering and from oppressive melancholy. Yet you know that the road to recovery is barred for you . . . You sink back, hopeless, disconsolate. End the song in deep bitterness. Sing very *piano,* very restrained, very *ritardando*: "Sie lassen mich nicht ruh'n". The pause between "mich" and "nicht" is not a pause for breathing: it is as if your heart stopped beating, as if you can scarcely bare to speak of anything so deeply painful.

Bind the two songs together by holding the tension from the end of the first song to the beginning of the second.

ALTE LAUTE

Kerner   *Schumann*

Years have passed. You are sitting, at the window, tired and broken. It is a beautiful spring day and you sit there in the warm sunlight. Your head is bowed with fatigue, your eyes are half closed. You feel life ebbing away from you.

The dull pressure in your heart, which like a bad dream has tormented you day and night, seems to lessen.

Here the prelude begins. You stand beside the piano with your head slightly bowed, your hands folded lightly together are lowered. Slowly you raise your head. The song of a bird penetrates your consciousness: You look upward. Your face shows that you are moved. Don't look straight ahead of you. Your expression must show that you are listening to something which comes from outside,—to the song of a bird. Sing with a breathy *pianissimo*—as if in a dream.

"Herz" is a call to your own heart,—sing it with a soft emphasis.

"Was hör' ich?" should be sung with mounting expression, more awake. More as if you were coming back to life. ("How is it possible? The melody of that life so long gone by, seems to sing to me from out of this bird's song! I thought that I had lost even the memories of my youth, but now they seem awakened again!")

Sing "Der Zeit, als ich vertraute der Welt und ihrer Lust" with a bitterness which has long ago changed into a smiling resignation. There is only a shadow of bitterness remaining in you. But what is the world and all its pleasures to *you*, whom long experience has made distant and wise? . . . It is a song which has faded away, a song which you can scarcely remember. Spin out "ihrer Lust" with a suspended *ritardando.*

Silenced is the song of the bird, silenced the sweet song of spring... Reality is with you again: "die Tage sind vergangen". Sing with a dark *crescendo,* very *legato,* in a beautiful musical line up to "dem Traum, dem bangen." *No forte* here! Sing it as if you were bent over, sick and tired. You try to straighten up, to get away from the frightening dream.

But no! You sink back again. You know there is no healing for you. Only a miracle could save you and there are no miracles on this earth...

Sing "weckt mich ein Engel nur" with an audible breath, *adagio,* dying away. You long for the coming of the angel, — and yet with the longing comes the knowledge that there is no angel who could save you. And yet — and yet, as long as the heart still beats, so long will one still dare to hope. You must be able to bring all these contradictory feelings to realization. Resignation, hopelessness, longing, bitter knowledge — and a slight ray of hope.

Your eyes have opened wide, — you look into the distance. Hold the "nur."

WALDESGESPRÄCH

Eichendorff   *Schumann*

The beautiful witch Lorelei is riding through a deep and silent forest. Where the trees become wilder and the rocks more rough, where the paths are no longer smooth and the sombre pines struggle amidst the rocks, buffeted by the winds, is her castle . . . Towering over high cliffs it looks down upon the Rhine. There is the home of the Lorelei. When the wind lashes the water until it breaks in wild surf and ships can only be guided around this perilous corner by the most trusty of pilots, — there she sits. In all her bewildering beauty she sits there upon her cliff and many are the ships which have crashed upon these rocks carrying to death the fishermen who have looked up too long upon the lovely but cruel face of the witch, Lorelei.

But on quiet summer days when the Rhine lies like a broad shimmering band of silk in the sunlight, Lorelei mounts her milkwhite horse and rides out through the dark forest. She hates the peaceful, silvery water. She hates the boats which pass so quietly and the smiling faces of the fishermen, who can now, in safety, marvel at her beauty. So she turns toward the silent forests riding slowly through the deep ferns, lost in her brooding thoughts.

A young man, carefree and gay, passes through the woods. Suddenly his horse stops, shaking and trembling. There before him on a white horse is a woman, lovely as a dream. Golden hair floats about her face, her eyes burn darkly and strangely. The young man does not feel the uncanniness of this strange apparition. With strong quiet hands he reins in his trembling horse and looks laughingly into the deep dark flames of her eyes. Adventure seems to beckon to him. How beautiful she is! How strangely and challengingly she looks at him! The blood rushes through his veins. Stormily, almost certain of his victory he addresses the lovely woman.

Begin the song with great fire and assurance. The accompaniment is the melody of his life — his free courageous assertiveness. Apparently he is accustomed to getting what he wants! At the moment, it is this beautiful and strangely seductive woman whom he wants. She seems to be a willing prey to his adventurous desire. But she answers him with words which seem to glide over him like the murmur of the swaying trees.

Her first phrases should be sung without expression. With half closed eyes sing, so to speak, over the head of the impetuous youth, gazing into the emptiness of space. Imagine that you are like the evil spirit of the sombre forest, the whispering voice of a dangerous wilderness, a wilderness in which ferns and clinging vines grow rank, where snakes under the thick moist leaves rear their heads awaiting their prey.

The warning—"O flieh', du weisst nicht, wer ich bin..." should be sung with the intention—not of warning but of luring him. The young man is adventurous, he does not fear danger, on the contrary he is intrigued by it. Perhaps others have been lost in the wilderness, their piercing cries for help ringing out like bugles through the forest, but he is sure of himself. He knows how to deal with danger. He welcomes it. And you, the clever Lorelei, know that if you but warn him of danger, he will never give up. His answer comes back with the same straight forward, gay melody of the beginning. He doesn't even listen. He is intoxicated by the beauty of Lorelei. With a violent desire to take her into his arms, he comes nearer, — then suddenly, in a flash, he recognizes her. He sees the witch of whom he has heard ever since his childhood, the witch of the fairy tales that were told him as he sat on his mother's lap beside the fire, the witch of whom the fishermen tell, as they sit mending their nets on the banks of the Rhine, the witch of whom young girls tell, as they sit together by their spinning wheels on winter evenings. The young lad had never really believed in her. "Fairy tales" he used to scoff, laughingly. But now he looks into the terrifyingly beautiful eyes of the fairy. He crosses himself, knowing that God alone can help him to escape from her hynotizing gaze.

Slowly you raise yourself, becoming from head to toe — the triumphant witch, Lorelei. "Yes, I am Lorelei. You know me well. You know my castle on the Rhine." Sing this with an icy triumph — and then break out into fierce scorn, repeating the impetuous words, which the young man had used when he first caught sight of you, when he was so sure of himself and so confident of an easy and successful adventure. Sing with cutting irony—"Es ist schon spät, es ist schon kalt" and end with wild and vicious triumph: "kommst nimmermehr aus diesem Wald." The repetitions of "nimmermehr" should be like the blows of iron hammers, like wildly rushing footsteps crushing their helpless prey in furious destruction. Keep your feeling of dark triumphant hatred until the end of the postlude. This fades away into the theme of the young lad, but it is only a recollection of his carefree laughter. You feel, and your listeners must feel it with you, that his laughter will die upon his pale lips even as the melody is fading away and the deep ferns will close around his helpless body like a web—and never more will the forest release the prey of the Lorelei.

STILLE TRÄNEN

Kerner   *Schumann*

You are talking here to another person who has never understood you. Perhaps it is to your beloved that you are talking. He is utterly different, he doesn't really know you. He is carefree. His nights are never disturbed as yours are, by grief and inner pain. Perhaps you are deeply wounded by his carefree lack of concern and his lack of understanding. Now on a brilliant morning he comes to you. From the way he walks, you see that he is refreshed. His eyes are smiling, his heart is light and sensitive to the beauty of the day. Lost in your unhappy thoughts, depressed by your sleepless night, you see him coming toward you across the flowered path . . . You are standing at your window. Your room, like your heart, is filled with shadows. But you know that he will never question how you feel within the depths of your heart. He is only capable of superficial feeling and so he will take it for granted that the smile with which you greet him comes from a contented heart.

Begin the song with a *crescendo* which develops from a subdued *piano* tone. All the glamor of the captivating personality of your beloved is in the broad *crescendo* up to "die Au". It is as if you are looking at him admiringly. A person who lives, so to speak, in darkness, will always admire and even unconsciously envy "the children of the sunshine". With the first sentences you are thinking: "There you are, young, glamorous, carefree, like a young God. Yours is the loveliness of the morning, yours is the blue of the cloudless sky. You have slumbered untroubled, never knowing that the same sky which greets you with dazzling sunlight has been clouded through the night. Rain fell steadily, but you did not hear its heavy drops upon your roof, you were lost in lovely and playful dreams!"

The first part of the song ends with: "viel Tränen niedergoss." In this first part the personality of your beloved has been the center of your thought. Now you return to *yourself*, to that self which is embittered and misunderstood. But you do not say: "Look at me, think of me, share my troubles with me, you happy one . . ." No, you say with bitterness: "You, who think you know me, what can you understand of one who is able to hide all her thoughts and feelings? How can you understand what it means to suffer through the whole night,

to shed burning tears with never any consolation, until dawn? You
see only the meaningless smile on lips which have learned to smile and
so you can never realize that there may be pain or despair or bitter
loneliness behind that smile . . ."

The interlude after: "stets fröhlich sei sein Herz" is the transition
between bitterness and triumphant realization. "I succeed in fooling
all of them. They believe my smile. And you, you my thoughtless beloved, you believe it too! Proudly I stand before you seeming untouched by your lack of understanding. I smile even if my heart is
breaking." With the last phrase — "sei sein Herz" return to a subdued *piano*. It is as if your triumph cannot really satisfy you. It may
satisfy your *pride* but your *heart* is nevertheless filled with misery. With
this last *piano* there should be a suggestion of desperate tearfulness.

The postlude expresses a surging longing to be understood. With
the last bar, *adagio,* you loose yourself in sombre resignation.

JOHANNES BRAHMS

1833—1897

VON EWIGER LIEBE

Wentzig   *Brahms*

The first verse describes an evening landscape, but through this description you must convey the prevailing mood of this song. You must anticipate the drama, of which you tell in the following verses...

Consider the story which has preceded this scene: because of her love, the girl has encountered difficulties. Whatever the cause may be — that has nothing to do with the song — she has been made unhappy by the people of her village, who could not understand her love and could not forgive her for it . . . But the lack of understanding and the unkindness which surrounds her, has never discouraged her . . . On the contrary: she has gained in strength through this very opposition. She holds her head high, before all of them . . . On the other hand, the young man whom she loves and who in the eyes of the world is unworthy of her love, struggles vainly against an overpowering impatience . . . This opposition seems to be too much for him — he can not endure that his beloved is made to suffer on his account. He wants to free her from the disgrace which this love has placed upon her in the eyes of the people who know her and are fond of her and are eager for her good . . .

Feel this atmosphere as you begin the song.

You describe a friendly evening. But it is overshadowed by melancholy. Sing the beginning absolutely devoid of sentimentality, but as if weighed down by something dark and oppressive. (Again and again I say — "without sentimentality". Sentimentality takes from any song its grandeur . . . And a Lied must have grandeur. You wouldn't want to put anything mediocre into either its words or music, would you? Verse and music lift the idea out from mediocrity — be very careful that you don't, through sentimentality, place it back within the drab light of the commonplace . . .)

For example when you sing "Nirgend noch Licht und nirgend noch Rauch, ja und die Lerche, sie schweiget nun auch" that is nothing tragic, but it is also not anything which should be sung without expression . . . Sing it as if under a shadow, with a melancholy which is devoid of sentimentality, — this is no contradiction as it may seem at first glance . . .

In the interlude give the impression that you see the lovers approaching from the distance. Do this very, very discretely: it is enough, if you raise your head a little and your glance seems to sweep into the distance. Sing the beginning of the second verse with a slightly increased tempo. "Führt sie am Weidengebüsche vorbei" should be sung with an expression of mystery: he leads her away from people, he doesn't dare to walk with her where others may see them. There is hiding, secrecy, fear, in this avoidance of others . . . The next phrase "redet so viel und so mancherlei" is again very significant. The young man's heart is so full. He is so unfree, so inhibited, so filled with fear before these malicious people, that he talks much and all around the subject . . . The interlude which musically is absolutely the same as the first, must be animated through an entirely different facial expression: you are the girl who is listening to what her beloved is saying. You must have an expression of listening, of anxious attention.

Now sing the verse of the young man with great vigor. You are filled with anger, filled with loathing — you say with short, hard words "it would be best to put an end to all this"—an end to the tormenting of his beloved, an end to his senseless fighting, for he is already weary of struggling . . . Sing the entire verse with ever mounting passion — a passion to end all that can no longer be tolerated . . . In the interlude which continues what the young man has so stormily and wildly expressed, you are still *he* — you are still seething with revolt, with the desire to break away . . . When the music — *poco a poco* —becomes softer and more hesitant, you very discretely go over into the feeling of the young girl.

Your facial expression becomes soft. It is as if you would still listen to the words of your beloved. With the change of key you are completely the girl, not only passively but actively. Sing "Spricht das Mägdelein, Mägdelein spricht" very delicately and with lovely expression. Now, when she really speaks, put all the great strength, which a pure and believing heart possesses, into your words. Sing very darkly and with great emotion, up to the interlude. During the interlude, you search for words with which to convince your beloved. (You haven't yet seen in his eyes what you are longing to see: the dawn of a new confidence, the promise that he will be true to you no matter what may happen . . .) Now you search for new words — and you can only repeat "Iron and steel" which symbolize for you the greatest possible strength and power. Sing with a great inner enthusiasm, with passion and great force to the end of the song. At the end sing in a lovely *ritardando* broadly and nobly: "unsere Liebe muss ewig, ewig besteh'n".

End the song standing very erect. In your eyes should shimmer a look of noble triumph: one must have the feeling that you have convinced your beloved, that nothing, nothing can ever separate you. That all suffering becomes small and insignificant before the greatness, the power, the infinitude of your love.

WIEGENLIED

Brahms

This folksong which is loved in every language, played by orchestras and by every solo instrument, sung by choruses and is a radio favorite, seems almost too popular to warrant any discussion. But too often one sings such a simple melody just by force of habit without really considering the poem . . . I certainly do not want to take from this song any of its captivating simplicity. Quite the contrary, the more simply and charmingly it is sung, the nearer it approaches the ideal. I only want you to consider with me the lovely simple poetry and through it to find new inspiration in this old beloved song, for one can create much which is new and beautifying when one looks into the depths even of simplicity itself . . .

"Mit Rosen bedacht, mit Näglein besteckt". . . The child is lying in its cradle which has a canopy made of gay material, as they do in German villages. Roses and carnations are embroidered on this canopy or woven into the gay pattern . . . You, the loving mother, are thinking — "Oh how I want to make life as beautiful as possible for my child . . . I should like to strew his way with roses and carnations..." Sing "Morgen früh' wenn Gott will" like a smiling prayer . . . You know that God does want your child to awaken early in the morning, so sing it confidently, filled with happiness and trust. Lift out the "wenn Gott will" very tenderly as if you said it glancing upward toward heaven . . .

In the second verse your desire to give the child everything which is humanly possible is still more emphasized. Now roses and carnations are no longer enough, oh no, the angels to whom you have called in your prayers, are standing around the cradle . . . Sing the "Englein" with a subtle delight — as if in your imagination you see before you the kindly angels who watch over your child. Sing "die zeigen im Traum dir Christkindleins Baum" as if it were a secret promise. "Schlaf' nun selig und süss" should have the sweetness of a violin tone. Sing it floatingly, delicately, ethereally. At the repetition sing *ritardando* and end very broadly, delicately accenting each syllable of "Paradies". Sing this word as if you yourself were seeing the gates of paradise opening before you, as if you were looking into the splendor of heaven with bated breath, in devout ecstasy.

DEIN BLAUES AUGE

Groth   *Brahms*

Imagine that you have been deeply hurt. You have loved someone with all your heart. You have given your whole being to someone
who has been the beginning and end of all your happiness. But you
have been disillusioned. The experience through which you have gone
has seared your heart and has devoured your thoughts, your peace, your
soul with a consuming fire. Now someone whom you have come to
love, in a very different way, stands before you. Her clear and innocent
blue eyes look up into yours. In her eyes is no flame, no, her eyes are
pure and bright. And you who have been so deeply hurt, long to sink
forever into the deep clarity of her gaze. It is not love which you
seek, it is not passion which you crave. It is peace and healing and forgetting. And that she can give you.

Begin the song with yours eyes cast downward, but at the first chord
open them. You should give the impression that at this moment you
are looking into eyes which question. These eyes do not waver. They
are quiet. They seek only to understand and to help you, to heal and
console you. Begin to sing with half voice, as if with awe: it still exists,
it is here before you — Peace . . . "Ich blicke bis zum Grund" —
every note must be sung with emphasis. These notes must be like slowly descending steps, as if you were slowly going deeper and deeper into
the coolness of her eyes. Sing "Du fragst mich, was ich sehen will"
with a somewhat lighter voice and answer her question with deep emotion, as if you were plunging into the very depths of the deep, deep
well of her eyes. Then you remember the past. You shrink back into
yourself, remembering the glowing eyes of the one who had wounded
you so deeply. A shadow of the passion which has brought you so much
misery floods through you. A shadow which you do not want to touch
you. You want to feel that passion has left you. You know that it
has. But something still smoulders within you as you recall the love
which made you so insane. It is pale — only a trace — an afterthought,
but it is there and it disturbs and pains you. Now you return to the
clarity of the eyes which are before you. Change the quality of your
voice, open your eyes (they have been closed before the shadow of
your remembrance). Look again deeply into the eyes before you (you
must give this impression). To bring the right quality of tone here
you must sing very correctly, tone by tone. Don't slide, don't scoop.
Make the most of the consonants and vowels. Prolong each vowel in
"Wie ein See so kühl". Every tone must be clear and very light. Before the last word "kühl" make a pause, sing the *k* with a breathy qua-

lity. Give the impression that you, your body, your whole being is sinking into the deep coolness of clear and velvety water. Imagine the green clarity closing over you. You sink into its coolness. Your facial expression should be one of soft ecstacy until the end.

NICHT MEHR ZU DIR ZU GEHEN

Daumer   *Brahms*

You are entangled and caught hopelessly in the web of an unhappy and passionate love. Sombre shadows brood heavily over this wonderful song. The accompaniment follows the voice as if with heavy steps — hesitant and undecided, as if seeking to hold it back, to hold it fast. Color your voice very darkly, sing steadily and with a sombre weight. For heaven's sake avoid any sentimentality. You are the victim of inner weakness, but this weakness is passion. It is a dark, glowing weakness which consumes you and makes you the victim of this love which will destroy you. Any sentimentality would lessen the grandeur of this song. Sing each syllable clearly. Paint, even in the first phrases, the picture of the lovelost being who with full knowledge and without any power of defense goes to his destruction . . .

Go over into a veiled *piano* at "und jeden Halt verlor ich". Lift out the word "verlor" like an anguished sigh.

The tempo becomes more animated: impatience, disgust, despair break out from you. Flight into death seems the only escape . . . Your expression should be suppressed, restrained, yet glowing. Tie the syllables to a greater extent than you did at the beginning of the song. Sing with a driving force and with sharp accents. But, at "und möchte doch auch leben für dich, mit dir"—a sacrifice to your conflicting emotions — you throw your whole being into this outpouring of your will to live. Slide the "und" in a broad *crescendo* to "möchte". Give this phrase an almost aria-like surge. Sing the repetition "nimmer sterben" as if through tears. It is as if you were saying—"Oh how radiantly happy I could be,—so happy, that I should never want to die—living for you and with you . . ."

The interlude is a reflection of your inner distraction.

You return again to the melody of the beginning: restrained and trembling, the words fall heavily from your lips. The accompaniment follows you as if with heavily creeping steps and rises and falls in *crescendi* and *decrescendi* which are like deep sighs . . . Give great significance to the words "ein klares". You must imagine that you have again and again questioned, wept, threatened and implored, but you have never received a clear yes or no — never an answer which might have settled your fate, might have lent you the strength to bear either happiness or misery . . . It is the uncertainty which has tortured you so bitterly, the terrible inability to see into her heart, which is worse than a "no" . . . With your expression paint the whole story of your love in the words "ein klares" . . . It must be clear to your listeners from what inner uncertainty your weakness arises. Sing it breathily, almost in a whisper and with a harshly colored "a". And now you storm on in a powerful *crescendo* — "gib Leben oder Tod mir" and sing as if with tears of despair: "nur dein Gefühl enthülle mir, dein wahres". Make this last word the climax of the song: stand very erect, with an expression of passionate questioning . . . You have never had a clear, true word in answer to your question . . . Now you ask again — and you will probably ask again and again in the future, until your love dies within you — and until you die from this love . . .

In the postlude further questioning discloses with an inner and crushing certainty, that the answer, if it were clear and true, would be a "No". . .

BOTSCHAFT

From Hafis by Daumer   *Brahms*

The wind rustles and whispers through the whirling leaves, to sweep down upon you, in a gracious swing and then glide away. You call out your message to the wind sending it forth as the messenger of your love. Sing very softly, floatingly and full of grace.

(Imagine that your doubts have all been dispelled, you have the assurance that your beloved loves you. All the torments of uncertainty have now become things of the past and all that was sombre before is now radiant . . .)

Give your voice a free, floating quality as if it will be borne away upon the wings of the wind. At "eile nicht hinwegzuflieh'n" sing in a broad line as if carried by the wind. Oh and you know that she will ask the kindly messenger, the wind, how you are faring . . . You are sure of it — so you can say, playfully and roguishly: "tut sie dann *vielleicht* die Frage?" and emphasize the "vielleicht" with a delicate humor

Tut sie dann viel - leicht   die Fra - ge

You say of yourself "my poor self"—but of course you don't mean this seriously—so sing it with an emphasis which is full of humor, as if with scorn for yourself. For such a long time you have been so senselessly unhappy, — you didn't believe or realize, how much your adored one loved you. But now you are so sure of her that you can speak of yourself scornfully as "the poor one" . . .

During the short interlude you prepare the message which you want to give to the wind. (You straighten up, your glance roams eagerly into the distance as if you wanted to call out to someone.) Sing with strong voice: "Sprich" and in the repetition of "sprich" in the following phrase, cut it very short. Breathe after the one short word, so that the following phrase will seem like a real message. Now you tell of all your sorrow, of all you have suffered for the sake of your beloved. But all this is over now. You look back upon it with a smiling scorn, you, who are now so happy and so confident of your love. Sing with an almost mockingly tragic emphasis, with a roguish scorn for yourself. At the repetition of "höchst bedenklich seine Lage" sing *ritardando* and immediately change your tone quality at "aber jetzo kann er hoffen". Sing this with a swing and with great joy but in strict tempo. Change your tone quality again at "denn du Holde denkst an ihn", sing this tenderly like a caress. Sing "denn du Holde" *ritardando* and "denkst an ihn" *a tempo*. The repetition is broad and filled with a joyful swing. Play with the word "Holde" so that it radiates the tenderness which lies in this caressing word. Hold the last "denkst" very long and end with a rapturous sigh: "an ihn". . .

denkst   an   ihn.

In the short postlude, have the idea of the vanishing wind — follow, with your delighted glance, the soaring messenger of your love.

DER TOD, DAS IST DIE KÜHLE NACHT

Heine   *Brahms*

The dream of love and life which one, even though dying, may still dream, is here so wonderfully and poetically expressed by Heine (who when he wrote it was lying fatally ill) that it seems almost incredible that it could be made still more beautiful through music. But the genius of Brahms has even surpassed the genius of Heine. Sing the poem, make of the music poetry, if you would do justice to this masterpiece . . .

For a long, long time you have been fatally ill. Within you is a deep yearning for death, yet life which from far away often still touches you, sings from the branches beyond your window . . . Begin very softly, with an unearthly quality, with a darkly colored timbre. All of your longing for death must sound through the words — "Der Tod, das ist die kühle Nacht" and your turning away from life—through the bitter "Das Leben ist der schwüle Tag". The life which once engulfed you in both happiness and misfortune is now far away from you, it seems like a sultry and oppressive dream from which you emerge into the coolness of longed for death as into the waters of a crystal spring . . .

Sing with a deep and darkly floating voice, almost in a whisper: "es dunkelt schon, mich schläfert". All the weariness of life lies in — "der Tag hat mich müd' gemacht". Sing this with emphasis but without any *forte* certainly. It is more a heavy sigh, with no trace of reality in it. But the day which has wearied you, throws its sunbeams across your bed: life speaks to you anew . . . Outside your window, a flowering branch sways in the breeze and from the bough of the tree comes the sweet song of a bird . . . Sing with a lighter voice quality, with somewhat more strength, with a dreamlike longing. The tree, the song of the nightingale — the old, well known song of love, — all this comes to you as if from a time, long, long gone by . . . It no longer makes you restless, it no longer makes you despair, it is like a long forgotten song, — you listen to it and it tires you sweetly, like a soft slumber song . . . Sing the *crescendo* with warmth and a longing which is beyond any feeling of torment . . . In the repetition you sink back, losing yourself again in the half sleep which leads you so comfortingly from this world to the other eternal one... Sing the end, fading away, as if in a dream. Hold this expression until the end of the postlude.

DER SCHMIED

Uhland   *Brahms*

The strong rhythm of this song conveys the motion of the swinging hammer, — a joyous and vivacious melody. Without any prelude you plunge into a full *forte,* singing in strict rhythm throughout the first verse. Build up the words with strong consonants. No *forte* tone can be truly effective here unless it is supported by very clear enunciation. Don't forget however, that every phrase must have one main word. While never diminishing the tone value or interrupting the rhythm, you must bring out the important point in every sentence. This song will become monotonous if you fail to do this.

Coming out of a warm *forte* make a *crescendo* at "Gassen und

Platz". Accent the second note of "Gassen". This *crescendo* does not mean that you should force your voice. Play with the words — increase the intensity and you have a climax!

During the interlude, your body (with the greatest discretion) shows the rhythm which dictates the character of the whole song. Your facial expression should radiate pride and happiness.

Begin the second verse *forte*. Your face reflects your delight! You see your beloved beside the forge. His face is dusty from his work, but how handsome he is! You pass him pretending that it is only an accident which brought you here. (Actually, how you have looked forward to this opportunity for seeing him!) You say to yourself — "He mustn't discover that I wanted to see him, I'll just pass by him, perhaps I can manage to see him out of the corner of my eye . . ." But oh! It must have given him a thrill to see you! He wants to attract your attention and hammering still louder, he makes the forge blaze more violently, and there he is — your handsome, marvellous young blacksmith, surrounded by flames!

Start "Am schwarzen Kamin" with strong emphasis and sing "da sitzet mein Lieber" with pride and delight. Then sing more subduedly as if you were telling your listeners a secret — "doch geh' ich vorüber."

The next two sentences have a strong *crescendo* on "sausen" and "brausen". Sing "sausen" with a long drawn out *s* and give the diphthong *au* an expression of something swinging vigorously . . . The word "aufbrausen" is again *crescendo* (many r's). You must give the impression through this word painting of actually *seeing* the soaring and surging flames which surround the figure of your beloved.

With the last words — "Und lodern um ihn" you stand very erect, your head is thrown back, your eyes show that you are radiantly happy. You *see* your beloved in your imagination. Hold this expression until the end of the postlude.

IMMER LEISER WIRD MEIN SCHLUMMER

Lingg   *Brahms*

You are dying. As you lie upon your bed, you are awakened out of a half slumber and look with longing out into the blue distance which is forever limited for you by the frame of your window. You can see a small patch of sky, a branch swaying in the wind . . . You have only one wish: to see your beloved once more before you die, — and you know that it will be very, very soon that you must take leave of this life. You are so weak and ill — even your deepest wish is only like a tormenting dream and does not have the power to rouse you to glowing desire . . .

Begin very *pianissimo,* with an unearthly quality. Sing floatingly as if in a dream. Sing as if you were halfway between sleeping and waking. At "zitternd über mir" hold the *z* a moment so that it sounds as if you caught your breath. Sing the repetition of "über mir" *ritardando.* Your expression remains the same — dreamy and unreal, until you sing "niemand kommt und öffnet dir". Now there is fear within you, fear that he might be there and yet go away because there is no one to open the door . . . Sing "ich erwach' und weine bitterlich" *crescendo* with deep despair. But never sing a powerful tone, be always subdued, feeling an inner weakness. Tears veil your voice, (how could one ever sing this song without real tears? Actual tears may perhaps interfere with the technically flawless flow of this song, but your expression can only give it inner life, if the song really grips you to your very depths . . .) The *forte* at "weine" is no real *forte* of power but a *forte* of expression . . .

The short interlude brings you back to the quiet resignation, to the soft surrender, which is now the melody of your pitiful life . . . Sing with the softest *pianissimo,* with an absolutely unearthly quality: "ja, ich werde sterben müssen" and then like a suppressed sigh—very soft, very unreal — "eine Andere wirst du küssen". You look into that life which so cruelly you must leave: you see your beloved before you, you realize that he will forget you, that the vital and wonderful life, which is ending for you, will begin anew for him, that love and happiness await him when you are gone. Your death seems something unspeakably cruel, at this moment you do not see in it a release from your pain, you see only your loss through it, of everything which might have been good and beautiful. Full of horror, you see yourself — cold and pale, a corpse which is the victim of destruction, while life smiles at others and another will kiss the man whom you love . . . Color your voice darkly at: "wenn ich bleich und kalt", sing it, so to speak, shrinking from yourself with horror, terror and repulsion.

Your veiled glance sweeps into the distance, turning away from the shocking picture which your tortured fantasy has created. Sing *accelerando* but very softly and with suppressed passion "Eh' die Maienlüfte weh'n". And now there bursts from you the despairing question: "willst du mich noch einmal seh'n?" Sing this with great dignity, overshadowed by the majesty of death... With the last atom of your strength you try to raise yourself (imagine this in singing) to call to him . . . Sing with an outbreak of passion "komm', o komme bald!" But you are too weak, you have demanded too much of yourself: you sink back exhausted, lifeless, perhaps — dying. Sing fading away, like a sigh: "komm', o komme bald" and imagine that with the last chord, you die.

DIE MAINACHT

Hölty   *Brahms*

While the beginning of this song is a description of nature, you
should not sing it as if it is only nature, which you are describing. By
this I mean that while you are singing of nature, you must sing of it,
overshadowed by the sombre feeling which must pervade the whole
song. You are a lonely and miserable soul, disgusted and disillusioned
by life and love. You begin to sing, under the shadow of your unhappy
experience. Your voice must be dark and veiled.

There should be a sweeter and lighter quality in "und die Nachtigall flötet" — a very silvery quality. "Wandl' ich traurig von Busch
zu Busch" is very dark and filled with sadness. With the next phrase
you raise your head slightly, looking up to the side (most discretely of
course) as if you see the doves upon an overhanging branch. Sing
"überhüllet vom Laub" in a repressed and veiled *piano*. You don't describe the doves with delight, on the contrary you look upon them with
disgust, with suppressed envy: "girret ein Taubenpaar sein Entzücken
mir vor . . ." You know that the delight of the doves, like all such
delight, will pass and disappear in the course of everyday existence. You
no longer believe in the sweet enchantments of nature, you are too
disillusioned, too lonely, too brokenhearted to feel any longer any desire. So you say "Aber ich wende mich" (But I turn away). This should
be sung with a very dark quality, filled with despair. Your head is turned toward the opposite direction, your eyes are cast downward. You
must prepare for the next phrase with your facial expression: you slowly raise your head, your eyes look into the distance as if you were seeing
something very beautiful, something of which you have always dreamed. But you know that it can never be anything but a dream, that it can
never become reality: "Wann o lächelndes Bild?" But there is no answer to your question, you know that there is no reality. And the lonely tear burns more painfully upon your cheek. Sing "Träne" without
sliding from tone to tone. Don't rob this song of its grandeur through
a weak sentimentality . . . Accent each syllable in "heisser". Breathe
after "Wang'" and sing "herab" through tears.

In the postlude, lonelier than ever, you disappear in the depths of
the quiet moonlit night.

SAPPHISCHE ODE

Schmidt   *Brahms*

This song is pervaded by the darkness and the mysterious beauty of
a warm summer night. It should be sung floatingly, with a dark quality

56

and with deep emotion, but without sentimentality. Avoid a too slow tempo — this song should be *moderato* rather than slow. The marking "rather slowly" is in my opinion, more a warning not to take the song too fast. Begin with a cello-like quality. Accent glowingly: "süsser hauchten Duft sie als je am Tage". "Doch verstreuten reich die beweg-ten Äste" should be sung with the utmost lightness, with a silvery and ethereal quality. Tie the word "Äste" over to "Tau" (in the way which I have explained in the Introduction, page 15). In the interlude (as throughout the whole song) the branches sway in the warm night wind. Take up the gentle rhythm with your body, follow it (very, very discretely) in your feeling, your expression . . . The first verse was a tender, compassionate description of nature, in the second verse your own individual experience floods your delighted observations. Sing "auch der Küsse Duft mich wie nie berückte" very darkly and passion-ately and give much emphasis to the word "Duft", sing this with closed eyes, losing yourself in this enchanting remembrance . . . Sing "die ich nachts vom Strauch deiner Lippen pflückte" with an impelling force. Yet you hesitate now, — it is as if you see before you the face of your beloved, as you saw it on that night — pale, unreal, consumed by a passion so strong that it made her weep. Sing "doch auch dir, be-wegt im Gemüt, gleich jenen" very subtly, with restrained delight, lost in the happy memory. The marking in the song indicates *crescendo* and *decrescendo* at "tauten"

I myself sing a *crescendo* with the first two tones and then go over into a *subito pianissimo* at the third tone. This of course is a matter of purely personal opinion but I have the feeling that the memory of those tears of delight is almost too much . . . , that you scarcely dare to relive this memory . . . That is why I make a *subito pianissimo*—but of course it is completely within the style of the Lied —perhaps even more "correct", if I may say so—to go on in a full *crescendo* . . . Sing the final "die Tränen" broadly with a soft swing.

In the postlude feel yourself sinking into the glow of your over-whelming memories . . .

AUF DEM KIRCHHOFE

v. Liliencron   *Brahms*

Perhaps you are in a strange city and knowing no one there feel very lonely. So you wander through the unfamiliar streets, oblivious of the bad weather which only makes your loneliness the more acute. Soon you have reached the outskirts of the town, and before you is a cemetery. You wander about between the graves, reading names which mean nothing to you, for you have never known anyone who could have been buried here.

The prelude gives the impression of the storm with its torrents of rain. The wind blows cold over the quiet cemetery and melancholy broods over the lonely graves like a sombre cloud. Take up the stormy music with your whole being: but realize that it is a storm which rages around you, it is not a storm of inner passionate feeling. Very solemnly you watch the uproar around you. You look about you as you would in real life if you were in the midst of a storm which you do not fear but which is nevertheless very unpleasant. Begin to sing forcefully, but with the same expression of serious observation rather than any pain or distress. Sing with an earnest but impersonal expression: "Ich war an manch' vergess'nem Grab' gewesen", and in the same way—"verwittert Stein und Kreuz, die Kränze alt". Sing this very distinctly and without sentimentality. Your glance is turned slightly to the side, as if you were looking at the graves around you. When you sing: "Die Namen überwachsen, kaum zu lesen" the realization of the transitoriness of everything which lives, sweeps over you. You look up, you look so to speak into the face of eternity seeing how mercilessly perishable is everything which was once human and which now rests under the old stones of this forgotten cemetery . . . Feel the horror which sweeps over you as you think: so completely transitory is everything, so completely transitory am I, like everything else around me, that even the names are obliterated, even that last trace of those who once lived and loved and suffered. Everything is a sacrifice to destruction so that nothing, nothing remains but a sunken grave, which no one loves or cherishes . . .

The stormy music of the prelude is repeated. But now it is the expression of your own inner feeling which engulfs you. Now you are gripped by the shocking realization of your own destructibility. Despair of life itself floods through you and makes you shudder to your very depths . . . Show by your facial expression, this change in your reaction to the stormy music. Show that the storm now does not just engulf you from the outer world but that it is within you, shaking you, raging within you . . . Sing with great force and an expression of helpless despair: "Der Tag ging sturmbewegt und regenschwer" and with an inner horror: "Auf allen Gräbern fror das Wort: Gewesen". Sing this with forceful rhythm and with very much emphasis. Sing each syllable of "gewesen" *sforzato* as if terrible footsteps trample everything into nothingness, obliterating forever everything which exists . . . Until now your glance has been rigid, looking into the distance. Now you slowly look downward, now with the change of key your fear is dissolved and changes into a feeling of peace and resignation . . . Sing the following phrases with a warm *piano* tone: "Wie sturmestot die Särge schlummerten". Accent "tot" as if gratitude were welling from the depths of your being. End with a soft *piano,* with great warmth of expression: "auf allen Gräbern taute still: Genesen". Accent "taute" very subtly. It must sound as if tears are running down your cheeks, tears which free you of your inner tension. Sing the word "genesen" like a deep sigh of release. Let the *n* sound and tie the first tone of *ne* to the next tone in a lovely sweep, like a prayer and let it be full of warmth.

In the postlude, feel the sombre chords as if you were hearing organ music, with devout feeling. Remain as if lost in meditation — your whole being breathes the one thought — "genesen"... (released ...)

WIR WANDELTEN

Daumer   *Brahms*

A quiet and lovely poetry pervades this friendly song, — a bright summer sky arches over the flowering countryside . . .

Feel within yourself, the light flowing melody of the prelude: your thoughts turn happily to the beauty of that day when you wandered with your beloved through the flowering fields—in perfect harmony, in deepest contentment. Begin softly, delicately, but with great feeling: "Wir wandelten, wir zwei zusammen". Never make it sentimental! Sing with simplicity, with warmth and a quiet dignity. Don't drag out the tempo, but never let it be fast.

"Ich war so still und du so stille" has an almost imperceptible *ritenuto.* Sing the *st* in "stille" very distinctly holding the two consonants for a second very discretely as if the memory of that beautiful experience makes you pause for a moment . . . Sing somewhat faster: "ich gäbe viel, um zu erfahren, was du gedacht in jenem Fall". This phrase should be sung lightly and vivaciously. Deep and overwhelming emotion should be felt in "was ich gedacht, unausgesprochen verbleibe das", sing it broadly with a soft *crescendo,* with the dignity of someone who experiences a love so deep and pure, that it seems like desecration to try to tell of it.

Was ich ge-dacht, un - aus-ge-spro - chen ver-blei-be das!

Sing "Nur Eines sag' ich" in a soft piano, lightly *ritardando.*

Beginning with "So schön war alles, was ich dachte" sing floatingly until the end of the song in a lively tempo. Close with a rapturous climax, in a broad *ritardando.*

in   der   Welt   kein   and'   -   rer   Hall.

NACHTIGALL

Reinhold   *Brahms*

In the prelude you hear the nightingale as it sings from the branches just outside your window. As if dreaming, you listen to the sweet song, which awakens old halfforgotten memories, lovelier far than all of the nightingale's songs . . .

Your first exclamation: "O Nachtigall!" is like a sigh. Sing as if you were speaking into the distance. Imagine that it is a lovely summer night and you are leaning at your window, lost in revery. Not far from where you stand, the little bird sings its sweet song from the thicket of flowering lilac. With your first words don't look straight in front of you but with raised head look slightly to the side. (When I give advice of this kind I feel that I must always repeat that everything which you do must remain within the limits of concert singing. You may never be "theatrical". The moment that you overdramatize, you have misunderstood me . . .) Give attention to the exact note values, if you should disregard this the song would take on a sentimental character which is entirely foreign to it. Sing "er dringet mir durch Mark und Bein" with a great swing, accented and with glowing expression. In the postlude you are still listening to this song, which so grips you. But your thoughts turn back to yourself: memories surge back upon you — the song of the bird fades from you... With a dreaming smile you sing: "Nein, trauter Vogel, nein". Sing this with the greatest delicacy, like a caress, giving your voice a light silvery quality. "Was in mir schafft so süsse Pein, das ist nicht dein!" should be sung with an inner driving force. You turn away from the song . . . The pain, the secretly sweet anguish which awakens in you, as you listen to the nightingale, was not enflamed through the beauty of the singing. No: it was the memory of a sound which once flooded your life with golden sunlight, it was this memory which touched your heart so deeply . . . Was it the sound of a beloved voice? Was it a word which enraptured you? Was it some noble music which has gone from you forever? Whatever it may have been: lose yourself in the memory of it. Sing broadly in a lovely mounting *crescendo* and with flowing warmth: "das ist von ander'n, himmelschönen" and sing with a great *ritardando — decrescendo*, fading away sweetly: "nun längst für mich verklungenen Tönen".

nun längst für mich ver-klun-ge-nen Tö - nen,

I take the liberty of advising something here which the advocates of strict correctness may forgive: to produce the word "längst" on such a high tone is rather difficult. If you find that it causes you trouble, I see no reason why you shouldn't sing "lang" instead of "längst". It will certainly help your tone quality . . .

Sing warmly with half voice, smiling as if in a dream — "in deinem Lied ein leiser Widerhall". The interlude of two measures is again the twittering of the bird.

You listen smilingly and end with a lovely *legato* in the most subtle *pianissimo*: "ein leiser Widerhall". Let the last chord fade away gradually. Holding the tension — let the song die away.

DAS MÄDCHEN SPRICHT

Gruppe   *Brahms*

This charming, roguish song should be sung in a very lively tempo. You are young, very much in love, engaged or perhaps married for a very short time. You are lighthearted. Life seems for you just playing and flirting. You have found in this new love the fulfillment of all your desires, all your dreams . . .

Perhaps you stand at your bedroom window watching with merry eyes the pair of swallows who flit so playfully by. They have built their nest in the thick vines which twine about your window — a nest hidden under the overhanging roof. How often you have watched and listened to these swallows. You have been witness to their games of love, their sweet companionship — yes, the two swallows have become your friends, for since you have never disturbed them, they trust you...

The lively prelude seems to describe the flitting about of the swallows. React immediately to this graceful music—look into the distance with an eager expression, smiling in delight. Sing smilingly, with a childlike curiosity, as if it were a secret question: "Schwalbe, sag' mir an, ist's dein alter Mann?" Accent "alter Mann" very facetiously but discretely:

you can't really take this question seriously — sing everything lightly, with a joking expression . . . (with this lightness you lessen the frivolity of this intimate question . . .)

You have watched the lovemaking of these swallows and have thought: "Oh they cannot be a couple which has been married for a long time . . . I think they are delightedly discovering one another and are always surprised anew, just like me and my beloved"... Sing with great significance "oder hast du jüngst erst dich ihm vertraut?" ("or have you been intimate with him just lately?") Accent "jüngst" and sing "dich ihm vertraut" in a smooth *ritardando* as you would tell a secret, with smiling understanding . . .

The interlude tells again of the flitting of the swallows, which you follow with your glance.

Sing the second verse mysteriously with an increasing intimacy. Be piquant with a playful sensuousness in singing: "Sag', was zwitschert ihr, sag', was flüstert ihr des Morgens so vertraut?" With the *forte* of the interlude you already give the answer in your next question: "Gelt, du bist wohl auch noch nicht lange Braut?"

Sing the ending *ritardando* with the abandon of one in love. In the postlude you watch the playful swallows smilingly.

FELDEINSAMKEIT

Almers   *Brahms*

An infinite peace pervades this wonderful song. From the very beginning until the very end you must be as if under a spell, a spell which can only be experienced in this completely disembodied sense, if, released from the limitations of his own being, one has in a moment of exaltation, become one with nature, one with the blue expanse of infinity... At the very beginning of the prelude you must lose yourself in this transcendent feeling. Sing in a soft *legato,* in broad tempo—yet never dragging and above all things never scooping or sliding. (Sentimentality would completely destroy the pure beauty of this song.)

At "von Grillen rings umschwirrt" be sure to give the dotted notes their exact value. Sing this very subtly with a light tone and then color your voice more darkly in "von Himmelsbläue wundersam umwoben" so that the phrases seem to enshroud you in a broad surge like rich cello tones. Feel yourself one with the blue of the heavens, lose yourself in it, feel the soft blue closing about you like a warm cloak of velvet...

The second verse again begins with a lighter, more silvery voice quality: "Die schönen weissen Wolken zieh'n dahin". It is absolutely essential that you feel the beauty of these words just as deeply as you feel the immortal beauty of the music: recite the poem, feel the word

62

painting, drink in the description of the white clouds, the deep blue heaven . . . Only then can you do justice to this song. Certainly: a singer with a lovely *piano* and faultless breathing technique can render the beauty of nature, in this glorious song, with light, delicate colors, but to endow this soaring spirit with warmth and feeling is only possible for a being who is itself capable of realizing this sublime beauty.

Sing "wie schöne stille Träume" somewhat more animatedly and with great warmth, *crescendo* and *decrescendo*—

wie   schö - ne—   stil - le—   Träu - me,

"Mir ist, als ob ich längst gestorben bin" should be sung as if with bated breath, very subtly and filled with mystery — it is as if you were listening to your own soul. In "gestorben" give each syllable significance, but discretely, *pianissimo*. You scarcely dare to speak of that which has given you this wonderful sense of exaltation, raising you above the course of every day existence and the commonplaceness of this too earthly life. Sing "gestorben" with a transfigured smile, in breathless rapture.

Submerge yourself again in the broad flood of warm sunlight and floating clouds in "und ziehe selig mit durch ew'ge Räume". Feel the soaring exaltation of this union with the infinite.

MEINE LIEBE IST GRÜN

Felix Schumann   *Brahms*

This song is often sung too fast. It should have a *tempo animato* but the meaning of the song should not be lost in a wild storming . . . It is a swaying lilac branch, it is the song of the nightingale, of which you sing and which have inspired you to poetry and music . . .

You are very much in love, you search for words with which to tell of your happiness. Plunge, so to speak, into the song — accent "Fliederbusch" with an emphasis of delight — mount from a soft *piano* into a lovely *crescendo*: "und mein Lieb' ist schön wie die Sonne". In the repetition you should also begin *piano*, singing "schön wie die Sonne" as if you are swaying dancingly in the warm glow of the sun.

Sing in quickened tempo "die glänzt wohl herab auf den Fliederbusch"— enunciating very distinctly! Broaden out at "mit Duft und mit Wonne" but without being at all *ritardando*. Sing this phrase with a broad surging sweep.

Make the interlude absolutely your own: feel the exultation in the music, the passionate driving force, from head to toe . . .

Begin the second verse warmly but with an inner restraint: you sing of your soul, giving it the wings of the nightingale, feeling the blissfulness of its flight, its swaying and dancing among the flowering lilac branches. You cannot sing of such delicate and poetic things with a bombastic *forte* . . . Sing the repetition "und wiegt sich in blühendem Flieder" lightly *ritenuto,* with a delicate swing — and feel the swaying motion with your whole being.

Go immediately into a livelier tempo at: "und jauchzet und singet" and end broadly with a surge of enthusiastic delight.

In the postlude feel again the driving sweep and let the quieting conclusion of the music die away before you break the tension.

THERESE

Keller   *Brahms*

In this song you are an experienced woman, with whom a youth is in love. You must sing with a charming superiority. You are rather amused and your rejection of the amorous boy is friendly and gracious . . . After all: it is never unpleasant to be adored . . . In your refusal there is still a certain enjoyment of the situation — a light, charming coquetry . . . Of course you have known for some time what the shy approaches of the lad meant . . . You have tried to overlook them in a friendly way, but his glances became more significant and you really have to put an end to the sweet nonsense. You know that you can best do this by making it clear to him that his love is childish and by being a little scornful of this "puppy love" . . . It will hurt him a little, perhaps, but it will heal him of his infatuation and make him able, again, to enjoy dancing and playing with his contemporaries . . .

The prelude is your amused question: "How dare you look at me, you bold boy?" This question, inquiring, ironical, reflective, must be clear, through your expression. Begin with great vivacity, with a quickly changing expression: "Du milchjunger Knabe, wie schaust du mich an". Sing the last words "für eine Frage getan" strongly *ritardando*. Be coquettish to the youth — be coquettish in a very feminine way, you want him to stop adoring you so, but the adoration itself gives you an exquisite pleasure . . .

Sing "Alle Ratsherrn in der Stadt" as if you were speaking to a child,—vivaciously, wittily, with superiority. Make a little pause before "stumm". Give a *sforzato* accent to the *st* and close the phrase with the same playful, tender coquetry, *ritardando,* as you did in the first verse.

But now you really must give an answer to the impetuous and passionate pleading of the boy's eyes . . . Now you must hurt him a little, wound his pride, for you know that that is the only way to get rid of him . . . Sing with a mocking and mysterious expression "Eine Meermuschel liegt auf dem Schrank meiner Bas' ". Sing somewhat more slowly, each word stressed with a humorous importance: "da halte dein Ohr d'ran" and end *pianissimo, ritardando*—"dann hörst du etwas". Hold the "hörst" and slide it downward in a light curve. Sing the last word "etwas" with much emphasis, laughing and piquant. During the postlude which fades away lightly with vivacity and grace, feel a smiling compassion for the poor boy whom you must embarrass — regretfully.

VERGEBLICHES STÄNDCHEN

Niederrheinisches Volkslied   *Brahms*

You must make this little scene very gay and full of life. It is unnecessary to give different colors to the voice, singing the part of the young man with a dark color. In doing this there is danger of making it like a caricature, which sometimes happens. It is absolutely enough if you give different expression to the two people . . .

Begin very dashingly, full of a bold confidence: "Guten Abend, mein Schatz, guten Abend, mein Kind". You feel absolutely certain of success. Sing very urgently, but be always confident of your own irresistibility. Your whole behavior should express your sureness of yourself. You stand very erect, with your head thrown back and with a superior expression, you sing laughingly and playfully . . . The answer of the young girl, which is sung with a very light quality, is haughty and rather scornful. Sing with a certain importance: "Mutter, die rät mir klug, wärst du hinein mit Fug, wär's mit mir vorbei" . . . But don't sing this with naivety. This girl is not naive. She is very sly and it amuses her to pretend that she is naive . . . So exaggerate mockingly: "wär's mit mir vorbei" . . .

The wooing suitor is apparently very much surprised by this unexpected resistance . . . . Sing the second verse as a really urgent avowal . . . You have now lost some of your superiority, you realize that you will really have to exert yourself a little to win this coy girl . . . Now you try arousing her sympathy. There is a saying that "sympathy is fertile ground for cultivating love". . . You will now put this into practice . . . Describe with heartrending misery (very humorously!) the cold night in which, without any pity, she makes you wait, the icy wind which whistles about your ears and freezes your heart . . . Yes, you even dare a warning: "If you make me stand here in the cold much longer — my love will freeze too — and then won't you be sorry???" And now your request that she open the door becomes stormier, bolder, more confident of success. (She really wouldn't let you freeze, you and your love . . .) But the girl has had enough of nonsense by now. If her coquettish rejection hasn't been clear enough until now, she will tell him in no uncertain terms that she just plain doesn't want him, that he doesn't at all please her, that he can freeze along with his love and can go to the devil for all she cares . . . Sing the last verse with great vivacity, full of wit and humor. Accent "Geh' heim zu Bett, zur Ruh'," very clearly, so to speak, hurling "zu Bett" into his face . . . Sing with great scorn "gute Nacht, mein Knab" giving the impression that you are turning away from the window to which your stormy suitor has lured you . . . I mean imagine that you shut the window in his face with great finality as you sing the last "Gute Nacht".

VENETIANISCHES GONDELLIED

Thomas Moore   *Mendelssohn*

Through this whole song must pulsate the trembling impatience of the romantic lover . . . It persuades, lures, seduces . . . You whisper secretly and hastily into the ear of your beloved — you entreat and promise . . .

The accompaniment throughout the song gives the illusion of the rocking of the boat in which you and your adored one, when the appointed hour strikes, will glide through the quiet, dark lagoon.

The prelude should be enlivened through your play of expression: imagine that you approach your beloved with great caution — awaiting with charming impatience the moment in which you may deliver your message to her.

Begin *pianissimo,* hastily, secretly: "Wenn durch die Piazetta die Abendluft weht" and sing in this way up to — "du weisst, wie die Sehnsucht im Herzen mir brennt" — this should be sung *accelerando* with passionate excitement. Give great emphasis to "brennt" and sing the repetition—"wie die Sehnsucht im Herzen mir brennt" *decrescendo* and *ritenuto.*

The interlude again brings to your thoughts the quiet rocking of the boat — satisfaction, fulfillment of all your desires . . .

Begin the second verse hastily, immediately with an *accelerando* — *pianissimo*: "Ein Schifferkleid trag' ich". . . You and she—together — have hidden from the world — no one shall discover your sweet secret. You meet each other in disguise—and the charming unreality of that great enchantress — Venice, becomes living in this scene: you come in the costume of a boatman, she is wearing veil and mask . . .

Sing with fire and with a seductive voice quality — "und zitternd dir sag' ich: das Boot ist bereit" in a whispered *pianissimo,* breathy, trembling, passionate—

The next phrase "o komm' jetzt, wo Lunen noch Wolken um-zieh'n" is to be sung in a broad swing with a lovely *crescendo* which flowers into a full *forte* at "Lass durch die Lagunen, Geliebte, uns flieh'n"—sing the repetition *decrescendo* but without *ritardando.*

In the interlude the tempo quiets down. Sing the last phrases in the sweetest *pianissimo,* very softly, *legato* and very seductively. Hold the *fermate* without making a *crescendo* and hold the tension of the song until the end of the postlude has died away.

NEUE LIEBE

Heine   *Mendelssohn*

Don't let the light and apparently facile flow of the music lead you astray in this song. A ghostly train of fairies rushes past you. What it augurs of good or ill you do not know. So you are in suspense throughout the whole song — in breath taking suspense.

The prelude casts the spell of the phantom throng, which seems to dance before you. Your facial expression is concentrated, your eyes follow the sparkling elfin train. Begin with a whispered *piano*. Be careful to follow the markings.

In the first verse do not sing the *fortes* with full voice. Both your voice and your body should give the impression of something floating and swinging as you sing — "läuten, ihre Hörner", etc. The branches which sway in the wind, the bugle tones wafted near and far, the bells — all become floating tones . . . End the first verse with a whispered *piano,* mysteriously.

The elfin train comes nearer. In the second verse you see them rushing on — you see clearly the white horses, so strangely adorned with golden antlers. They come quickly as if borne on by a driving storm. Your expression becomes animated. You see them now as if they were just before your eyes. Sing "rasch wie wilde Schwäne kam es durch die Luft gezogen" with full voice. Emphasize "wilde", "kam", "durch".

wie wil-de Schwä-ne kam es durch die Luft ge-zo-gen,

Hurl the word "Luft" into the music with a half speaking tone. One must have the impression that you are quite paralysed as you stand there in the quiet moonlit forest watching the storm of approaching fairies as they fly wildly through the night like a flock of white swans.

In the third verse you go back to the restrained *piano* of the first verse. The fairy queen smiles at you: it is as if lightning had struck you. Your eyes follow her. Glancing back as she vanishes, her look seems to hold you fast. Your voice must convey the impression of this enigmatic and disquieting smile. Sing each individual syllable clearly and be careful not to slide them together. Each tone must be clear cut.

Out of your amazement and bewilderment you ask warmly — "Galt das meiner neuen Liebe?" Yet no, you are not sure, there is something evil which lurks in the queen's smile, she seems to you like the demon Lorelei, whose smile enchains and kills . . . The pause after "Meiner neuen Liebe" is one of inner horror. Terrified—the fateful question—"oder soll es Tod bedeuten" is built up from a *piano* whispered through fear.

Breathe after "Tod" consciously and intentionally. Thrust out "bedeuten" with sharp emphasis. Retain a tense and questioning expression until the last tone of the postlude.

AUF FLÜGELN DES GESANGES

Heine   *Mendelssohn*

It seems rather superfluous to explain this charming song which has become such a favorite throughout many lands—but how could one speak of Mendelssohn without including just this one in the wreath of his lovely songs!

Throughout the song, the accompaniment has the quality of a harp and the whole song is pervaded by a dreamlike and romantic quality which you must never fail to retain. It is a flowering and glowing fantasy which created these verses—it is a lovely and romantic melody which encloses them in a shimmering frame!

Begin with swinging phrases, enunciating distinctly but never destroying the soft graceful line. Sing "dort weiss ich den schönsten Ort" with an expression of mystery. The *crescendo* at "die Lotosblumen erwarten" should not be *forte*: you are speaking of very delicate and mysterious flowers, so you must sing with charm, with a gentle *crescendo* and *decrescendo*.

In the second verse the phrases can be made very effective through discrete word painting: in "Die Veilchen kichern und kosen" sing "kichern" half *parlando* and "kosen", on the other hand, softly spun out. In "heimlich erzählen die Rosen" exaggerate the *h* in "heimlich", this helps to bring out the quality of mystery in the breathy *pianissimo*. "Und in der Ferne rauschen des heil'gen Stromes Well'n" should be sung with dignity in a broad floating line. Sound the word "rauschen" with a *crescendo* and *decrescendo* giving it the effect of the flowing and ebbing of surf.

Begin the third verse with a livelier tempo—passionately animated yet with the quality always restrained as if telling a secret. At "und Lieb' und Ruhe trinken" sing *ritenuto,* emphasizing the *r* in "Ruhe"—and lift out this word in a gently mounting *crescendo.* When you first sing "und träumen seligen Traum" it should be *accelerando*—in an outburst of desire—in the repetition sink back again into unreality, singing *diminuendo* and *ritardando.* The very last "sel'gen Traum" is barely whispered—let the words die away— holding the tension of the song even after the two final chords.

HUGO WOLF

1860—1903

AUF EIN ALTES BILD

Mörike   *Hugo Wolf*

The flowing melody of this song which is written with such deep religious feeling is pervaded by the inexpressible simplicity of an old holy picture. A picture to which, standing in a church — remote from the world, you would look up, as a soft half light, falling through the high window, transfigures the faces of the Madonna and the playful Christ-child . . . A picture before which you would pause with devout attention, in the wide halls of renowned museums . . .

Be one with the flowing organlike melody of the prelude — enter into the stillness of the church . . .

Sing with a lightly colored voice, softly and tenderly but without any sentimentality. In the interlude after—"der Jungfrau Schoss" your glance widens: the realization sweeps over you that the tree, which rises green and filled with life at the edge of the forest, bears within its trunk the wood from which the cross of suffering will be built. Hold the tension of this phrase over from the word "wonnesam" to the sigh of "Ach" and continue to hold it through the whole interlude, as if the phrase were not interrupted . . . For the inner connection between the two phrases is not broken: the music of the interlude is realization, prayer, and deepest thanksgiving . . . Sing the last phrase extending it broadly with a dark voice quality, vibrantly as in a helpless protest against so much suffering.

In the postlude you look into distant space — your whole being pervaded by devout and humble devotion.

DAS VERLASSENE MÄGDELEIN

Mörike   *Hugo Wolf*

There could be no more expressive tone painting of boundless emptiness, of complete abandonment, than the short prelude of this song. It is as if one really sees the pale griefstricken girl entering the door with dragging steps. *You* are this girl. The house is cold, everyone still sleeps. But you, the servant, must arise in the early dawn and go to your work. Everyday it is the same work, life has become an endless purposeless monotony since your beloved abandoned you so faithlessly.

Begin the song with a so to speak empty *pianissimo,* lightly colored, glassy. The syllables fall almost reluctantly from your pale lips — sing without expression until "Feuer zünden". Warmth and light come into the music. You look into the play of flames which you have lighted on the hearth. Imagine that your glance, unconsciously attracted by the brightness of the flames, is held fast, staring as if hypnotically transfixed upon them... Sing *piano*: "Schön ist der Flammen Schein"—sing it as if you feel the beauty without being really conscious of it—as if you say this almost unconsciously. So don't give any expression of delight to this phrase, but sing it with *almost* the same emptiness as the beginning. Give only a light emphasis to "schön" — sing more softly perhaps but not with full awareness. "Es springen die Funken" has a light *crescendo* and *decrescendo*—

es spring - en die   Fun - ken;

Sing the triplet distinctly,—only in the painting of the music does life seem to awaken in the leaping flames—your voice itself keeps the quality of great emptiness. Retain this expression through the interlude until suddenly, as if awakening, you become animated. Sing with passion, through tears: "Plötzlich da kommt es mir, treuloser Knabe" and end, becoming again quieter, in the softest *piano* —"dass ich die Nacht von dir geträumet habe". Sing this with an expression of painful happiness, as if you relive the dream which brought back to you, so deceptively, the lost ecstacy of love. Hold "geträumet" on the note of E a little, sing this word with subtlety—feel: you only really live in your dreams—only a dream can bring to you the happiness, which in reality has abandoned you... In the following three measures the dream fades into the cold grey light of the dawn. Sing now "Träne auf Träne dann" with the palest *pianissimo,* but tears tremble through your voice —the emptiness with which you dragged yourself into the cold, dark kitchen (at the beginning of the song) is flooded with grief and longing, flooded by burning tears released through the memory of your dream . . . The word "stürzet" is a strong and dramatic word but the musical line is quiet here. Yet just this apparent contradiction (which for Wolf would seem very strange) between word and music gives the greatest possibility for expression: you are so unutterably exhausted — you have wept so much, suffered so much, rung your hands in such despair — alone in your comfortless room . . . You are no longer capable of violent outbursts of passionate grief . . . You say only the *word,* stammering with lifeless, pale lips, a wild word... Try to bring this to expression: paint the elementary outburst in the word "stürzet" (consonants! darkly colored *ü*, breathy piano tone). End the song in hopeless resignation. The last outcry "o ging' er wieder!" is a stifled sob. The grey day closes around you like the walls of a prison, from which there is no escape.

AUCH KLEINE DINGE

Tuscan Song translated by Heyse   *Hugo Wolf*

Like careful fingertips touching something fragile and precious, is the exquisitely subtle mood of the prelude. "Kleine Dinge" are alive in the uppervoice of the accompaniment and the delight in them in the bass voice. Feel the lovely play of delicate thoughts — reflect it in the expression of your face: it is as if someone had doubted that there is pleasure to be found in little unimportant things . . . Even during the prelude your smile should imply: "oh—but don't you see how enchanting little joys may be? If you can only learn to *see* them, then you will enjoy them!!!"

There is no *forte* in this song — scarcely a noticeable *crescendo*. Sing with a light voice, with a warmth which arises from delicate delight, not from the deep well of your emotion. A light *parlando* runs through the whole song. Speak to your listeners as if you wanted to convince them, as if you wanted to convert them to your opinion. Be one with your audience, make them a part of your song, of your singing, of your argument. Bending slightly forward — speak to them as if you were among them, not separated from them by the feeling: I am the singer, you are my audience . . .

Give a warm emphasis to "können teuer sein", making a slight pause before "teuer". This pause should be scarcely perceptible, just enough to give value to the word. When you speak of pearls which it is hard to pay for ("schwer bezahlt") sing with a rather roguish importance—as if you say: "could there be better proof that pearls are precious? One can scarcely buy them . . ." Each fresh comparison is a new idea so you must begin anew with each one . . . Give especial emphasis when you sing of the rose. This is the crowning point of all your examples — you love this beautiful, noble flower very specially. Sing with great warmth and loving delight—"Denkt an die Rose nur". Close with a warm tenderness as you would in speaking of a being very dear to you and sing with a delicate *ritardando* — "und duftet doch so lieblich . . ." (Avoid any sentimentality! Sing each note very clearly and without scooping.) In singing the last words: "wie ihr wisst", you should bend slightly forward toward the audience and sing directly to them. Your facial expression says: "Do you see? Am I not right?" Hold this expression until the end of the postlude.

UND WILLST DU DEINEN LIEBSTEN STERBEN SEHEN

Tuscan Song tr. by Heyse   *Hugo Wolf*

You are a very young lover. You kneel before her whom you adore, looking up at her as you would at a beautiful picture. With a harplike quality the accompaniment flows through the song — it is the accompaniment which is the surging language of your heart, while the singing voice mingles with it and soars above it with a silvery lightness.

Begin with a restrained and veiled piano. You sing with intoxication, your words fall from your half closed lips, heavy with passion, which, being transmuted into words, becomes a dreaming play . . . Make a slight pause before "sterben" then sing it with an ecstatic emphasis.

Slow and sustained (♩ = 54)
(*Langsam und getragen*)

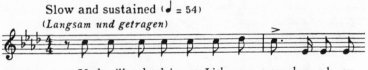

Und willst du dei-nen Lieb-sten ster-ben seh-en,

Make a *crescendo* at "du Holde" sliding the two tones upwards in a forceful curve. Tie the word "Holde" to the next phrase as I have explained in the introduction.

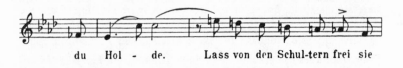

du Hol - de.   Lass von den Schul-tern frei sie

Breathe however, after "Holde" without interrupting the connection and sing "Lass' von den Schultern" like an expression of wild delight. Emphasize "frei". The phrase "Wie Fäden seh'n sie aus" is again a restrained, vibrating *piano*. Sing very quietly, with a clear *pianissimo,* as if in delighted playfulness: "Wie gold'ne Fäden". Observe carefully the *crescendi* and *decrescendi*—Hugo Wolf always give the clearest of directions . . . "Ungezählt" is the climax of the song—sing it broadly and ecstatically and with a lovely *crescendo*:

Gold-fä - den, Sei - den-fä-den   un - ge-zählt,

Whisper the last phrase and sing a *pianissimo* vibrant with passion at "schön ist, die sie strählt". Your eyes are half closed, — lingeringly, the words fall, slowly and heavily, from your lips.

IN DER FRÜHE

Mörike   *Hugo Wolf*

Like heavy steps emerging out of the darkness of night is the accompaniment's underpainting of the voice. You are exhausted — a sleepless night has brought no peace to your troubled thoughts, to release and quiet you. Slowly the first grey light of dawn spreads over the heavens — but you still struggle for the healing forgetfulness of sleep. Sing with dark voice, with heavy weariness. Sing devoid of strength, with resignation until "an meinem Kammerfenster". The following measure seems to be the sombre memory of all the comfortless darkness with which the night has enshrouded you—the sleepless one, as with a black cover. Sing on in the same heavy tempo, although the recollection of the disturbing, despairing thoughts which have tortured you, makes your voice more animated, more expressive. Go without any binding from E to F at "verstörter Sinn" carefully avoiding any expression of softness.

At "und schaffet Nachtgespenster" sing in the same way (from B to C) and give the word "Nachtgespenster" a quality of uncanninness. Make the most of the consonants: lift out the *sp* and sing a dark, restrained *piano*. With the change of key your facial expression becomes relaxed and peaceful. The morning sun sends its first rays into your room—and with the coming of light the sombre, tormenting thoughts of the night leave you. New faith, new hope awaken in your heart. Your voice loses its dark and trembling restraint. Sing in a clear *pianissimo*: "Ängste, quäle dich nicht länger, meine Seele". Like warm sunlight your voice must break in upon the dark mood which has held you captive, — angelic, overflowing with warmth, pure and clear. In the underpainting of the accompaniment is the sound of bells and over the bells, which greet the new dawn, flows the melody of your voice. "Freu' dich" is like a bright fanfare. With the fading *pianissimo* of the last phrase your hands are folded together in a prayer of thankfulness.

GEBET

Mörike   *Hugo Wolf*

This song should be sung with the utmost simplicity. It is the inner prayer of a simple person, but a person of great wisdom and understanding. In order to make it living for you, yourself, you must follow the organlike prelude with your own thoughts. Anticipate the opening phrases of your prayer in thought and feeling so that when you begin to sing, you repeat in word and tone what you have already experienced in your heart. Sing simply but with the deepest sincerity and warmth. Sing very evenly and without sentimentality.

Be imperceptibly more animated as you sing: "wollest mit Freuden und wollest mit Leiden mich nicht überschütten!"— and then go back into the sustained tempo (without ever dragging!) at "doch in der Mitten". Sing this with the indulgent smile of one who looks back upon a long life which has brought him every kind of experience: he has known joy and sorrow, from jubilant happiness has fallen into the deepest disillusionment. Now he has attained wisdom: no longer does he want great happiness which may change to desperate grief . . . So sing with a smile of deep understanding: "doch in der Mitten liegt holdes Bescheiden". With the quality of a violin tone the lovely accompaniment delicately rises and falls, carrying your request as if with ethereal tones to heaven. Remain motionless until the postlude fades away.

GESANG WEYLA'S

Mörike   *Wolf*

Orplid, that land of longing, that island of dreams — always remote . . . Who does not carry in his heart an Orplid? Who has not experienced looking far, far away — beyond the line of the horizon, to where this land may lie, — the land of untroubled joy, the land of fulfillment, the land which Schubert's "Wanderer" sought with sombre longing, yet realizing that he would never find it . . . The land which Mörike and Wolf make appear before you as a lovely reality — far, far away, yet near, real, yet like a dream . . .

The harplike accompaniment with solemn arpeggio chords carries the hymn of greeting to Orplid, the island of fabulous loveliness. In singing this whole song you should be moved by deep and noble feeling. Begin with a soft, mysterious *pianissimo*, as if in a dream — reality recedes. Far away behind undulating veils of mist, in a rosy aura, you see the longed for island . . . Sing with a continuously mounting *crescendo* which develops slowly, very slowly from the beginning *pianissimo* up to the outcry "Kind!" All the infinite tenderness of your yearning adoration lies in this word "Kind". . . (The tides which with never changing constancy roll in from the sea in broad dark waves upon the island, become silvery white flashing surf from which its radiant cliffs rise in virginal purity . . .) Sing the word "Kind" with an inner trembling. Sing it with a broad exhalation, carefully, with a caressing delight. Notice the accompaniment: here for the first and only time, it becomes the melody, separating from the upper tones of the solemn arpeggio chords and soaring upward with your voice — like the surge of surf — to the radiant word "Kind". Hesitant and *decrescendo* the short surge of melody becomes again the accompanying harp. Sing the next phrases *pianissimo,* mounting very carefully. If you cannot sing the phrase "Vor deiner Gottheit beugen sich Könige" in one breath—and only do this if you can give full power to "Könige"—it is better to breathe before "Könige". The word "Könige" must be lifted out as the emphatic climax of the song. Sing each syllable with broad and ecstatic emphasis. Close broadly *ritardando.* Your face should have an expression of exaltation, you stand erect, your glance is directed into the distance, to where the land of your dreams rises from out of the mist — your own longed for "Orplid".

ER IST'S

Mörike   *Hugo Wolf*

The flickering play of spring sunshine, the singing of birds, fleecy white clouds floating amidst the blue of the heavens, dance through the accompaniment. Begin to sing with jubilance, like a bright fanfare —gay, dazzling, very vivacious . . . Sing "wieder flattern durch die Lüfte" very distinctly and with a bold surge. In the next phrase change your timbre, singing softly, *piano,* very sustained and with a restraint filled with mystery. Sing with delight —"Veilchen träumen schon, wollen balde kommen". Sing "Horch" very short, as if you were really listening attentively,—stand tensely, listening with concentration and expectation. Begin "von fern ein leiser Harfenton!" *pianissimo.* Let the last sustained tone mount in a powerful *crescendo*—tying it to the jubilant outburst "Frühling, ja du bist's" by breathlessly holding the tension. Don't break the mounting effect by a noticeable interruption! Note the dot at "ja". Sing the two outcries sharply and clearly like a fanfare.

From the *fermate* at "du" at the end of the song slide up to the last "bist's". Feel the sweet tumult of awakening nature—the lavish, overwhelming bliss which sounds and sings through the postlude. Follow the music with your whole being . . . Feel the mysterious stirring and sprouting in the restraint at the ending of the accompaniment.

DER GÄRTNER

Mörike   *Hugo Wolf*

The lively gallop of the beautiful princess's horse beats in a joyous dance through the whole accompaniment of this song. Feel immediately the quality of this graceful prelude: your facial expression should be animated, reflecting delighted expectation and concentrated attention — as if you really see the beautiful princess approaching, seated upon her noble snow-white charger . . . Sing in strict rhythm without any sentimental slurring. Paint in tone the lovely proud woman on her flawless, spotless steed . . . Lift out the phrase: "Der Sand, den ich streute" with a warm surge. It is you, you yourself who scatter the sand upon her way so that her horse may not be in danger from the rough road . . . Without altering the tempo or the strict rhythm, sing this one phrase softly sustained and with warmth of feeling. But again at "er blinket wie Gold" it is from the distance that you are watching in admiration . . .

The prancing horse bearing his beautiful rider, approaches nearer. It seems like a wonderful, dreamlike adventure that she should really come nearer, that she is actually there—near you, as you stand upon her way, overwhelmed and enchanted . . . And boldly you call out your wish to the princess, as one would in a dream, without fear or hesitation . . . Oh but your wish is not so presumptuous as to allow you to meet her glance . . . Oh no! You do not look into her beautiful face—you look only at the rose colored bonnet which rises and falls with the rhythm of her gallop, going up and down behind the high green hedge that separates your path from hers . . . The hedge which separates two worlds—the world of reality and the world of your dreams . . . It is to this hat that you call out your wish—"Throw me a feather—but secretly, so that the princess may not know about it..." Sing this in a whisper with a quality of mystery, with a restrained *pianissimo,* as if you have an understanding with the hat, this servant of her beauty—as you are the servant of her garden . . . Sing: "Und willst du dagegen eine Blüte von mir" with delicate feeling, and sing "Blüte von mir" in a soft *ritardando.* Go over immediately into *a tempo* and in a *crescendo* rise to a jubilant *forte* at "Nimm tausend für eine"... You feel so rich: the garden is blooming in extravagant profusion, and what could be more worthy of her beauty than your wonderful living flowers, all of which you would pluck to adorn her, your adored one. But she rides past you. The dancing nodding bonnet throws no feather as a secret token of love. With sadness your glance follows her—your lovely princess... Sing the last repetition "Nimm alle dafür" *pianissimo* and *ritardando.* What had been a daring demand becomes a silent question, humble and modest . . .

In the postlude you see her vanishing, like an apparition—farther and farther the white horse bears her away—and you stand there, alone among your flowers.

MAUSFALLEN-SPRÜCHLEIN

Mörike   *Hugo Wolf*

Here you are a playful child who doesn't realize that a mouse trap is not such a delightful experience for the harmless little mouse who is approaching. So in happy expectation you dance around the trap, singing your gay song.

Sing like a child, very lightly and playfully. (Be very exact with the note values!) Slide "nur" to "kecklich" in a very quick upward slur and sing "kecklich" very *staccato.*

Become very mysterious at "heute Nacht bei Mondenschein" sing the three repetitions each time with an increased expression of childish secrecy. Breathe audibly after each "Mondenschein" in order to make the word very important. Sing "Mach' aber die Tür fein hinter dir zu" like a sudden outcry, *pianissimo* but with urgent significance. The "hörst du?" are short, bold, smiling. "Dabei hüte dein Schwänzchen" should be laughing and childish and the repetition "dein Schwänzchen" quite *parlando* in a teasing tone which brims over into a merry cry. In the short interlude you (the child) spring about the mousetrap in a boisterous abandon (in your imagination!). In "Nach Tische singen wir" you rock back and forth, *legato,* but without disturbing the tempo. The two "ein Tänzchen" are like awkward little jumps. But you haven't had enough fun yet in frightening the poor little mouse with the mouse trap . . . The cat must come too . . . With unconscious cruelty this thought suddenly occurs to you. You interrupt your jumping about. With raised shoulders and a comically threatening facial expression you try to imitate the hissing of the cat. Sing very short syllables and let the *w*'s hiss and the *tt*'s spit . . . Sing "Meine alte Katze tanzt wahrscheinlich mit" smiling, in childish delight, and sing the word "Katze" very short and glaring. The three "hörst du?" should be sung in different ways: the first is a very short cry, in the second prolong the "du" as if in a secret warning, in the third—short separated words as if with a shuddering horror and remain standing very rigid—in childish fear.

RICHARD STRAUSS

1864—1949

RUHE, MEINE SEELE

Henckell   *Richard Strauss*

The dark threat which hangs over you, sounds in the heavy chords of the prelude, which, ascending like deep sighs, dissolve and soften and are the preparation for the delicate entrance of the voice. Feel the dark foreboding in the chords of the prelude. Look into the distance with wide open eyes, searching, prepared, composed . . . Begin singing very softly and in a slow tempo. Paint the deep stillness all about you, paint the deceptive quiet which surrounds you. Sing with a lightly colored voice almost without expression.

Lift out "Sonnenschein" with a delicate emphasis making it the climax of the mounting phrases. Sunshine is all around you, sunlight floods through the dark leaves, through the darkness of your thoughts... Sing with deep emotion, as if with a sigh of relaxation: "Ruhe, ruhe, meine Seele". Sing this as if you were speaking to a weary child, as if you wanted to sing it to sleep . . . Sing "deine Stürme gingen wild" with a restrained expression making a pause before "wild"; it isn't necessary that you breathe here, but hold the pause between the two words as if your heart has stopped beating. Sing "wild" in a strong *sforzato*. At "hast getobt und hast gezittert" sing with restraint, with half voice, suppressed. Note the two *sforzato* signs at "gezittert". Go over into a powerful *crescendo* at "wie die Brandung, wenn sie schwillt". Feel the tumult in the accompaniment, feel its roar within yourself. You stand very erect, with flashing eyes, offering your free brow to meet the challenge... Sing throughout with a dark timbre, very heavily and with full power: "diese Zeiten sind gewaltig, bringen Herz und Hirn in Not". Sing this storming on impetuously, as if pursued. Hold "Not" sustained with undiminished force, then break it off very suddenly and abruptly. Now as if remembering yourself you return to the mood of the beginning: "Ruhe, meine Seele". Sing this softly (but for heaven's sake without sentimentality) but sing it with great feeling as if you were laying a quieting hand upon a feverstricken brow . . . Sing diminuendo, very softly and tenderly—"und vergiss, und vergiss"—accenting each syllable, making each syllable significant. Close with a dark *pianissimo*, your glance directed into the distance, your expression rigid—"was dich bedroht". Understand this rightly: there is no really deep assurance in this song. You force your impetuous heart to rest—but the threat remains—you know that something dark and evil and tragic awaits you... Give all the significance of which you are capable to the word "bedroht". Make one realize: there is danger before you—no matter how courageously you disregard it, it is there, it awaits you, it will strike you down... It waits and threatens . . . Sing from out of your deep realization: "und vergiss, was dich bedroht".

Listen to the postlude, in which the play of sunlight enchants you yet again, comfortingly, quietingly — yet deceptively . . .

ALLERSEELEN

v. Gilm   *Richard Strauss*

All Soul's Day, the day of the dead—the day on which one thinks of all that is gone, of all that has been and will not come again . . . With the first phrases of the prelude, memories sweep over you. Feel the sweet, yearning, violin quality of this melody, follow it with closed eyes, surrendering to the lovely melancholy of remembrance . . .

Consider the situation from which the poem and the song have arisen: Life has separated you and your beloved — your dreams have never been fulfilled. Perhaps you see each other often, but always among others who perhaps are watching and listening . . . You have learned to approach one another, before the world, like two strangers... But in your heart still burns the old memory, it will not pass, in spite of the greyness of everyday life which separates you . . . But to-day, on the day of the dead, by accident you are alone together. With overwhelming power the old longing sweeps over you, the old love which will not die. Defiantly, you say: even the dead have a right today to that which *was* . . . Have we not also the right, for once, a single time, to say to ourselves—even if it be only with a look—that we have not forgotten, that we both know what longing means?

In this feeling of overwhelming longing enter into the lovely prelude of this song.

Begin *piano* and with tender significance: "stell' auf den Tisch die duftenden Reseden". You want the flowers of autumn around you, the flowers which have the fragrance of something which is passing . . . Autumn is within you and within your beloved: you are no longer young — you have both had to go through a long life — apart... All the flowers of spring have withered for you, the glowing roses of summer have faded — but the last blossoms of autumn still remain in the garden . . . Emphasize the "duftenden Reseden" — give a yearning delight to the word "duftenden". Sing "die letzten roten Astern trag' herbei" very evenly and softly, without sentimentality. "Und lass' uns wieder von der Liebe reden" should be sung with a shy reserve, — but overpowered by your memories — sing with a warm surging *crescendo*

— "wie einst im Mai". Begin with restraint, *piano*, — "Gib mir die Hand, dass ich sie heimlich drücke" and sing with an outburst of passion: "und wenn man's sieht, mir ist es einerlei . . ." Oh you have concealed your love from the world and from yourselves for such a long, long time! Today, on the day of the dead, you feel a burning desire within you to tell for once, what you feel, for once — to be yourself . . . Sing softly in a warm *crescendo* — "Gib mir nur einen" and in *subito piano* — "deiner süssen Blicke". You want, so to speak, to sing on with full tone, but the memory of the sweet look overcomes you and you sing this phrase like a long drawn sigh. Close softly and tenderly —"wie einst im Mai". Begin with a new surge: "Es blüht und duftet heut' auf jedem Grabe"—sing it darkly and with the warm timbre of a cello. And now go with great significance, with fire and enthusiasm into the great outburst which ends the song so magnificently: "ein Tag im Jahr ist ja den Toten frei — komm' an mein Herz, dass ich dich wieder habe, wie einst im Mai". Do not rush these phrases: take a deep breath before "komm' an mein Herz"—give yourself time, broaden out, sing with an inner significance. Sing "dass ich dich" with great emphasis and mount to a noble *fortissimo*

komm an mein Herz,— dass ich dich wie - der ha - be

The first "wie einst im Mai" is to be sung broadly and with abandon, still completely under the spell of passion, with flowing expression. The second "wie einst im Mai" is like a sigh of remembrance. The whole resignation of the "today" lies in this vanishing, fading away of expression and tone. Sing very subtly, with an inner trembling—and hold the tension of the song until the last chord dies away.

TRAUM DURCH DIE DÄMMERUNG

Bierbaum   *Richard Strauss*

This whole song is pervaded by a deep blissful contentment. No driving passion ever interrupts the quietly flowing melody which sways and rustles like dreamy boughs in the soft evening breeze. The rhythm rocks softly and gently but without any sentimentality. Be careful not to be too slow in tempo. There should be no hurrying in this song but neither should there be any dragging, only a quiet ambling toward the lovely goal.

With the first measure of the introduction enter into the melody with your whole being. Lean, very relaxed, against the piano—feeling the peaceful happiness of this man who wanders through the beautiful spring evening toward the arms of the beloved woman and the deep communion of complete harmony.

It is most important here to, so to speak, *paint* the words: color your voice darkly but without making it heavy. There is the silvery shimmer of evening in the beginning of this song. See before you the quiet landscape: the meadows overhung with the grey veil of mist upon the far horizon—the last glow of the setting sun, and above—the first pale stars . . . Make the most of the consonants — let the *w* sound in "Weite Wiesen" — the *s* in "Sonne" and sing the word "Sterne" with an expression of restrained ecstacy. To look up into the starry heavens is to look into inconceivable beauty. Feel this beauty — express it in singing the word "Sterne" as if with a caress. Make a soft *crescendo* at "nun geh' ich hin" and a *subito piano* at "schönsten Frau". (You are so overwhelmed by her loveliness that you can only voice in whispered tones the emotions which pulse so hotly within you.)

From a soft piano at "Weit über Wiesen" develop a *crescendo* bringing out the word "Busch" in a full and dark quality of tone. Close the phrase —"von Jasmin" with a slight *ritardando*. Give these two words a quality of enfolding, as if the boughs of jasmine were closing like a bower around you and your beloved. Now you are near her, near her home, deep in the bushes, where she awaits you. With the change of key take up again the quietly flowing movement of the beginning. Color your voice darkly and softly. Merge each word with the next one so that in a discrete *crescendo,* but without any *accelerando,* the ascending melodic line expands in a beautiful soft curve to "der Liebe Land". Feel the magic quality which draws you on, feel the sweet compulsion which as with hands of velvet, leads you to where beauty and love await you. Imagine that with the last word—"Land" the gates of bliss open upon you: before you lies the blue, mild light of the serene evening, of the blessed land in which love dwells. Sing with a *subito pianissimo* with the greatest softness of expression — "in ein blaues, mildes Licht". The following phrases are to be sung almost unconsciously as if in a dream, in quiet and blissful reminiscence. With a light *ritardando* (without dragging) delicately emphasize each syllable and end with the finest *pianissimo,* holding the last word "Licht" and letting it fade away as gradually as possible.

BEFREIT

Richard Dehmel   *Richard Strauss*

Someone who knew Dehmel well once told me that he wrote

this poem upon the death of his wife. This thought has made the song so poignant for me, that I mention it even though I cannot absolutely guarantee its truth.

Surely there can be no more beautiful, no more composed or inspired leave taking than that described in this wonderful poem. To see with clear eyes that a beloved being must die and have the strength of heart which speaks from out these words truly indicates an unusual grandeur of spirit.

Imagine this situation: you and I both know that death will soon part us. I know that very soon I shall lose you and you know it too,— so well, that it would be vain to deceive you with comforting words, as one ordinarily does — charitably and painfully . . . Yet here the terrible grief is lessened by a complete understanding of the situation: you know and I know, what will come. We both want to look toward the last moment with quietness and composure. You speak with her, who is fatally ill — your beloved, of the last moments which will be granted you together. Every hour is now like a farewell, so the last one will not be different. No tears shall desecrate this moment.

Begin singing very tenderly: "Du wirst nicht weinen, leise, leise wirst du lächeln", sing "lächeln" with an expression of infinite sweetness. You know she will be so brave, so indescribably wonderful. She will smile, — once again you will see that smile which you have so loved . . . Sing with quiet warmth until—"Blick und Kuss zurück". Then your glance sweeps around (very discretely) — it is as if you see your home before you, the home in which you have been happy together. Sing in a slightly increased tempo: "unsere lieben vier Wände, du hast sie bereitet" — and with a broad surge — "ich habe sie dir zur Welt geweitet". Oh! our home was our world. We needed nothing more for our happiness than these four walls, which enclosed our bliss . . . Sing "o Glück" as if it were joined to the previous phrase, holding the tension over from the last word "geweitet" to the next "o Glück" in a broad *crescendo.*

In the interlude your heart which had overflowed with happiness and gratitude for all the years which you have known together, is quieted. Sing with an inner trembling but with great restraint — "dann

wirst du heiss meine Hände fassen und wirst mir deine Seele lassen".
(You, yourself — your beloved body must go from me, but your soul
will be mine forever. We shall never be parted, never . . .) Sing
with great love and tenderness: "Lässt unser'n Kindern mich zurück".
You leave them with me, you give them to me as a precious heritage
— and I will care for them in your name . . . Sing flowingly and
with deep feeling—"Du schenktest mir dein ganzes Leben—ich will
es ihnen wieder geben—o Glück". Again tie "o Glück" to the preceding phrase, it must, so to speak, flood out from this phrase.

In the interlude the realization comes to you that the hour of separation will soon strike. Your face becomes clouded, you look far into
the distance, with wide opened eyes as if you are looking into the face
of eternity. Sing with held breath: "es wird sehr bald sein, wir wissen's
beide"—but go over into the broad and free tone to which you have
forced yourself in order to make it easier for her, who is dying . . .
Sing with a great *crescendo*: "Wir haben einander befreit vom Leide,
so gab ich dich der Welt zurück". This sentence is the most significant
of the whole song. Sing it as the great climax, with consecration and
exaltation. The world which is above the earthly world, the all embracing eternity, has led you together into its eternal orbit. Your earthly paths must part. But with the realization that you are only a small
part of an endless whole, you have mastered the grief of separation.
So, with a freed heart you recognize the wisdom of the infinite and give
her back to that other world from which her soul floated down to meet
and love your own . . . Sing "so gab ich dich der Welt zurück" very
slowly, very restrained, with deep significance and solemnity.

wir ha - ben ein - an - der be freit ___ vom

very slowly

Lei - de   so gab' ich Dich der Welt ___ zu - rück

Begin *pianissimo* "dann wirst du mir nur noch im Traum erschein-
en". Let there be a feeling of mystery here, sing it like a promise which
transcends earthly things, like an exhortation, an inner plea . . . From
here until the end, the song mounts with a great line — prepare for it,
don't expend yourself, save your strength for the very end! For this
reason sing "und mich segnen" with half voice, sparing both force and
expression here . . . Begin the widely spun "und mit mir weinen"
piano and close with a radiant *fortissimo*. Tie the last "o Glück" to this

phrase again, letting it break forth like a sobbing sigh of pure and exalted passion. Hold the last "o Glück" very long—letting it fade away — and hold, for some time, the tension of this song.

MORGEN

John Henry Mackay   *Richard Strauss*

The clouds upon the landscape before you — perhaps also the clouds which shadow your life — will one day vanish . . . You know that — you have faith in the future. You disregard the darkness of to-day and look with confidence toward tomorrow, which will again bring you sunshine, sunshine in the lovely landscape which you love so much, sunshine in your heart . . .

It is with this feeling that you become one with the prelude.

To make such a long prelude living, both for yourself and for your audience, without becoming theatrical, will only seem difficult if you approach the development of your expression "from the outside". (I can only repeat again: only that will be effective which is truly felt. In the end you must always be sincere,—warmth which is simulated may be, for a time, convincing to your audience, but your listeners will very soon fathom the empty shell of your feeling and cease to be yours . . . You must yourself feel deeply what you are singing, must draw your audience with you into the flow of your emotion, you and your listeners must be *one* in the enjoyment of what you have to give . . .)

Project yourself into this scene and let your own thoughts follow the prelude. Think: "everything is dark around me, to-morrow I know the sun will come again . . . We will be one again, you and I and we will go hand in hand, down to the beach and will stand there in silence, feeling our inner happiness, our inner understanding . . . I await that lovely morning, I await the beauty which will come to us, bringing us completion". Think these or similar thoughts, while the piano sings what you are feeling . . . Then you will find the right facial expression, you will know: how you should raise your head, how your eyes should close, how a smile should play about your mouth. And you will also find the right feeling with which to begin singing: quiet, consciously happy, with deep feeling. Give your voice a quality of lightness and softness. Sing without haste—but for heaven's sake never drag this song. It is absolutely lacking in sentimentality, it should flow in a great soft line. There should be an emphasis of exultant warmth in: "Glück-lichen" in the phrase—"den ich gehen werde, wird uns, die Glück-lichen". Sing "inmitten dieser sonnenatmenden Erde" very evenly. Your glance should be lowered slightly with the falling of this line: "sonnen-atmenden Erde" is, so to speak, a closing phrase. Look up as with a new idea at "und zu dem Strand, dem weiten"—sing this a trifle faster. (It seems almost dangerous to say this: it is not really *accelerando,* only a little more animated. The phrases must always be alive, must have a swing, they cannot just stand there woodenly, like a row of toy soldiers . . .) Pause after "wogenblauen", sing it with the sweetest *pianissimo,* paint here in tone the overwhelming blue of the shimmering sea. Sing "und langsam niedersteigen" very distinctly. Feel the climbing down, in the broad accents of the music. Now, in your thought, you are standing alone with your beloved upon the beach as if enclosed in the blue infinity. Feel the blissful solitude all about you—alone with your beloved as if in the whole world no other being existed. Everything about you fades away, you float on a lonely star through the infinity of the universe. Sing vibrantly, with restraint, under the enchantment of perfect bliss: "Stumm werden wir uns in die Augen schauen". Sing this very evenly in a floating line without dragging it. Wait before you sing—"und auf uns",—the longer you can hold the tension here, the better it is. You would break the magic of the spell if you should go ahead too quickly. Sing *pianissimo,* with great significance. Lift out the word "Glückes", letting it enfold you like a golden cloak. Remain withdrawn into your thoughts until the end of the postlude dies away.

DIE NACHT

v. Gilm   *Richard Strauss*

The description of the night is here a very unusual one: it is pictured as a thief, who steals all color from the world. Feel the uncanny slinking of the dark thief, and the strange tension of this song, which Strauss has brought to so great an effect in an apparently very simple melody . . .

The first measure of the prelude already conveys the throbbing of heart beats. Feel immediately the mysterious threat which seems to hang over all nature. Your face is clouded, your glance is directed into the distance with a tense and excited expression. Sing as if you were watching someone: "aus dem Walde tritt die Nacht, aus den Bäumen schleicht sie leise". Sing with half voice, with great restraint. "Schaut sich um in weitem Kreise" should be sung in a great surge — and after a short pause connect it like a cry of warning to "nun gib Acht". It is better not to breathe before "nun gib Acht", but make a pause, change your expression, lift out this warning. Sing with increasing fear: "Alle Lichter dieser Welt, alle Blumen, alle Farben löscht sie aus" and sing "und stiehlt die Garben weg vom Feld" with a light timbre, almost between the teeth, enunciating very distinctly.

Everything is *piano*—there is no loud tone, only suppressed fear, suppressed horror. The following phrases—"alles nimmt sie, was nur hold"—to "Vom Kupferdach des Doms weg das Gold" should be sung each time with a mounting *crescendo* and each time with a discretely increased *accelerando*. The interlude is the sweeping of your glance as it sorrowfully confirms the destruction about you. Sing very softly as if trembling with compassion and horror—"ausgeplündert steht der Strauch", but change your expression immediately at "Rücke näher, Seel' an Seele". This should be sung urgently, imbued with fear, *crescendo* and with more animation. In the next phrase—"o die Nacht, mir bangt, sie stehle dich mir auch" sing again *diminuendo,* very sustained and soft. Make a slight pause, without breathing, before and after "mir bangt" so that these words will stand alone. You say "I am afraid"... Emphasize this, say it very distinctly, and with intensity. Sing "stehle" in the most delicate *pianissimo* with great restraint, as if under a spell of petrifying fear. Your heart stops—you sing: "dich—mir—auch" torn apart, breathlessly but with restraint. Hold the anxious tension until the end, look into the distance with wide open eyes as if you see something fearful before you. As you emerge from the song it must seem as if a spell of horror falls from you—you must give a sigh of relief—and with you—the audience.

CÄCILIE

Heinrich Hart   *Richard Strauss*

Think of the story which has led up to this song:
You are an artist, a creative being who lives upon heights unknown to the average person and who can not accommodate himself to the commonplace things of everyday life. You have fallen in love with a woman who can not understand you, to whom your whole behavior—your free ways, are absolutely foreign. But you love her and you keep on hoping that you may awaken her soul as you see it in your dreams...
This song is an outburst of impatient passion, a plea for understanding, a plea and an explanation. Sing with great fire, with great power of conviction, with passionate intensity. With the very first chord of the prelude you must be the young, impetuous artist, the rare person who is blessed with genius. Stand erect, with flashing eyes, with raised head. Begin "Wenn du es wüsstest, was träumen heisst von brennenden Küssen" with a reckless vehemence—but sing *piano,* with restraint (this is not a contradiction, you must find the right quality for this effect). Sing the triplet very distinctly and with strongly emphasized consonants—

Wenn du es wüss-test, was träu-men heisst von brennenden

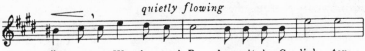

quietly flowing

Küss-en, von Wan-dern und Ru - hen mit der Ge-lieb - ten;

Sing "von Wandern und Ruhen mit der Geliebten Aug' in Auge" with a very soft and quiet flow. At "und kosend und plaudernd" sing a light *ritenuto*—have an expression of dreaming enchantment, very tender and devoted. But immediately sing very dramatically again and emphasize "wenn du es wüsstest, du neigtest dein Herz". The accompaniment now resumes the melody of the beginning—react to it as if it were a new beginning with an expression of being in complete harmony with the stormy music of the accompaniment. Begin now with a sombre countenance, full of secret persuasion, fevered and urgent: "wenn du es wüsstest, was bangen heisst in einsamen Nächten"—oh! you would tell her, how horribly alone you are in the night, how you long for comfort and for her presence, how lonely you are, how neglected you feel . . . Paint the gruesomeness of the lonely night "umschauert vom Sturm", paint with the consonants, color your voice darkly and mysteriously . . . Flowering from out of this sombre picture of which you tell her, is your renewed plea—"wenn du es wüsstest, du kämest zu mir". Sing this with a kind of grandeur. You are no humble pleader, no, your demands have great force behind them . . .

Again the melody of the accompaniment bursts in upon you with a majestic *forte*: take it up as if with wings, plunge your whole being into the storm of the music, be completely one with it. Sing with grandeur and overpowering force—"wenn du es wüsstest, was leben heisst . . ."

Now you come to the greatest argument of all: first you tried to convince your beloved by describing all the joys of love of which you know—that they might charm her to dream, to wander and to rest... Then you tried to excite her sympathy by describing your abysmal loneliness, your forlorn condition, your longing . . . But now you tell her of the greatest, the best and truest thing about you: you tell her what it means to live above everyday life—near to the clouds, near to God, —to light . . . Sing with a great surge, full of pride and with the enthusiasm of genius—"wenn du es wüsstest, was leben heisst, umhaucht von der Gottheit weltschaffendem Atem . . ." Raise yourself above the world in this last verse, sing with radiance, withdrawn, uplifted... Break off the "zu seligen Höhn" and sing broadly, with great emphasis:

"wenn du es wüsstest" and then very quickly and vehemently—"wenn
du es wüsstest", in order to close with exultant force with "du lebtest
mit mir"

zu se - li - gen Höhn, ____

wenn du es wüss - test, wenn du es wüss-test,

Sing this with great triumph giving the impression that your
beloved, overpowered, will follow you, wherever you may call her . . .
Retain the expression of inner enthusiasm and exhaltation until the end
of the postlude.

ZUEIGNUNG

v. Gilm *Richard Strauss*

In this song you are a man who has gone through life enjoying
everything which it could bring you, to the fullest extent. You have
never questioned whether what you did was right. It gave you pleasure—that was all that concerned you! Life is to be enjoyed . . . But
then you met a woman from whom you learned what real love could
mean—and life was changed for you.

Perhaps this song is a letter which you write to your beloved, who
for the time being is far away from you. Perhaps she has asked you if
you really love her,—if you are thinking of her—if her love can really
satisfy you, you, who have known so much, who are so experienced,
who have always gone your own way . . .

You answer her questions,—her burning anxiety . . .

The prelude begins with a great sweep. The words "teure Seele"
are rather unusual. In just these two words they tell the whole story
of your feeling:—you are dear to me,—"du bist mir teuer" means much
more than just "I love you". "Teure Seele" is a wonderful way of expressing a very great and deep devotion. You must convey this in your
singing of these words. "Liebe macht die Herzen krank" stands like
fate before you. You look into the eyes of fate. Fate has sought to make
you know so deep a love, that it will make your heart sick . . . Now
far away from your beloved you are ill and miserable. Yet even this

terrible feeling is a blessing to you because it is born of the radiant happiness which the realization at last, of true love, has brought you. "Habe Dank" should be sung in a veiled *piano*. It is as if you were to say to God—"Thank you". Only with the deepest reverence could you say this. So it must be here.

The second verse begins with a livelier tempo. The recollection of your past life comes back to you, with all its glittering joys, its complete abandon, its gay surrender. You gave your life, your days, your nights, without asking for any deep inner exhaltation or inspiration. To your beloved you have confessed everything in your life before you came to know her. She has understood, and her understanding has been like a benediction. It is as if she had laid her hand upon your brow saying—"What you have done is not wrong. I understand you. It has not hurt you. You are you and I love you as you are". The second "habe Dank" is filled with exuberant enthusiasm. Here you thank the understanding and forgiving friend.

The expressive *crescendo* of the interlude should be mirrored in your eyes. You feel a new world opening before you. This world you have entered hand in hand with your beloved. It is a world of inner freedom, a world of the utmost beauty. You feel a door opening before you into this world, as a church door opens before a believer. So you enter into the sanctuary of her love. It is she who has wrought this change in you, who has opened this way before you. All that was wrong in you has vanished as if under the spell of a holy blessing. And you, rising from out of your past into this new and better life, feel free and clean and pure as you have never felt before. The embrace with which you took your beloved into your arms was an embrace free of all desire. You have found fulfillment in knowing that she loves you. So you sing the last "Habe Dank"— after the last exultant and ecstatic chords which introduce it, as a climax—filled with exhaltation. The last tone should be held until the very end and broken simultaneously with the piano chord.

STÄNDCHEN

von Schäck   *Richard Strauss*

This charming song has a quick and stealthily gliding quality. Sing *piano,* not forgetting that you *whisper* something to your beloved, secretly, hastily . . . The accompaniment leaps and skips about with the quality of a mandolin. You stand in the dark, pressed closely against the wall just outside her window—your light play, your hasty words, soar through the open window where your beloved is listening . . . You are filled with impatience, you are young and you are terribly in love—you have a lust for adventure and enjoy the sweet secrecy as much as your love and your glowing desire . . .

Begin "Wach' auf, wach'auf, doch leise, mein Kind" with great vivacity, sing "um keinen vom Schlummer zu wecken" with a graceful swing. So to speak, hurl the word "keinen" into the quiet window... Close this verse with a light piquancy: "Nur leise die Hand auf die Klinke gelegt" should be sung with a secret laugh and clear emphasis and should be bold and lightly playful. Keep a similar expression in "zu mir in dem Garten zu schlüpfen". Paint the next phrases with a seductive vivacity: "rings schlummern die Blüten am rieselnden Bach und duften im Schlaf, nur die Liebe ist wach." Sing "und duften im Schlaf" with a sensual expression as if overcome by glowing desire. Emphasize "duften" with a seductive, charming *ritenuto,* very softly and passionately "nur die Liebe ist wach". Imagine in the short interlude that the girl comes down the stairs to you with stealthy haste. You are a little quieter now: you know that she will be yours—she is here beside you, she has answered your call . . . In your imagination you draw her into the shadows of the silent Linden trees . . . Sing in a warm dark tone "sitz' nieder, hier dämmert's geheimnisvoll". Paint the lovely summer night, which envelops you, with soft and glowing tones. With "die Nachtigall uns zu Häupten" begin a new idea. I mean: don't sing in the same mood as you have been singing; don't sing "unter den Lindenbäumen" in the same way as you sang "die Nachtigall uns zu Häupten" . . . Change your expression, enliven it, be full of your triumph, sing sensually and glowingly—"von uns'ren Küssen träumen". . .

During the interlude your glance roves about: "What shall I say? How can I put into words what I feel, what I wish for, what I desire? The nightingale, the lovely bird who knows so well longing and how to sing of it, will dream of our kisses;—and see the wonderful rose sending out its fragrance as it glows darkly in the shadow of the Linden tree—it will shimmer more glowingly in the early morning because it has heard how much we love each other, how much we enjoy each other and belong to one another". . . End this song with great passion, sing lavishly with a surrender to singing which should be like the surrender of love.

Hold the "hoch" in "hoch glühen" which is the climax of the song, through two measures. Instead of making a free *fermate* hold it just through two measures, the accompaniment plays the measure twice. (I have sung this song with Strauss and he always repeated this measure). In this way there is no interruption of the flow of the song, no break in the accompaniment.

Emphasize the consonants in "Wonneschauern der Nacht" very distinctly. Hold the expression of enchanted ecstacy until the end of the postlude dies away.

HEIMLICHE AUFFORDERUNG

John Henry Mackay   *Richard Strauss*

Imagine the situation from which this song was born. You are near your beloved amidst many people. You have a sweet secret between you,—no one shall know how much you love one another, how much you long to be alone together. It is a gay party. There is smoking and drinking. The mood is overflowingly happy and carefree. Immediately take up the prelude with vivacity: you are happy, radiant, inflamed by wine and love. Begin with a powerful *forte*: "Auf, hebe die funkelnde Schale empor zum Mund"—sing this freely and joyously with a kind of recklessness and lust for life which one feels when one is "mellow" with wine. At "und wenn du sie hebst, so winke mir heimlich zu" sing with restraint but with the bold and unveiled passion of one in love.

A signal has been arranged between you: if he winks at you secretly he wants to tell you: the hour will come soon when we shall meet in the garden—wait for my sign . . . Sing in a soft swing "dann lächle ich und dann trink' ich still wie du". Emphasize the *t* and the *r* in "trink'", give this word a kind of abandon and reckless extravagance. Sing in the same way to "das Heer der trunk'nen Schwätzer", break off this last word suddenly and sing very lightly—half laughing "verachte sie nicht zu sehr" (Why should you despise them? They are happy just as we are. They perhaps have only wine to make them happy, but we have our love. We have the sweet delight of secret happiness which is more intoxicating than all the wine in the world . . .) Sing the "Nein" broadly and swingingly, filled with joy and laughing delight. Continue with the same mood through "Und lass' beim lärmenden Mahle sie glücklich sein" . . . With "doch hast du das Mahl genossen, den Durst gestillt" sing suddenly with a restrained quality as if telling a secret. Be quieter in tempo now—paint in soft words how the lovers leave the other noisy drinkers, becoming rather slow at "festfreudiges Bild". Hold the tension between the last word "Bild" and the next "und". Of course you can breathe here—but nevertheless connect the idea of the last phrase with the next one as I have explained in the introduction p. 14. Sing the word "und" in a long spun out *ritardando* but then go over immediately into *a tempo* at "wandle hinaus in den Garten zum Rosenstrauch". Sing this very glowingly, very passionately, but with restraint. At "und will an die Brust dir sinken eh' du's ge-hofft" sing with full voice, warmly and flowingly as if completely lost in the broad swinging phrases. The song now presses on until "der Rose Pracht"—sing this as the climax, letting it flow from you in a complete surrender. The last "ersehnte Nacht" dies away in an intoxi-cated *pianissimo*. Remain standing withdrawn until the end of the song.

GUSTAV MAHLER

1860—1911

LIEBST DU UM SCHÖNHEIT

Rückert   *Gustav Mahler*

This whole song should be sung with very soft and broadly sustained tones. Build it up very carefully! A song, in which the musical phrases are repeated, must, like a song with verses, be worked out with especially loving care.

The two measures which precede the song are like a question: How can you love me? What can you find in me which is worthy, worthy of your love? Perhaps you seek beauty: Oh! I am not lovely enough for you . . . Begin with a soft *piano*, singing with a slight hesitation: "Liebst du um Schönheit"—and answer in a quickened tempo—"o nicht mich liebe!" Go over into a broad but soft *forte* at "Liebe die Sonne". Your delight over the all pervading beauty of the sun—the source of all light,—radiates through your voice. With "Liebst du um Jugend" immediately change your timbre and your facial expression. A slight resignation sounds through your voice as if you would say: "My youth is so short, it goes so quickly by. If you loved me for my youth, your love would be bounded by time". Sing in a soft *piano*— "Liebe den Frühling". In the accompaniment is an *arpeggio*. Like the tones of a harp, the accompanying chords are interwoven with your voice. Give it, in harmony with the accompaniment, the soft shimmer of spring's eternal youth!

In the short interlude your thoughts ask: "What is it? For what can he love me?" Sing with a half smile: "Liebst du um Schätze?" (This question isn't intended seriously. You know very well that he certainly can't love you for your "riches"). Toss off this question rather playfully, giving it and "Liebe die Meerfrau, sie hat viel Perlen klar!" the romantic shimmer of a fairy tale. Now change the quality of your voice completely at "Liebst du um Liebe?" The more lightly and playfully you sing "sie hat viel Perlen klar" the more effective can you make the dark pervading warmth with which you end the song. Don't forget the *subito piano* at "liebe" which again, borne with the rapture of spring by the harplike *arpeggios*, conveys a hesitant expectation, a humble inability to believe . . . "Liebe mich immer" should be very much emphasized —and now, breaking out into a passionate confession, you sing: "Dich lieb' ich immerdar". Feel in the postlude the blissful answer of the lover.

ICH BIN DER WELT ABHANDEN GEKOMMEN

Friedrich Rückert   *Gustav Mahler*

Here you are a person who, of your own free will, has withdrawn from the world. You live in great peace amidst a beauty which brings you fulfillment and freedom from all desires . . . In the endless beauty of deep solitude . . .

In the prelude feel within you and all about you the peace which comes with withdrawal from the world. It is only with hesitation that your thoughts return to the world, emerging from the depths of inner contentment, free of all desire.

Begin in the softest *pianissimo* as in a quiet dream. Make a slight *crescendo* at "Welt", in this way giving emphasis to the important word of the phrase. Sing "mit der ich sonst viele Zeit verloren" thoughtfully and with melancholy. "Sie hat so lange nichts von mir vernommen" should be sung with the utmost simplicity. Listen to the delicate flow of the interlude with an expression of contemplation. In the next phrase "Sie mag wohl glauben, ich sei gestorben" sing with a silvery quality, lightly, without expression. In the short interlude bow your head slightly, following the melody of the accompaniment. With the *arpeggio* chord raise your head and sing "Es ist mir auch garnichts daran gelegen, ob sie mich für gestorben hält"—thoughtfully but with a smile. Make a *crescendo* with a slight *ritenuto* at "gestorben". Listen to the interlude which leads you from the smile of contented contemplation into the delicate *parlando* of the next phrase: "Ich kann auch garnichts sagen dagegen". The realization that your seclusion is like death, like being extinguished and passing away from the world of others into the silence, makes you solemn. Sing with soft emphasis but not at all sadly—"denn wirklich bin ich gestorben der Welt". The word "Welt" is the high point, the important idea in this phrase. Build toward this climax. Sing "wirklich" without any sentimental sliding, accenting both syllables clearly. Sing the end of the phrase in an impetuous tempo (but very discretely). The following interlude seems in the first two measures to express the hustle and bustle of the hectic world, whose echo presses in upon your solitude,—the echo of your reminiscent thoughts . . . The next three measures bring the wonderful, peaceful melody of your solitude. Sing now softly and darkly as if lost in your dreams: "Ich bin gestorben dem Weltgetümmel", sing these words with closed eyes as if enraptured by the sound of the words, of the music, of your own voice . . . In the next phrase go over slowly from the dark cello tone into a clear and silvery *piano*: "und ruh' in einem stillen Gebiet". Clarity is all around you and within you—sunlight, the freshness and coolness of mountain heights . . . Sing with pride and with emotion: "Ich leb' allein" and then with quiet delight—"in meinem Himmel". Avoid most carefully any sliding or scooping in singing— "in meinem Lieben". Sing it *pianissimo*—with each tone standing out clearly and with a soft purity . . . Feel the sigh of delight in the interlude, and sing with an expression of exquisite rapture: "in meinem Lieben". End as in a prayer with warmth and blissful ecstacy—"in meinem Lied". The word "Lied" is the climax, the conclusion, the magnificent finality. Sing it as if losing yourself in sublime beauty. Hold the expression of enchantment until the ending of the postlude.

UM MITTERNACHT

Friedrich Rückert   *Gustav Mahler*

In this song the words "Um Mitternacht" are sung ten times. Immerse yourself in the meaning of the poetry and in the inexpressibly beautiful music and you will be able to sing "Um Mitternacht" with a different expression each of the ten times. I remember having sung this song once as a young beginner in Hamburg—boldly and with no real conception of it . . . After the concert I asked a distinguished musician how I had sung it. I am afraid I was quite confident of my success . . . Smiling at me, he answered: "You sang "Um Mitternacht" ten times!" . . .

The night of suffering from which this exalted song arises, is the night of decision, of destiny, of deepest resolution. Begin with a deep sadness. You are completely alone. You are *Christ* alone in Gethsemane, struggling, praying, feeling your loneliness as never before... The night which surrounds you seems silent and empty. Its sad melody flows through the song in unchanging harmony. As if in deep meditation the bass voice of the accompaniment descends slowly, step by step, this theme being repeated by the upper voice.

Begin *piano* with a dark timbre, with great nobility and a feeling of consecration. Your face has a searching expression,—feel the misery which is consuming you as you watch through the long hours of the night, finding no answer to your question. Sing with deep significance: "um Mitternacht hab' ich gewacht und aufgeblickt zum Himmel". Be careful to avoid here, as throughout the whole song, any sliding or scooping. Both the words and the music have a noble grandeur which must not be destroyed through the banality of sentimentality.

With each syllable emphasize the descent in the words "kein Stern vom Sterngewimmel" and sing a deep cello tone: "hat mir gelacht um Mitternacht". While the vast universe lies as an open book before the eyes of Christ the God, it is locked against Christ the struggling human being, for him it is only firmament, only blue infinity . . . Tormentingly the painful question pierces through you: "How can it be, that in this hour of need, the universe is locked against me?" But there is no answer, there is only silence all about you . . . Above the worlds your searching spirit rises—as with wide spreading wings it soars upward: "Um Mitternacht hab' ich gedacht hinaus in dunkle Schranken"—sing this with surging grandeur, with impelling force in a more flowing tempo and sing the following "Um Mitternacht" with a majestic quality. It is as if you yourself rise up, feeling: I am alone, but my solitude is noble and I have chosen it . . . I seek no further for an answer from the stars, my question reaches far beyond them to where the limitless darkness is like a final barrier, a gateway between these worlds and the great beyond—there must be an answer!

But in spite of all struggling, and searching questioning, the night remains silent and empty . . . The accompaniment rages as in tortured anxiety through your outburst of impassioned complaint: "Es hat kein Lichtgedanke mir Trost gebracht um Mitternacht". Let this "Um Mitternacht" fall as if through tears of deepest grief.

Again the desolate wastes close about you. Your thoughts now turn back to yourself, wearied of flight into the endless silence . . . Perhaps you may find the answer within your own heart—perhaps the wisdom of your heart is so great that it alone can give the answer which you seek . . . Sing as if secretly questioning: "Um Mitternacht nahm ich in acht die Schläge meines Herzens". But no, within it is only the raging of torment and pain. There can be no answer for you: "ein einz'ger Puls des Schmerzens war angefacht um Mitternacht". Sing this with impetuous and sombre bitterness. Your questions penetrate more deeply within you. What you now say is so great and strong that it can only be expressed with the most complete and sincere simplicity . . . Sing very simply, pianissimo, but with the majesty of the purest soul, which has dwelt within a human form: "um Mitternacht kämpft' ich die Schlacht, o Menschheit, deiner Leiden". Sing a warm flowing *crescendo* and *decrescendo* at "o Menschheit, deiner Leiden". And yet you, the human Christ, do not know whether you can bear such suffering. Sing with pain and impelling power—"nicht konnt' ich sie entscheiden mit meiner Macht um Mitternacht". The word "entscheiden" is extended through three measures—it is important that it be sung powerfully and without being hindered by having to consider breath control. If you have difficulty in this, divide it as follows:

The melody of the night enfolds you anew: empty, silent, quiet... With the descent of the harmony your head is lowered. Slowly you raise it, your face transfigured through the inner realization: "um Mitternacht hab' ich die Macht in Deine Hand gegeben". This should be sung with mounting grandeur. From out of the night of questioning, from out of the darkness of midnight, you soar into eternal light, into the radiance of realization. Casting off the limiting chains of humanity, you become again divine—one with God, the Father, Lord of heaven and earth—"Herr! Herr über Tod und Leben, Du hältst die Wacht um Mitternacht!" Sing until the end with steadily increasing power. You must experience here the power of exalted enthusiasm which is more than vocal force.

This overwhelming song can, in my opinion, only be placed at the end of a program.

THE CYCLE

The interpretation of a cycle is, it seems to me, the ideal form of Lieder singing. Without the interruptions of applause one can with complete inner absorption maintain the tension which encloses a long series of songs. And even if the songs are absolutely different in mood and each song demands the same flexibility in changing expression as does a group of unrelated songs, still one sings a cycle within one frame. It is one fate, one life, one single chain of experience, of joys and sorrows, which, when united, seem indivisible.

This is a very great task for a singer.

Before beginning to study a cycle, immerse yourself with your whole being in the figure into which you will transform yourself, to whom you will give life with these songs. You must love this figure of your cycle, you must be one with it, be happy and sad with it, live and die with it . . .

When I mention not being interrupted by applause as an advantage, I do not mean to say anything against applause as such! Oh no: the artist needs the response of his audience, he needs confirmation, he needs the intoxication which comes with the feeling that he is understood . . . He doesn't want to experience the exaltation of these hours alone, he wants to sense the deep communion, which comes of feeling one with his audience. He would like to take them all to his heart, knowing that they understand and like him, that they enjoy his singing as he enjoys this feeling of participation. It is applause which makes this possible.

In a cycle in order to illumine the figure whom you represent, you must explore it psychologically. Through song sketches you must portray a human being, you must build up and conclude a human fate. It requires enormous concentration to attain this goal.

Applause between the single songs would destroy the inner absorption. But so—without interruption—you hold fast within yourself as if by some magic power, that which enables you to mould creatively, through a long series of songs, a human fate. It is for you to make certain that you are not interrupted by applause: hold your listeners bound as under a spell. Stand motionless between the single songs—permit yourself no relaxation. Hold the mood of the song which you have just ended until the beginning of the following one. The intervals between the songs can only be very brief—you will soon develop an instinctive feeling as to when to pause and when to continue. When a cycle is completed, the breaking of the spell, under which you have sung it, leaves you in a state of exhaustion which seems almost unbearable. But it is the wonderful exhaustion which the creator feels when he has completed a work of art and realizes: it is good—I have given it life with my own breath—my own heart pulses through it—I have given it my own soul.

AN DIE FERNE GELIEBTE

Jeitteles   *Beethoven*

As you begin to study "An die ferne Geliebte" you will see that the songs which the poet sings to his beloved, telling of the beauty of spring and of his love and longing for her, are set within the frame of a beautifully simple melody which in its warm and glowing flow gives them a shimmering loveliness apart from their intrinsic quality. The real inner feeling floats through the *frame* of this melody. Here you, the lover, tell of your yearning love. The songs themselves are like flowers which you send to your beloved who is far away. You have placed them within a lovely wreath and sent them as an expression of your devotion.

Begin with full voice and sing the first three verses in a warm floating line. Begin the fourth verse: "Will denn nichts mehr zu dir dringen" *piano,* with a wistful restraint. Put your whole heart into the phrase—"Singen will ich, Lieder singen". Make it very clear that it is *here* that you begin to sing the songs themselves. Until now it has been your *heart* which spoke, now it is your *imagination* which is creating the songs for your beloved, because, as you say in the fifth verse, music dissolves the distance which separates you and makes your spirits one. Feeling how near your beloved seems, as you sing to her, a great joy overwhelms you: at "und ein liebend Herz erreichet" your tempo quickens. With the beginning of the songs be different: the lover who gazed into the distance with melancholy longing, has now changed into the creative artist. Inspiration is now the source of your singing, it is no longer a matter of morbid and passive longing.

Begin the first song—"Wo die Berge so blau", lightly, *un poco allegretto*—the voice must have the quality of soaring. The distance which at first seemed grey and sombre, because it separated you from your beloved, now becomes light and filled with radiance. Beyond is sunlight and the fog seems but a veil from out of which rise the blue mountains . . . After the first "möchte ich sein" which should be sung quite lightly, you pause for a moment in your thoughts: deep in your heart burns your longing—and those words have again awakened the realization of your loneliness. With great emotion, hesitantly, almost tremblingly you repeat: "möchte ich sein" . . . Now it is as if you listen to the lovely melody which is floating through your creative mind —almost mechanically verses rush through your thoughts—but the musical line is stronger, becoming "song"—and the words are only like a whispering sigh. Sing very *pianissimo* the phrases—"dort im ruhigen Tal" and let "möchte ich sein" almost fade away—in a sigh of longing. But then pull yourself together, you don't want to be lost again in melancholy, you want to send the flowers of your thoughts to your beloved. So you continue to compose. Twice—caught by the significance of your words—you pause. First at "innere Pein". Notice the *sforzato* before the repetition: it is as if something grips your heart, sing "innere Pein" with passionate feeling.

The second pause is at "ewiglich sein". This should be sung as a climax with breadth and longing.

The next song is filled with joy and should have a floating quality. You have made up your mind: these should be lovely and light, unburdened songs. They should make her happy, make her smile. Your impatient, glowing heart must be quieted. So begin with a lightly colored voice. Notice carefully where you must sing a light almost *staccato* melody and where the *staccato* changes into a soft *legato*. Realize that you want and intend to be light and unburdened and without any sentimentality, but again and again your imagination is overwhelmed by the words or the music, as they bring the image of your beloved before you so vividly, that you cannot restrain your feeling. Always color your voice more darkly in the *legato* phrases. For instance: "Seht ihr Wolken sie dann gehen sinnend" is *staccato*. But now in your imagination you see her walking there and the next phrase, full of emotion and longing, changes from *staccato* to a warm *legato*: "in dem stillen Tal, lasst mein Bild vor ihr entstehen"—then you pull yourself together and are again light and *staccato* in—"in dem luft'gen Himmelssaal". This changing interplay continues through the whole song. The *staccati* should not be exaggerated, sing them lightly and without any hardness.

At the end of the last verse: "Meine Tränen ohne Zahl"—lift your gaze toward the sky—there in the deep blue of the heavens, the wind-swept clouds, the flying birds, you find inspiration for your wreath of songs. It is as if the fresh wind has lifted from you clouds of melancholy—you feel refreshed, elated, filled with optimism. Sing "Diese Wolken in den Höhen" with your head thrown back, vividly and filled with enthusiasm. Your voice must have a quality which conveys courage, adventure, delight. It is as if you stand there at the top of the hill, where in the beginning you had sat, sad and discouraged . . . Now the wind blows through your hair, your eyes sparkle, your blood pulses hotly through your veins—. Now you are able to sing a lovely harmless little song about nature and the pair of swallows under your roof. Your voice should be light and playful: "Es kehret der Maien, es blühet die Au". You tell, how everyone who loves, will find a companion in May, just as the happy swallows do. The natural climax of the song would be to end it with the blissful thought: "and so we shall be united". . . But you cannot say this. You realize that the song must end with disharmony: Everyone else is united, only I am caught here while my beloved is far away! Darkness overshadows you again. Slowly you sink back and tears pour down your cheeks. Sing with a long *ritardando*: "und Tränen sind all' ihr Gewinnen".

In creating these songs you have unburdened your heart. You are not happy but you are less miserable than you were. You feel sure that your beloved will be delighted to receive these songs which were inspired by your longing for her and this thought gives you satisfaction.

The frame closes around your songs. Now it is again your heart which speaks: sitting on the hilltop in the glow of evening, a feeling of peace pervades you. Sing with a quiet dignity: "Nimm sie hin denn, diese Lieder". Your voice is rich and warm. Give it a quality which may convey the loveliness of this scene: "Wenn das Dämmerungsrot dann ziehet"—. Feel the beauty of these words and the incredible beauty of the musical line. Spin out the *ritardando* in a soft *pianissimo* to—"Bergeshöh". The words "und du singst" should be in broad *adagio*, filled with a glowing delight. You picture your beloved in all her loveliness singing the songs which you have written for her—this is an overwhelming thought! Continue very simply and spin out the *cres-*

cendo: "nur der Sehnsucht sich bewusst" with *ritenuto* up to a *subito piano* at "bewusst".

The following melody is until the end like a joyful hymn of re-union. You cannot be together in reality, but you are united in soul and in spirit. Sing this whole verse exultantly and feel the victorious delight which the music expresses until the very end. The *diminuendo* in the postlude is like a smiling greeting, like caressing, happy thoughts.

DIE WINTERREISE

Wilhelm Müller   *Franz Schubert*

This cycle is certainly one of the most beautiful which has ever been written. Its origin has been so well described by Newman Flower, that I quote him directly:* "Müller was brilliant in the tone painting of his words. He had a rare sense of humanity. He set down with the most natural ease the atmosphere of a life. 'I can neither play nor sing,' he wrote. 'But when I compose my poem I sing all the same and play as well. If I could express the tunes that come to me, my songs would please better than they do now. But, patience. There may be found a sympathetically tuned soul, which will discover the tunes in the words, and give them back to me.'

"Unknowingly he found that soul in Schubert. The last twelve songs in the Winterreise cycle show the gloom gathering about him, the infinite sadness which, with the end of all endeavor approaching, had taken its hold on Schubert at the time he composed them. Müller died in September, 1827; Schubert was to set his last songs and pass on little more than a year later. The last Winterreise songs are an epic in sadness, the blending of two moods of beauty—both in verse and in music—overshadowed by death."

This cycle begins with the last phase of an unhappy experience of love. The lover has come to realize the worthlessness of his beloved and knows at last that the love which was the greatest experience of his life, has been squandered on one who was incapable of appreciating the unique gift of true love and faith. The girl had playfully accepted her lover's pledge and then without any compunction had broken his heart. He struggles to escape from his devotion to her. He tries to leave the surroundings where he has been so deeply wounded and be-trayed. This cycle—through twenty four songs— leads step by step to utter dissolution.

Newman Flower: *Franz Schubert, the man and his circle,* Tudor Publishing Co.

GUTE NACHT

Imagine that you are this man who is on the verge of complete disintegration. It is a cold winter night. A clear moon brightens the snow covered world with its cold white light. You have decided to leave during the night—for if you left in daylight, you might see her, from whom you are fleeing, and perhaps if you should see her again you would weaken and would not find the strength to go. But you can no longer bear the torture of being near her. You will lose your mind if you cannot escape from her.

You pass her house. You remember desperately how full of hope and budding happiness the spring had seemed to you. Your love had seemed to bring fulfillment . . . The girl appeared to be devoted to you. Her mother had not opposed your marriage. Now the whole world has changed for you.

Begin the song with great bitterness. In the first lines you should convey the personality of this lonely and desperate man. Your voice, your words, are filled with scorn as you sing—"Das Mädchen sprach von Liebe, die Mutter gar von Eh'. . ." Change to an expression of grief with "Nun ist die Welt so trübe."

The third verse has a slightly quickened tempo. "Lass' irre Hunde heulen" should be sung with a kind of desperate contempt. "Die Liebe liebt das Wandern" should convey suppressed scorn. Sing it *piano* and emphasize the consonants sharply. Give a very slight *crescendo* to: "Von Einem zu dem Ander'n, Gott hat sie so gemacht". Perhaps in one of the sad quarrels which were the prelude to the end of all your happiness she has said to you—"What do you expect? I cannot love you forever. God made life that way, you cannot blame me..." and now again you recall her flippant answer to your pleading. (The interludes between verses should always be considered as if you were singing them yourself. Your facial expression must reflect the music as if it were floating from your whole being. The listener must have the impression that the cycle is just being created at this moment—that it is *you* who write the poems, *you* who compose the music . . . Re-creation means: created anew . . .)

Your face should have a soft expression of deep sorrow as you begin the last verse. Prepare for it. Look downward during the interlude and then when the key changes slowly raise your head gazing before you. Imagine that you are passing her home, that you are passing the window behind which she is sleeping, oblivious to your grief and misery . . . You walk softly lest you disturb her carefree slumber . . . This last verse can quite rightly and effectively be sung with deep bitterness but I always sing it with the utmost tenderness, delicacy and subtlety. There is here so much opportunity for outbursts of bitterness and desperation that from the standpoint of building up the cycle I think it is better to sing this verse very *piano*. It is as if you don't want to touch the wound in your heart by speaking roughly to your beloved even in your thoughts . . . Sing "sacht, sacht die Türe zu . . ." with a breathy *piano*. End with an expression of infinite pain: "an dich hab' ich gedacht"—especially in the repetition—as if you were saying: "you cannot know how I thought of you—leaving you . . . You don't care. You only think of me with indifference. But my thoughts are so tender, they float through your window to lie like roses at your feet . . . But you do not care . . ."

DIE WETTERFAHNE

You have left the house of your beloved. You have left her village. But you have no thought of where you are going or what you want to do. You want only to forget, but there is no road which leads to oblivion and peace. One who is possessed will always try to escape from that which possesses him. But it is in vain that you try to escape, for you are possessed by love and this love will not set you free. It holds you bound relentlessly to the one place . . .

A grey and stormy morning finds you again at the very spot which you are seeking to avoid . . . Staring at her house with burning eyes, you subconsciously follow the weather vane as it veers about in the wind.

In the prelude is the violence of the wind, but the violence of your own thoughts is also there. You have lived through so much agony—your thoughts are confused. It seems as if the vane—rattling and squeaking in its mad whirling,—scorns you, scorns the innocent belief which you had in your beloved . . .

Begin this song with an expression of deep bitterness, of driving force. Avoid sliding,—every note, every syllable must be clear cut and devoid of any weakness or sentimentality. Sing strongly until "Ein treues Frauenbild". Then change to *piano*—as if you were telling a secret—"Oh how terrible it is that our hearts can be so weak as to become the victims of changing moods and whims! They flutter as if the wind were tossing them about, but secretly . . . softly . . . "

You do not blame your beloved for leaving you to marry another man. You only blame her parents. It makes it easier to think that it was they who forced her to give you up . . . You blame their fickle hearts which are like toys in the cruel wind. Sing "was fragen sie" with *crescendo* until you end in a desperate *forte* with "eine reiche Braut". The repetition is sung in the same way. Your facial expression should reflect the violence and desperate hopelessness which engulfs you so completely.

GEFROR'NE TRÄNEN

Wandering without any goal along the icy streets and snowswept roads, you feel the tears upon your cheeks, frozen by the icy wind. The first *staccato* chords of the prelude are like heavy, weary, staggering steps, while the *decrescendo* (softly *ritenuto*) is the wakening awareness of reality.

Tears which you weep, without realizing it, become the conscious expression of your inner pain. Sing the beginning very *legato* and without expression, sing from out of utter emptiness, from a feeling of inner cold, as if your deep pain is submerged beneath the frozen crust of complete hopelessness.

In the short interlude after "dass ich geweinet hab" your icy numbness changes. Bitterness wells within you . . . Sing with suppressed passion, with mounting dramatic expression until the end—"des ganzen Winter's Eis" which should be sung broadly. In the postlude you sink again into yourself, wandering on, lonely, without any goal.

ERSTARRUNG

Your wandering has changed into flight. Flight from this terrible emptiness, flight from the aimlessness which yet drives you on. You have been shaken out of your lethargy by the cold wind which blows over the frozen fields. With the quickened tempo of the prelude, you must give the impression of being driven on. A slight bending forward may be helpful in giving this impression but the principal thing is and will always be: FEEL that you are driven on, FEEL the cold wind. If you can do this, your expression will be convincing. I must always repeat: *only that is convincing which is truly felt.*

The two phrases—"ich such' im Schnee vergebens nach ihrer Tritte Spur, wo sie an meinem Arme durchstrich die grüne Flur" should be sung *legato*. Your remembrance of that happy time is here stronger than any thought of the present. Sing these phrases touched by the soft glow of reminiscence, but at the same time with animation as if you were increasing your pace. Imagine that your steps take on increasing vigor as you hurry on, while your eyes searching mechanically, sweep over the broad expanse of white snow. But your feeling is pervaded by the glow of memory: "wo sie an meinem Arme durchstrich die grüne Flur." So your singing here must be soft and *legato*.

In the next verse you return to reality, to passionate desire, desperate grief. Sing it with dramatic fire. Note the two *crescendi* at—"bis ich die Erde, die Erde seh". Feel the passionate restraint in this. There is brooding insanity in this bitterly glowing restraint.

In the next verse go back to the sweet *pianissimo* of remembrance, a *pianissimo* which is, so to speak, moist with tears. Note the *sforzati* at "Blumen" and "erstorben", but sing them discretely. Feel the colorless emptiness in the word "blass". Paint it with the consonants and with a very light *"a"* as if you were using water colors. Sing *ritenuto* to the end of the verse.

The *crescendo* and *forte* is the transition to the more passionate expression of the next verses. "Wenn meine Schmerzen schweigen, wer sagt mir dann von ihr?" Your grief for your lost beloved is now almost a joy, since it gives you a feeling of contact with her . . . Your heart seems dead but perhaps it may yet melt like the frozen brook, and the vision of your beloved which it holds may be borne away on the flowing water . . . Feel the self torturing pain in these words, this poetic picture, this stormy melody.

At the end the song fades into *decrescendo* and *ritardando* as if you yourself are breaking down under the tormenting power of your imagination. Convey the impression of complete exhaustion. Don't forget the little *crescendo* and *decrescendo* at the last "dahin".

DER LINDENBAUM

You seem to be going around in a circle. You try to get far away but the vicinity in which your beloved lives draws you back like a magnet—with the result that you seem only to wander around and around. So you find yourself back again at the old gate where you have so often sat in the shade of the old Linden tree.

In the midst of your restless wandering you pause as you suddenly find yourself beside the well under the old tree. You have forgotten all about the winter and its cold. You have forgotten your grief. A quiet peace pervades you, as if at last you are at home. The first verse should be sung with the greatest of simplicity, with warmth, very *legato*.

Begin the second verse a little more excitedly. At "vorbei in tiefer Nacht" darkness again pervades you. Your need to continue in your wandering is like a sombre compulsion. Sing this sentence with this thought. Yet the Linden tree holds you back. It holds you with a mysterious strength. Sing "Da hab' ich noch im Dunkel die Augen zugemacht" *pianissimo* with an expression of surrender... Now the branches speak to you through their rustling: sing this, full voice, as if the wind were swelling through the treetop. Sing "komm' her zu mir Geselle" entreatingly. But no: you tear yourself away from your dreams, you will not listen to the tree as it calls you back . . . Sing with dramatic force, deeply moved: "die kalten Winde", etc. Bring to a highly dramatic climax the last sentence: "ich wendete mich nicht". Make use of the consonants and sing with sharp accentuation, thrusting out the "nicht" as if you were tearing yourself loose from hands which seek to hold you back. You must give the impression that you are tearing yourself away, never more, no, never more to return again.

But the compelling song of the tree is more powerful than your decision. It comes to you in your dreams. Sing the last verse with a quieter melancholy and give the last words: "du fändest Ruhe dort" an alluring *pianissimo*, full of mystery.

WASSERFLUT

The important thing here is to be able to bring to life passionate feeling within the framework of a very austere melody. The rhythm must never be broken. The vital connection with the musical phrase can never be sundered. The more rhythmically you sing, the more you will succeed in bringing out the austere character of the song . . . Sing very quietly and make a glowing *crescendo* at: "durstig ein das heisse Weh". Accentuate the consonants sharply and stress the triplets. Sing "Wenn die Gräser sprossen wollen" very tenderly. Sing "weht daher ein lauer Wind" with a broad sweep. Your phrasing must be floating like a breath of wind.

To give too many details or too much advice for this song might lead to destroying the greatness of line. The interpretation here really needs no explanation.

AUF DEM FLUSSE

The beginning of this song is pervaded by an icy clarity. The prelude conveys the impression of heart beats throbbing beneath the ice.

Sing the first verse as if you are lost in quiet contemplation, without much expression. It must be sung with exact rhythm and strict attention to the value of every note.

In the second verse "In deine Decke grab' ich" your emotion overflows. Your facial expression is one of dreaming, your voice should be filled with deep warmth. At the end of the verse: "windet sich ein zerbroch'ner Ring" you are overcome by grief. (Emphasize the consonants in "zerbroch'ner"!) The throbbing heart beneath the ice seems like your own heart—life flowing beneath a crust of numbness—flooding passion which threatens to burst through the icy surface. Sing the four repetitions of "ob's wohl auch so reissend schwillt" each time with increased drama—with a swelling *crescendo*. End with vigorous force.

RÜCKBLICK

Again you are in flight, again you are trying to escape. Your wandering has led you back to the very place which you have wanted to avoid. You are drawn back irresistibly, but again you tear yourself away. You have hurried on through the old familiar streets. Everywhere you feel that you are scorned.

The prelude gives the feeling of storm and senseless racing ahead. Begin with a suppressed but passionate *piano* and at each "Eis und Schnee" and "die Türme seh" sing a surging and stormy *crescendo*. Note the *sforzati* at "Krähe" and "Bäll'." Sing this verse distinctly, almost *parlando,* and close with a *legato* at the last "jedem Haus" which leads over into the more measured tempo of the second verse. Reflect in your voice the change of key, sing with a softly flowing *legato*, in a lovely warm *piano*. Paint with both word and tone: the little town, the feeling of spring, the murmuring brook, the Linden tree . . . Sing the phrase: "da war's gescheh'n um dich Gesell" with a strongly exhaled *pianissimo* as if beneath tears of remembrance of all the loveliness which you have lost.

Again the key changes and with it your voice quality. Again restlessness seizes you. Each time, from out of suppressed misery, rises the *crescendo* which leads into a *forte*: "noch einmal rückwärts seh'n" and "ihrem Hause stille steh'n". In the repetitions both voice and tempo quiet down: sing *legato* and with a yearning expression. Don't exaggerate the repeated *sforzati* (zurücke, wanken)—sing them discretely.

The last "vor ihrem Hause stille steh'n" fades away in a veiled *piano* strictly in *tempo*.

IRRLICHT

This song is like a short dramatic scene. Sing it as such. Give this song a very individual character. Color your voice more darkly and sing with an heroic expression. Give the song a broad, strong swing as you would an aria. Begin very quietly with strong accentuation. Sing with exact rhythm, give each note its exact value. "Jedes Leiden auch sein Grab" should be sung with great warmth of feeling.

You know that your end is not far distant and with it the end of all your grief.

RAST

Your staggering steps (heard in the prelude) have lead you to a place where you may rest.

You must convey the picture of the tired wanderer who with complete indifference, feels himself driven on by the raging storm, wandering wherever the wind may drive him . . . Sing the *pianissimo* in "der Rücken fühlte keine Last" with a kind of bitter pleasure, but in the next phrase: "der Sturm half fort mich wehen" make one feel the power of the storm. This is not a power which comes from you, yourself. It is a power which is aiding you, which you must express. So be careful here: the feeling of your inner exhaustion must not be lost through the *forte* of this phrase. (Perhaps I may make this clearer by saying—the first sentence is like a deep inhaled breath—*piano;* the second like a released exhaled breath.)

Begin the second verse very quietly. Enunciate the consonants in "So brennen meine Wunden" sharply. Notice the sudden *piano* after the *crescendo*: your wound is so painful it even hurts you to mention it . . .

"Auch du, mein Herz" is filled with bitterness, as if you were saying scoffingly: "generally you are so courageous . . . But now in the quiet of repose you feel within you the gnawing worm which will consume you." Sing these lines very distinctly, with a brightly colored quality, making the consonants pointed and sharp. Close with a broad and dramatic *forte*.

FRÜHLINGSTRAUM

You are lying in the house of a collier where you have found shelter. You simply cannot wander any further, you must be patient and gather some strength. You are alone, you awaken out of the half sleep of deep exhaustion. The prelude conveys the dreams which fleet so entrancingly through your half waking thoughts.

The first verse should be sung with a quietly floating quality, as if you were still under the spell of your lovely dream. Then with your awakening comes grey reality: it is dark and cold and ravens circle ominously about the roof . . .

You must feel within yourself this awakening to a barren and sombre reality. Sing with force and with a feeling of deep pain. But you are sick and exhausted, you do not have sufficient strength to face reality, so you sink back, forgetting your gloomy surroundings and your eyes are caught by the weirdly formed and incredibly beautiful flowers frosted upon the window pane . . . Sing this whole verse *pianissimo* and *legato*. And so, with a tone carried upon your breath and with a fading smile, you sink again into your dream.

Sing the verse: "Ich träumte von Lieb' und Liebe" as you did the first one, with animation.

After your first dream you awakened to the sombre reality of the *outer* world. But now your heart awakens to the reality of your *inner* loneliness. You are so bitterly alone . . . You think of your dream which can never become reality . . . But so long as one may still breathe, so long will burn within one a spark of hope, however unfounded it may be. The last verse is to be sung with a feeling of the deepest depression, yet a warm surge of hopefulness floods through you at the words: "noch schlägt das Herz mir warm".

A melancholy self derision flows through "wann grünt ihr Blätter am Fenster?" The last sentence should be sung as a sigh which gradually fades away. You are again half sleeping, half dreaming.

EINSAMKEIT

You have pulled yourself up from your utter exhaustion and have wandered on, but you are oh! so wretched and weary. There is within you only a complete emptiness, a quiet which is not peace, a resignation which is only the result of your exhaustion and in no sense recovery . . .

The first verse should be sung without expression to "und ohne Gruss". With the following *crescendo* you straighten up, the force of your grief returns to you and even if it is only with the vigor of complaint—nevertheless your heart glows again.

DIE POST

The foolish heart will always hope, even when it knows that any hope is futile. So when the mail coach is arriving, you listen even though it isn't reasonable to do so.

The rhythm of the horses hoofs, the gay call of the post horn have awakened you from your sad dreams. Quite against your will, you go to the window, asking yourself—"What is the matter with my heart, why should it beat so violently?" Accent "hat" in "was hat es" and sing the repetition with a sudden *piano*. (Accent "hat" here also.) The mute bar before the next phrase is your own sad realization that it is very foolish of you to expect a letter. Now you sing subduedly and with resignation—"Die Post bringt keinen Brief für dich". Give a slight *crescendo* to "was drängst du denn so wunderlich" and play with the consonants in "drängst". There must be a delicate charm in the repetitions of "Mein Herz, mein Herz?" Imagine that your heart is like a bird which is eager to spread its wings. There must be a soaring and a sweeping quality in your voice and it should have a very slight vibration. Then the repetition of "Die Post bringt keinen Brief für dich" has more inner strength, and you sing it with a mounting *crescendo*.

During the interlude you listen to the posthorn and at the same time you listen to your heart. You understand this restless beating, you understand the never ceasing voice of your memories. Sing "nun ja, die Post kommt aus der Stadt" softly and give a *crescendo* of desperate remembrance to "wo ich ein liebes Liebchen hatt'. . . ." There is again a mute bar. Here it is your question to yourself—"but why am I so foolish? I know there is nothing for me to expect and yet I feel this burning longing. Oh I know, I understand: the coach comes from her town, perhaps they know how she is . . . Perhaps they know of what she is thinking . . . Oh my heart, my heart—don't fly away like a bird. Be still, my heart". End the song stormily and with a broad *forte*. Breathe very shortly and quickly before the last "mein Herz" and sing it as if it were a challenging call.

DER GREISE KOPF

This song, like "Irrlicht" is to be sung as a dramatic scene. Begin it with grandeur—in a broad line, and enunciate clearly. There is a sharply accentuated *crescendo* at "dass mir's vor meiner Jugend graut." (Be very careful to give the exact value to each note!) Make a *sforzato* at "graut".

The next phrase—"wie weit noch bis zur Bahre" should be like a soft, long drawn sigh.

Begin the second verse in the same way as the first, broadly and with grandeur, but sing it more softly, as if you were thinking while you are singing—"can this really be possible? How can this happen to others but not to me?" End the song with intense feeling. Accentuate sharply each syllable and consonant.

DIE KRÄHE

Imagine this situation: for a long time a black raven has been circling about you. It has seemed like an evil and sombre shadow about your head. Feel the weird atmosphere of uncanniness which surrounds you and pervades your being . . .

Sing the first verse as if you were inwardly benumbed, without any feeling. Your steadily flowing voice is filled with bitterness: "Meinst wohl, bald als Beute hier."

Exhausted, resigned, surrendering, you sing "nun es wird nicht weit mehr geh'n" and your bitter despair over the ruining of your life bursts out in the final sentence: "Treue bis zum Grabe".

The greater the restraint with which the beginning of this song is sung, the more effective will be the wild outbreak at the end.

LETZTE HOFFNUNG

The *staccati* which begin in the prelude and continue to the end of this song are leaves falling in the autumn wind.

Do not sing *staccato*. Sing steadily as if with held breath. There is a light *ritenuto* at "oftmals in Gedanken steh'n".

The restrained anxiety with which you look up at the leaf, as if your fate would be determined by whether it stayed or blew away, has in it a trace of insanity. So you should sing with a rather unnatural stiffness. Notice the *crescendo* and *decrescendo* at "Ach und fällt das Blatt zu Boden". Don't sing this *too* forcefully. It should be a kind of tone painting—a falling leaf blown about by the wind. This phrase must lead over into the insane whisper of "fällt mit ihm die Hoffnung ab". "Fall' ich selber mit zu Boden", should be sung with great force (although the musical notations are the same as in the previous phrase) as if you are really breaking down. Then change your timbre and sing with deep emotion with a full dark tone: "wein', wein' auf meiner Hoffnung Grab."

These last phrases should have a broad sweeping grandeur and should pour out like cello tones.

IM DORFE

Your restless wandering has led you to a sleeping town. The dogs bark, chains rattle. Unrest, beginning in the prelude, runs through the whole song up to "ist alles zerflossen." Sing this with a slight scorn as if you were comforting yourself by saying: "These people live in harmony together and share all that is good or bad. It is only I who am lonely and alone . . . But everything is transitory even joy and sorrow—why should I envy them?" And yet your heart beats, warning you secretly. Certainly there is nothing which is not transitory, but these people whom you do not know, have enjoyed what was denied you. And they will always find again their dreams of happiness—and hope, and hope . . . Sing these phrases with an expression of longing, giving your voice a bright and silvery quality. You are playing here with the dreams which other people experience and long for, you are singing of something floating and intangible. Give the words a light floating quality. With the passing of your dreams, reality again overshadows you. You are driven away by the barking of the dogs who, mistrusting the unknown wanderer, surround you.

Sing with great bitterness and with a broad line, until the end. One must have the impression that you turn away, slowly wandering on, engulfed by the darkness of the night.

DER STÜRMISCHE MORGEN

Dawn, red like fire, has broken through the windswept clouds. The cold wind has aroused you. Once again you feel the will to fight. You would like to fight against yourself, against your own weakness, your own self destruction . . .

The short prelude gives the setting for your stormy beginning.

Plunge, so to speak, into this very stirring melody, singing with vigorous accents. Your whole being is filled with animation, your eyes sparkle, you stand erect and defiant. You see your own heart in the image of the world ravaged by storm, it is cold and numb like winter itself. But at this moment it doesn't make you sad. As in exultant madness, you feel yourself one with the uproar of nature. These strange rather touching alternations between deepest depression and a surging will to live hold nothing surprising to the psychologist: on the contrary it is a well recognized symptom of mental illness.

The following song "Täuschung" is the bridge which leads back from this state of inner exhilaration to the sombre urge toward self destruction.

TÄUSCHUNG

The friendly, dancelike melody of the accompaniment is the confusing shimmer of the Will o' the Wisp, which you are pursuing. Sing with an expression of mystery, as if you are under the spell of a power which you must obey. When you sing: "und seh's ihm an, dass es verlockt den Wandersmann" make it obvious through your facial expression that you are *consciously* following the Will o' the Wisp. (It will help if you open your eyes wide, then half close them and sing with a light irony,—as if you were saying: I know you, don't think for a moment that I don't know that you are deceiving me.)

"Ach! wer wie ich so elend ist" is an outburst of deep pain. Sing this with a darkly colored timbre and then go over into a *piano* of re-

strained anguish. Emerging from the *pianissimo* you proceed broadly
and heavily with "die hinter Eis und Nacht und Graus". Now you are
again in your dream, the doors of a warm house seem to open before
you and you find the soul of your beloved. Sing these phrases softly as
though you were dreaming, then suddenly you find reality again and
sing with bitterness—"nur Täuschung ist für mich Gewinn."

The melody of the Will o' the Wisp returns in the short postlude.
Aware of what you are doing and so without any hope, you again follow it.

DER WEGWEISER

You have wandered here and there over the ice covered countryside, but no others ever travelled along your road . . . You stand at
a crossroads beside a signpost. With a tired glance, you look up at it
and considering which road you would choose, you realize that you
never choose the broad roads which others take, the roads which lead
toward cities . . .

The prelude conveys your thoughts, your realizations, your intro-
spections. The beginning of this song should be sung with a quiet
thoughtful expression. The repetition "durch verschneite Felsenhöh'n",
to the end of the first verse is sharply accentuated. The turbulent soaring of the music suggests the recollection of your conflicts and the dangerous and threatening icy road. But your thoughts only turn there for
a moment, immediately they swing back to yourself. The great
"warum" ("why") faces you and you raise your head singing with a
very light, *pianissimo,* floating tone and in an almost childlike way:
"habe ja doch nichts begangen". Note the *sforzati* at "törichtes" and
"in". The "in" however, should not be singled out, "Wüsteneien" is
the important word in this phrase. Bring together the force of the
music and the meaning of the sentence. Give a *sforzato* to each syllable.
But you must do this very subtly. It seems almost dangerous to suggest
this, for anything which is dependent upon the subtlest and most delicate feeling is very difficult to explain . . .

Begin the second verse in the same way as you did the first, lost in revery. At "und ich wandre sonder Massen" you are overcome by restlessness. This should be sung *crescendo* with driving emotion. After the
last "suche Ruh'" open your eyes wide for here you realize that there is
only one thing which can bring you rest and peace: Death! Sing with
a whispered *piano,* your glance fixed rigidly upon some distant point—
"Einen Weiser seh' ich stehen unverrückt vor meinem Blick" then go
over into a great *crescendo* with "eine Strasse muss ich gehen . . ." as
this realization closes upon you—inescapably. In the repetition the
crescendo does not again reach a *forte* climax.

The song ends with a feeling of quiet surrender. Hold the last "zurück" as long as possible, letting it fade away gradually.

DAS WIRTSHAUS

In the prelude, your wandering steps halt before a gate. Looking up you realize that your way has led you to the entrance of a cemetery. With a gesture of finality you open the gate.

Whenever I hear this beautiful music, I see before me a little woodland cemetery in a German village, to which I used to go every year in days long gone by, to visit a cherished grave. Over the gate of this sanctuary, long forgotten by the world about it, was written in simple black letters on old and weather beaten wood—"Here dwells the peace which the world does not give."

It is with this feeling that you must now (in your imagination) enter the cemetery.

Sing with great earnestness and a feeling of deep solemnity from the beginning to "in's kühle Wirtshaus ein". Be careful to avoid any inexactness here, do not make any *portamenti,* don't "scoop". The more purely, the more clearly and the less sentimentally you sing here, the nearer will you approach the ideal. This music is too uplifted, too heavenly beautiful, to be reproduced without the utmost reverence.

Bring out as much as is possible without exaggeration, the *ü* in "müde Wanderer" and "kühle Wirtshaus". Feel the painting of tone in these words.

The next sentence—"Sind denn in diesem Hause" should be sung with a veiled *pianissimo.* "Bin matt zum Niedersinken" is like a sigh. Lift out the word "matt"—but do it without any force. You can, if you do it with the greatest care, make an almost unnoticeable *portamento* at "zum Niedersinken"—but I am almost afraid to mention this, it is such dangerous advice: for it can only be done with the very acme of subtlety! "Bin tötlich schwer verletzt" is hardly more than breathed, it must be very restrained, sung, so to speak, with a fading heart beat.

In the short interlude your eyes become alive, a shadow crosses your face. Color your voice darkly. You tremble with pain: "du unbarmherz'ge Schenke, doch weisest du mich ab?" and the next sentence "Nun weiter denn..." is to be sung with the deepest resignation. Your voice becomes empty, light, colorless. The next "nur weiter" should have a delicate *crescendo* but one lacking in any force, as if with a sigh of despondent resignation. The last bar is *ritardando.* Sound each syllable distinctly giving the impression of tired feet which wander on.

In the postlude you turn away and again wander on, purposeless, without any goal.

Once again you pull yourself together, once again you find the power of defiance. Life has closed for you the door to happiness. Death has refused you. What can be left for you? Yet once again your heart quickens, rebellious, ready to fight . . .

Your bearing should express the change which has come over you: you stand very erect, as if you were facing the fate which has so sense-lessly destroyed you . . .

From the very beginning of this song a great differentiation must be made: you cannot sing "wenn mein Herz im Busen spricht" with the same force of tone and certainly not with the same expression with which you sing "sing' ich hell und munter". Your heart speaks to you in sombre tones, secretly, whispering. So you must sing *piano,* with a sorrowful expression. Then sing "sing' ich hell und munter" *forte.*

The same applies to the next phrases: "Höre nicht, was es mir sagt" is secret, with suppressed fear, *piano.* "Habe keine Ohren" is loud, ac-centuated, shrill. The following two phrases are again to be done in the same way.

The last verse is strongly rhythmical, loud, bold, challenging. It is as if one who is afraid of himself, whistles or sings loudly in order to drown his fear.

DIE NEBENSONNEN

But this moment of surging energy was only a deceptive one . . . Now you have sunken into further depths of melancholy. You can no longer struggle with either the world or yourself . . . Your thoughts seem befogged. Soon you will be lost in darkness and consumed by a horror which is worse than death . . .

I have often been asked what is meant by the three suns. This is a matter of opinion of which there are several. One might say: it is a foggy evening and the setting sun penetrating through the fog in a strange mirage, gives the illusion of three suns.

A great musician has the conviction, which sounds convincing, that by these three suns is meant: faith, hope and love. Faith in the beloved, in any kindly fate, has passed. Hope is dead. Only love remains and will not die. If only it would also die . . . Only in a complete inner emptiness can lie release! Much as I value this wonderful interpreta-tion, I cannot entirely accept it for my own. Why should we search for a logical explanation? The man who wanders so tragically through this cycle until spiritual dissolution engulfs him, thinks and feels with the soul of one who is ill. It doesn't seem strange to me that he sees before him the illusion of three suns . . . If you create the inner vision of three suns in your feeling, they are there *for you*—and with you—for your audience . . .

The restrained prelude is your glance as it falls upon something strange and wonderful: from out of your sombre thoughts you see the shimmering suns. Sing this simple flowing melody in a mysterious, floating, light *piano*. Be rigid, as if you were staring at something, be restrained as if under the enchantment of some spell. You must prepare in this song for the last song, which follows it. Disintegration through self destruction is your horrible fate. Prepare for this. This is the only way in which I can explain it: sing "Die Nebensonnen" *uncannily*. Your audience must experience the same cold shiver which you feel. The *forte* which develops with a *crescendo,* is very difficult to sing. ("Und sie auch standen da so stier")

The three suns are there before you like a wall, tremendous, shining over you with cold splendor. Retain the same rigid, uncanny, motionless bearing (in voice, carriage, facial expression) up to "doch in's Angesicht". Now take the *crescendo* to the next phrase with your whole being: a wave of pain floods through you. You think of the two eyes of your beloved which once lighted your way . . . "Ach neulich hatt' ich auch wohl drei, nun sind hinab die besten zwei . . ."

Beside the sun in the heavens shone the eyes of your beloved, which were like suns to you, but you have lost them, in darkness they have been extinguished for you. Sing this phrase veiled in tears, repressed, softly. Your eyes which have been closed, open again in the short interlude and numbness comes back into your face.

End the song with the same lifeless expression of uncanny rigidity with which you began it.

DER LEIERMANN

In this song the greatest lack of expression is the acme of expression . . . Stand very stiffly, your expression should be one of absolute emptiness, your eyes should be half closed. Words fall from your lips in uniformly light tones, without any accents.

You have been repudiated by both life and death. Senselessly you sway along the road without either goal or purpose. Madness which has followed you along your way has spun its web about you—inescapably, impelling you to become the companion of the poor old man, who, deluded and deranged, grinds away on his organ, amidst ice and snow, without any reason, for no one.

Bursting out in suppressed derision at yourself you call to him: "Won't you turn your organ to my songs?"

With a slight *crescendo,* you stagger toward the old man, the poor old fool, at whom dogs bark and whom human beings avoid . . . Darkness has fallen upon the ice round about you. Darkness engulfs your figure. You are lost in nothingness, submerged in emptiness . . .

DIE SCHÖNE MÜLLERIN

Müller   *Schubert*

The young miller has said farewell to the master in whose mill he has been working and has once again set forth upon his way as a wandering apprentice.

I remember from my childhood these lads, who, covered with dust and often hungry and exhausted, used to pass our home which lay on the road between Hamburg and Berlin. I see these young figures vividly before me, when I picture the miller boy of this cycle, but he must have been a very unusual one. For he is shy and sensitive and there is the soul of a poet in the dreamer who loves to wander through the world, enjoying its beauties with open eyes. There is the soul of the dreamer who is destined to be wounded, for it is too sensitive, too vulnerable, too unprepared for the bitter disillusionments of life . . .

But at the beginning of the cycle, a radiant sky still shines upon his road. He strides along his way, free from care, with a gay song upon his lips.

Das Wandern

Begin with a buoyant *tempo* as if you were wandering along briskly and were enjoying looking around you. You sing of the things which most concern you: of your world, which is the long country road stretching out before you, white and shimmering: the gaily chattering brook, whirring windmills, grinding mill stones. In each verse you should picture differently the things which you describe as you wander along, singing happily. Give your voice a light, mysterious quality as you speak of water, for the murmuring brook has always had a rather strange attraction for you, sing gaily and with a quickened *tempo* of the tirelessly turning wheels and with a whimsical clumsiness of the dancing, ponderous stones. In the last verse your recurrent farewell to the master and the mistress is without any sadness, even free of any regret. You are just a young apprentice, you work where you find a mill and go along your way singing happily.

WOHIN

You wander through forests and meadows and over wooded hills, wherever your path may lead you. Somewhere, sometime, you know you will come upon a mill and find work and good friends. So you wander on confidently,—filled with the joy of living. But suddenly your footsteps halt: you hear the murmur of a brook—and there, before you, you see a fresh mountain spring gushing out between the stones. Splashing gaily, it dashes down the hillside toward the valley. With your eyes you follow the silver shimmer of its falling waters. It is so lovely here on the crest of the mountains and you feel so fresh and free. The wind plays through your blonde hair and cools your moist brow. But the brook seems to lure you, strangely,—its rippling murmur seems to say: "follow me!"

Begin this song as if you were listening to something which is far away. You should have an expression of excited concentration as if it is something strange which you hear. Sing "ich weiss nicht, wie mir wurde" in a restrained *piano,* as if with amazement. "Hinunter und immer weiter" should be slightly *accelerando* as if driven by a power which you must obey. (One must immediately sense in this song the peculiar connection between you and the brook which becomes your friend and companion, your counsellor and finally your grave.)

The brook becomes wider, its rippling more distinct—and you follow its course, led on as if under its spell. Sing "ist das denn meine Strasse?" as if you are confused, ask this as a confused child would,—with uncertainty and amazement. But sing "du hast mit deinem Rauschen mir ganz berauscht den Sinn" joyfully and carefreely. Your romantic imagination enjoys this strange feeling of being led away from your path. The flow of your romantic imagination sweeps on: it must be water sprites, lovely alluring water sprites who sing their seductive songs to you . . . Sing this lightly, with a feeling of mystery but smiling as if in play, your thoughts take the form of verses. You wander happily along the brook, knowing that sometime, somewhere, it will lead you to a mill . . . Let the end of the song fade away, as if the wandering figure of the young miller merges with the blue distance.

HALT

Take up immediately, in a happy mood, the lively tempo of the prelude: you see before you a wonderful mill, and after the freedom of your wandering the thought of working appeals to you again. Begin with joyful exitement: "Eine Mühle seh' ich blinken" and sing— "bricht Rädergebraus" with a surging *crescendo* like a billowing wave. "Ei willkommen, süsser Mühlengesang!" is a warm greeting—sing it vivaciously, with radiant happiness. Seeing the freshly painted house, with its windows flashing in the sunlight, you take it to your heart. Sing with overflowing joy. And gratefully you think of the stream, whose seductive murmur has led you here. Sing with delicacy and with a smile "Ei Bächlein, liebes Bächlein, war es also gemeint?"

DANKSAGUNG AN DEN BACH

Now you have found your mill, you have work which you enjoy, and a place in this lovely house in which you feel at home. For all this you have your brook to thank, which led you away from your intended path . . . But it seems, you have still more to be grateful for: the miller has a lovely daughter . . . And you have fallen very much in love with her . . .

Begin with great warmth but nevertheless with an expression of delighted roguishness: "war es also gemeint, mein rauschender Freund?" "Gelt, hab' ich's verstanden" should be sung as if you share a secret with the brook. Let the word "gelt" stand alone, making a short pause after this word so that it stands as if separated from the question. "Hat sie dich geschickt oder hast mich berückt?" should be sung very softly and shyly. Your poetic imagination would so gladly let you believe, that it was the wish of the lovely miller maid which sang to you from out of the rippling of the brook. But you know that it can't be so . . . And your acceptance of reality is smiling and filled with expectancy... Sing "Nach Arbeit ich frug, nun hab' ich genug für die Hände, für's Herze" happily and with the confidence of youth which is able to see everything around it in a rosy light . . . Make a slight pause before "Für's Herze", sing this rather whimsically and with a tender boldness and close with "Vollauf genug" as if you wanted to say: yes, it is enough, but I know that something far lovelier awaits me . . .

FEIERABEND

But your impetuous heart puts an end to your ruminating contentment . . . You are young, you are healthy, you crave love and close companionship. With great zest you throw yourself into your daily work,—you want to show her, how you woo her with your whole soul, how you want to belong to her, to work for her, to spoil her and to love her . . .

Take up the *melto allegro* of the prelude, stand very erect, with flashing eyes, as if ready to struggle and determined to win. Begin with glowing impatience inpetuously and forcefully: "Hätt' ich tausend Arme zu rühren". Sing "was ich hebe, was ich trage" almost with despair, but there should be no tragedy in this. It is the despairing impatience of one in love, which to those, not concerned, has something almost amusing. Be a little quieter in tempo at "und da sitz' ich in der grossen Runde"—but don't drag the tempo. Color your voice more darkly when the master says "euer Werk hat mir gefallen", sing this with a broad ponderousness as if you want to imitate the words of the master. Then immediately color your voice more brightly at "und das

128

liebe Mädchen sagt". Sing the first "Allen eine gute Nacht" *pianissimo,* —see before you the lovely girl, how she stands at the door, smiling, delighting everyone with her friendly greeting. But the *sforzato* in the accompaniment is the piercing thought: but she says it to everyone, she is indifferent to me, for her I am only one of them—she sends me no special greeting . . . Sing the second "allen" with a pained expression. The accompaniment breaks in dramatically upon your word and you again sing with the same passionate impatience as at the beginning of this song. Sing the last "dass die schöne Müllerin" slightly *ritardando* and piano, delicately and very longingly. End with great feeling and a dreamy yearning: "merkte meinen treuen Sinn". With the two final chords of the postlude, you awaken again to the uncertainty of reality.

DER NEUGIERIGE

You are a shy boy and the love for the miller girl which has filled your heart so suddenly and so overwhelmingly has made you still more shy. You have found no friend among the other miller boys, your heart is too heavy with your love, you cannot be carefree and gay as they are. So you become lonely and strange. You have never played or danced or drunk with the others in your free time, no, you have gone your lonely way, always near the brook. To-day you are again beside it. Your heart is filled with love, with hope and shy expectation. If only you could be sure that your love has its echo in the heart of the maiden! You thought you saw a happy answer in her eyes, but perhaps you only imagined that she looked at you lovingly . . . If only you knew whom you could ask! Being too shy to ask her yourself, you long for some confirmation. But to whom could you go? Certainly not to her father or to the other boys . . . So you sit there alone, immersed in your inner loneliness.

In the prelude is your question: whom could I ask? You look hesitantly about you. Your face has a dreaming expression. Sing with a tender softness until "ich erführ' so gern". Then there comes a subtle change: you explain to yourself why neither the flowers nor the stars will give you an answer. You are not a gardener and so you cannot understand the voice of the flowers. The stars are too high above you, how could you hear their melodies? But there is always your friend, the brook. He will answer you. He spoke to you as you were wandering along your way. He brought you here, he will know . . . He will tell you if your heart is right,—your heart which tells you that she loves you . . . You listen to the short prelude—and to the silence of the mute measure—. But the brook gives no answer. Begin now with a soft reproach—*molto lento* and *piano.* Sing with a beautiful floating *legato.* The dreaming smile should never leave your face. You are so hopeful, you are almost certain that your heart does not betray you. If you were really afraid of the answer you wouldn't ask your question in such a dreamlike way. You would be more urgent and passionate.

"Ja, heisst das eine Wörtchen" is filled with happiness, but don't sing it too loudly. It should be like a soft, happy sigh. Make a slight pause before "nein" in the next phrase, as if you hesitate even to *think* that there might be a possibility of a "no". . . . The crescendo in "die beiden Wörtchen schliessen" is like a soft surging wave and subsides into a breathy *pianissimo* in "die ganze Welt mir ein" and in the repetition of it.

In the interlude you are again listening to the brook. But the waters only sing their own melody,—there is no answer to your question. Imagine that you bend down nearer to the brook as if you want to tell it a secret or are urging it to share a secret with you. ("Will's ja nicht weiter sagen . . .") Hiding your face from the outer world as you bend down over the softly murmuring brook, you dare, for the first time, to voice your inner hope, to ask the question which is burning within your heart: "sag' Bächlein, liebt sie mich?" Make a lovely climax at— "liebt" but don't sing it too loudly. Intensity of expression is here much more effective than a booming *forte* . . . The repetition of the last phrase should be sung as if you are overwhelmed by happiness. Even saying aloud that she may love you, even just saying it, makes you tremble with joy. Your expression should remain unchanged until the end of the postlude.

UNGEDULD

Your trembling, throbbing heart beats in a stormy tempo through this song. Sing with a firey impetuosity, and very distinctly. The lively animated tempo and the exact rhythm of the dotted notes continue without cessation from the beginning until the end of the song. The more rhythmically you sing, the more you will succeed in bringing out the feverish impatience of the throbbing heartbeats. In each verse from out of the surging restlessness there blooms, in a broad line and with great feeling, the confession of your devotion: "Dein ist mein Herz und soll es ewig bleiben".

(By the way, I always sing only three verses, the first, second and fourth.)

MORGENGRUSS

Shyly and humbly you approach the window of your beloved. It is a lovely warm summer morning and you long to greet her and look up toward her window. But she vanishes behind the curtains, after convincing herself with a hasty look that it is you who stand expectantly upon her threshold . . .

But the look which she threw you could not have been unfriendly, for you begin the song in a mood of happy animation. Sing whimsically and gaily: "Guten Morgen, schöne Müllerin". You don't really mean seriously the question "Verdriesst dich denn mein Gruss so schwer? Verstört dich denn mein Blick so sehr?" You sing this more in a teasing way and add roguishly "so muss ich wieder gehen".

The second verse should be sung with a tender intimacy. In the shy purity of your heart you look without any desire to your beloved: "o lass' mich nur von ferne steh'n". Sing pleadingly—"du blondes Köpfchen, komm hervor" and then very rapturously—"ihr blauen Morgensterne". I have always omitted the third verse, but if you sing it, sing it softly and dreamily.

The last verse is somewhat more lively in tempo, very fresh and soaring. End the song *piano,* softly, with a slight *ritardando*.

DES MÜLLERS BLUMEN

You bring flowers to her bedroom window and plant them where they may bloom in the light of her eyes . . . This song flows along in a lovely *moderato*—avoid throughout giving too equal emphasis to every syllable and in this way making this beautiful song monotonous. It is important that you recite the poem, so that you get the feeling of these floating phrases in speaking and so make it easier to achieve the same effect in singing them. Lift out the important word in each phrase with a discrete emphasis and sing toward it and away from it with a softly floating swing. "Ihr wisst ja was ich meine" should be very *pianissimo* and should be sung with a subtle delicacy.

In the third verse the musical phrase continues while the verbal phrase must make a slight pause. Make this necessary pause very discretely without disturbing the musical line as explained in the introduction.

Sing the last verse deeply moved. With the flowers you give her the tears which you weep because of her, of her who seems so far beyond your reach. Sing very softly and with inner trembling: "der Tau in euren Äugelein, das sollen meine Tränen sein, die will ich auf euch weinen".

TRÄNENREGEN

This song must be sung with deep emotion. Feel the subtle poetry in both the words and the music. With the beginning of the prelude feel the dreaming enchantment of the moonlit night. Sing very tenderly, in a swinging *legato* and very distinctly. "Wir schauten so traulich zusammen hinab in den rieselnden Bach" should be sung as if in your thoughts you bend down over the brook. Give an especial significance to "rieselnden Bach". It is the brook which has lured you to this mill—the brook to whom you now feel close in an hour which may perhaps be decisive for your whole life: you are alone with your adored one,—the magic of the quiet moonlit night envelops you,—perhaps you will find the courage to ask the question which will decide whether your life is to be one of joy or grief . . . Sing with a dreamy delight: "Der Mond war auch gekommen, die Sternlein hinterdrein".

Sing the second verse with a somewhat more animated tempo, with restraint but with glowing feeling. There is a surging warmth and a tender restraint in "Ich schaute nach ihrem Bilde, nach ihren Augen allein". You are so young and shy. You don't dare to look into the face of your beloved as she sits beside you, no, you look down into the brook in which her beauty is mirrored . . . Sing with a rapturous, dreamlike quality: "und sahe sie nicken und blicken herauf aus dem seligen Bach"—you believe the brook is blissfully happy because it holds the image of your beloved within its water . . .

Begin the third verse as if with a mysterious astonishment: "Und in den Bach versunken der ganze Himmel schien . . . " You see the deep blue heaven with its brilliant stars reflected in the brook. Heaven and water seem mysteriously interwoven, the earth seems extinguished, you yourself seem to soar over the strange picture of the heavens, over the brook and the image of your beloved,—between stars and clouds . . . This vision grips your thirsty, impressionable, vulnerable, poet's soul. Confusion sweeps over you—the beauty of this moment is too great, too much for you. You lean down toward the brook and see its waters, like a luminous veil, rippling on over the image of your beloved, over heaven and its stars . . . "Und über den Wolken und Sternen da rieselte munter der Bach". Sing this with delighted amazement but at the same time with restraint. And sing mysteriously, calling and yet listening: "und rief mit Singen und Klingen: Geselle, Geselle! mir nach". Lift out the two words "Geselle, Geselle" like a call, sing them separated from the continuing musical phrase and give them a quality of uncanniness. The brook is calling you . . . Does it call you away from here? Does it want you to follow it and wander on along a carefree road, away from the girl whom you love and in whose hands rests your fate? Or does it call you down? Does it want you to be lost in the reflected image as it closes over you.

This moment decides your fate . . .

In your confusion you do not understand the warning of the brook . . . You do not obey its admonition—you stay . . . But instead of taking the girl into your arms, as she perhaps expected and hoped you would, you bow your head, and tears of confusion fall from your eyes...

The girl's nature is a completely prosaic one, the overpowering emotion of the youth at her side is to her something foreign and beyond her understanding. Yes, she looks at him with a mixture of scorn, compassion and fear. He seems uncanny to her. Suddenly she gets up and the only thing which she can think of saying in this hour of enchantment is the very prosaic remark: "es kommt ein Regen, ade, ich geh' nach Haus..." ("It's going to rain, good-bye, I'm going home") Sing this *piano,* rather impatiently, but a suggestion of fear and a little scorn should sound through it. In this one sentence you must convey the picture of the girl: an unromantic, commonplace nature, coquettish, a little superior, scornful but at the same time almost superstitiously fearful of anything which is at all foreign to her. And that the miller lad, this dreaming, unworldly poet, certainly is . . .

In the postlude slowly bow your head as if you, the miller boy, withdraw into yourself.

MEIN

But one day you found the courage to ask the question which has burned in your heart for such a long time . . . The answer made you unspeakably happy—the answer was the longed for "yes". . .

Perhaps no one had ever before spoken to the girl in the way you did. Perhaps your lovely and poetic soul found the right words with which to touch her heart, the small and commonplace heart of one who can only feel superficially, but which you in your flowering imagination have clothed with beauty and worth . . . Perhaps in this moment she had loved you as much as it was possible for her to love . . . Happiness flooded through you like a stream of gold—the whole world seemed to whirl around you blissfully. In the uproar of your emotion, you are confused and helpless as never before in your life . . . You would like to hold fast the current of time, to change the whole everyday world into one resounding soaring symphony which would sing only of your joy and on the wings of its song would waft your ecstacy to the sun itself . . .

This song should be given a very quick tempo. It is like one breathless avalanche of word and tone. Immediately take up the storm of the prelude, plunge with your whole being into the flaring music. But don't sing loudly. Begin with exalted excitement. Build up! . . . The first *forte* is at "mein" and sing the following "mein" which is broadly spun out, with full and exultant power.

The whole middle part of the song should be sung with great restraint, but quickly as if in a rapturous whisper.

Without slowing the tempo, end with an exultant *fortissimo.* Hold the tension until the end of the postlude.

This song is a very difficult one. It will take a long time before you can give it quite the right form. To convey vehemence of expression and yet be at the same time restrained is especially difficult. But you *must* accomplish this, for otherwise this whole song will become an undifferentiated *forte* and will lose its essential character, which must be one of blissful confusion. It would become commonplace and that is something which should be very far from the miller boy . . . Try to imagine singing as if you are intoxicated—imagine that your whole body sways, as it would for example if sitting in a soaring swing, you become one with its motion. So let yourself be carried by the swing of these phrases. The whole world is your swing . . .

PAUSE

It is as if weariness overcomes you after the tumult of the first overpowering storm of happiness. You seem to be in a dream. Now that your beloved has said "yes" there should be nothing which could oppress you . . . You should now be deeply contented and completely happy. But the burden of joy is almost more than you can bear and in the depths of your soul is the fear which you won't admit even to yourself, that such happiness cannot really be lasting . . . Why should you think this? Why can you not enjoy your happiness completely? You feel the true nature of your beloved, you see her superficiality, and even if you do close your eyes and try with your whole heart to believe in her,—there is still in the depths of your soul, a kernel of unrest . . .

Begin the prelude quietly looking up. Your facial expression should convey a deep awareness of your happiness, your smile is full of contentment and devotion. (Don't drag this song, the *tempo* is *moderato* and it should not be made sentimental!)

Sing quietly: "meine Laute hab' ich gehängt an die Wand" and sing: "ich kann nicht mehr singen" with suppressed passion. An inner amazement sounds through the words—"Ei, wie gross ist wohl meines Glückes Last". Always in your life you have found words and when alone have been able to express in poetry whatever moved you. All the suffering of your young life became poetry, but now happiness makes you mute . . . This seems very strange to you and fills you with amazement.

Sing the beginning of the second verse with great tenderness. You speak to the lute as if it were your friend. It has always been with you. It has accompanied you in all your wanderings, its tones have carried your complaints and all your yearning songs . . . Now it seems as if you are separated from a beloved being, who is silent at the moment when you long to hear its voice . . . As with a delicate touch, your words stroke the lute—"nun, liebe Laute, ruh' an dem Nagel hier". Sing very delicately "und streift eine Biene mit ihren Flügeln dich".

Here again you must understand how to paint with word and tone: sing this line with a gentle swing, making the bees which buzz around its strings, seem alive . . . "Da wird mir so bange und es durchschauert mich" should be sung *ritenuto* with a strange and restrained anxiety. Your glance is clouded during the short interlude. Look as if you were searching in the distance, auxiously questioning. The query "Warum liess ich das Band auch hängen so lang?" must have an uncanny quality. You fear something, but you will bury your head so that you cannot see it, you refuse to recognize that there is something which you should fear. You haven't the make up of a fighter. For you there can be no challenge, you will never look into the face of fate with flashing eager eyes as so many young people of your age would enjoy doing. No, you want to hide in order to protect your sensitive soul . . .

Listen again to the distance from which seem to come disquieting voices . . . Strangely you sometimes seem to hear a sigh trembling through the strings of the beloved lute . . . It makes you shudder . . . Sing with restraint and heavily, the pressing question: "Ist es der Nachklang meiner Liebespein?" How you wish it might be . . . But you are not sure,—very softly, trembling and with great restraint you ask the fatal question: "Soll es das Vorspiel neuer Lieder sein?" (Remember, that in the past it has only been pain, loneliness, longing which has brought you songs . . . In happiness they have never come to you . . . What you want to say is:— or will I again be abandoned and lonely and filled with longing and so again be able to sing my songs?) The new songs bode nothing good . . . It is a premonition of grief and pain which trembles through you. And yet you love your songs . . . Even though they be born from pain you love them and in your happiness have missed them. So in the last repetition of the question—"Soll es das Vorspiel neuer Lieder sein?" let there be a subtle expression of pained happiness . . . Even though grief should overwhelm you,—you will still have your songs . . .

MIT DEM GRÜNEN LAUTENBAND

This is one of the few songs in this cycle (and in any case the last one), which has a carefree quality. You have thrust aside the lurking premonition—you are living completely in the happy present . . . Your loved one has been with you and has seen the pretty green ribbon which was tied upon your lute. She was eager to have this ribbon, to decorate her dress and her hair . . . Everything about your beloved gives you delight. That she will rob your lute of its adornment in order to place the ribbon upon your hair, is like a command for you. You take the ribbon from the lute and send it to her. Green is her favorite color . . . Green is becoming to her . . . This green which later becomes the hated color (the coat of the hunter with whom the unfaithful one betrays you, is green) now seems the most beautiful color in the world to you, because she loves it . . . (Perhaps she has said that she loves green because she has already flirted with the handsome hunter lad . . . Perhaps it is a tragic farce that you the poor miller boy, share her preference for green . . . Perhaps she is already laughing the evil laugh of heartless scorn . . . Who knows? . . .) Sing this song with freshness and as if you are free of every care. You are filled with optimism, you sing playfully and whimsically. Avoid any suggestion of heaviness here, sing with warmth of feeling and with inner delight. End the song with a happy confidence.

DER JÄGER

The realization that your beloved is not averse to the attentions of the hunter has struck you down . . . For you could not burst out in the violent passion which speaks from this song if you were entirely sure of your beloved. This is no jealousy which is only born of anger at the daring of one who pursues the girl, whom you consider yours . . . No, it is the jealousy of the man who fears that he might lose his beloved to the other one.

The whole song should be sung with a wildness which is entirely foreign to the nature of the gentle miller boy. But the shock has been too great. You have been torn too suddenly from your dreams, which were almost unbearably beautiful. You have been wounded to the quick. Sing the whole song from beginning to end in a violent tempo. It is especially important to enunciate distinctly in this song. In singing you must *recite* this song . . . End with great bitterness, with trembling contempt: "und treten und wühlen herum in dem Feld, die Eber, die schiesse, du Jägerheld". This shuld be sung between the teeth with a distorted expression almost through tears of rage.

EIFERSUCHT UND STOLZ

But from the hunter who seems scarcely worth your contempt you turn back to your beloved: you can no longer deny to yourself that she is the guilty one, that it is she who has betrayed you and has turned her fickle heart to the hunter . . . It is a sign of your great inner loneliness that you now take refuge again with the brook, the one friend to whom you may confess your feelings. You see in its vigorous flow, the wish to revenge you . . . You believe that the brook, your friend, wants to pursue the hunter who has robbed you of your happiness . . . The splashing waves which at the beginning of the cycle when you were still carefree and happy, sang a gay song of wandering to you, now sing the words of your heart, that heart which was once so good and kind but has now learned to hate and longs for revenge.

Begin the song with deep excitement. Sing with marked accentuation noting the dotted notes exactly. They again give the impression of the throbbing of your heart. (Don't neglect them!) Sing "kehr' um, kehr' um," with violent passion. "Ihren leichten, losen, kleinen Flattersinn" should be sung as if with suppressed pain. It is rather touching that you still try to think of the failings of your beloved as a whim, which springs not from ill will but from the fact that she is really nothing more than a child and so to be excused . . . You want to deceive yourself, to excuse what cannot be excused . . . But you love her so much—you still can't believe that she is really lost to you,—not yet . . . Sing as if you were telling the brook a secret: "Sahst du sie gestern Abend nicht am Tore steh'n" and sing "Wenn von dem Fang der Jäger lustig zieht nach Haus, da steckt kein sittsam Kind den Kopf zum Fenster 'naus," with the somewhat reproachful tone of an older person who is annoyed by the follies of youth . . . Sing in the same way "Geh' Bächlein hin und sag' ihr das." You must talk in a very intimate way with the brook as if it were really an understanding being. Sing "Doch sag' ihr nicht, hörst du, kein Wort" in a whisper almost *parlando,* cut the "nicht" very short and lift out "hörst du". Sing softly and very *legato* "von meinem traurigen Gesicht", pour your whole grief into these words: all your despair, your bitter disillusionment must resound through them . . . Sing "sag' ihr" as if you were considering what message you would give the brook for your beloved—and sing "Er schnitzt bei mir sich eine Pfeif' aus Rohr" as if it were a sudden decision. Sing this with a bitter smile of superiority, as if you wanted to give the impression that you are quite superior and haven't the slightest intention of taking the unfaithfulness of your beloved as though it were a tragedy for you . . . Give the impression of still greater indifference in "und bläst den Kindern schöne Tänz' und Lieder vor", sing this with a swing as if you wanted to make her think that you too have an urge to dance . . . End with an expression of wildness, singing through tears: "sag' ihr's, sag' ihr's" . . .

DIE LIEBE FARBE

A sombre longing for death sounds from out this sorrowful song. The color green (the color which in Germany is used for hunter's coats) becomes for you a fixed idea: you have realized what a tragicomic role you must have played in the eyes of your beloved, when you admired this color with her and agreed that green was your favorite color too . . . Perhaps (you think with the burning distrust of one who has been deceived) it has given her a malicious pleasure to hear you in all your innocence rave about this color, which she loves because of her dashing hunter ... The insignificant episode of the hour in which she asked you for this ribbon attains a torturing significance for you, it pursues you, it scoffs at you, it makes you restless and embittered, you who were such a short time ago the gay and charming, innocently happy young miller lad ...

In the prelude emerge as if from sombre thoughts, slowly lift your bowed head and look into the distance with a pained and forlorn expression. Begin to sing in a soft voice as in a dream, beneath a veil. In this verse sing "mein Schatz hat's Grün so gern" each time with a mixture of pain and scorn. Color your voice darkly, sing exceptionally *legato* and very quietly. At "eine Haide voll grünen Rosmarein" sing a *subito pianissimo* and end the first verse with bitterness: "mein Schatz hat's Grün so gern".

The second verse is somewhat more animated. Sing with sombre scorn: "mein Schatz hat's Jagen so gern". Sing *crescendo* until the end of the repetition of this phrase, then sing *subito piano*—"Das Wild, das ich jage, das ist der Tod". Close very softly, with tragic bitterness: "mein Schatz hat's Jagen so gern".

Begin the third verse in a whispered *piano,* trembling, through tears. This whole verse has no *crescendo,* no *decrescendo,* it flows in a sad monotony as if through tears which smother your voice. Try here to unite the realism of the expression with the melodic line of the song. End with a breathy sigh, through tears. Remain standing quiet and rigid until the postlude dies away.

DIE BÖSE FARBE

You cannot escape from the obsession: the color green pursues you, mocks at you, will kill you ... Your mind begins to be confused. Your delicate and sensitive soul cannot withstand the bitter disillusionment that has come through the realization that this love, this torturing love could be destroyed. Wherever you might flee, the color green is there ... The forest, the fields, the banks of the brook—everything glows at you with this malicious green, driving you into madness.

Take up the wild storming of the prelude with your whole being: stand a little bent as if on the point of running away, your facial expression is confused, you give the impression that you are being hunted ... Sing with great violence, like a cry of fear: "Ich möchte flieh'n in die Welt hinaus, hinaus in die weite Welt" and whisper with an expression of insanity—"wenn's nur so grün nicht wär' da draussen in Wald und Feld ..." The next phrase: "Ich möchte die grünen Blätter all' pflücken von jedem Zweig" is again like a cry of fear—und "ich möchte die grünen Gräser all' weinen ganz totenbleich" is again whispered uncannily, insanely, mounting into a *fortissimo* outburst at "bleich". The short repetition "weinen ganz totenbleich" should be sung very accentuatedly, storming on. Again begin *piano*: "Ach Grün, du böse Farbe du, was siehst mich immer an so stolz, so keck, so schadenfroh, mich armen, armen weissen Mann?" Sing this with suppressed trembling, with the fear of the madman who believes that he is pursued. Looking around with an expression of shyness, sing: "armen, armen weissen Mann" as if through tears. You feel so small, so worthless, beside the pompous, selfconfident hunter, who looks still handsomer in his green coat . . .

The next verse should be sung with an entirely different expression: with great warmth and emotion, with the whole wonderful humility of a pure heart. Only at the end make a slight *crescendo* at "das eine Wörtchen Ade". The next phrases should be sung in very strict rhythm (you should of course always sing rhythmically . . . When I mention it especially, I mean that the rhythm should be emphasized . . .) It is as if with quick, stealthy steps you hasten to her bedroom window only to see her, her who has made you so unspeakably unhappy . . . But what you see grips you with pain: about her brow is tied the green ribbon . . . The ribbon from your lute which you have given her and which she now uses to adorn herself for another . . . Sing with wild vehemence, with an expression of madness: "O binde von der Stirn dir ab das grüne Band".

End the song with the same violence, singing—"Ade, ade, und reiche mir zum Abschied deine Hand, zum Abschied deine Hand" as if running away, as if running straight to your death.

TROCK'NE BLUMEN

Your longing for death has now changed into a determination to die . . . Imagine that you are sitting alone, as always, in your little room . . . In your hands you hold the dried flowers which she had once given you and which you have cherished, perhaps laying them between the pages of your old Bible . . . Now you take them in your hands as if they were a precious legacy—as if in this hour of leavetaking from all earthy possessions, you must decide what is to become of your belongings, as you would about a great and important estate . . . But there is no one worthy of receiving these flowers, which have been your most cherished possession, a token of the short period of happiness that now lies shattered about you . . . You cannot part from them, even in death, so you must take them with you to your grave . . .

Begin already in the two measures of the prelude, to feel the tired resigned, powerless movement with which you would take the flowers in your hands . . . Raise your head slowly as if emerging from a deep dream. Your glance is veiled, withdrawn from reality—you are only alive now in the consideration of the withered flowers in your hand . . . Sing with deep melancholy, very softly and in a veiled *piano*: "Ihr Blümlein alle, die sie mir gab, euch soll man legen mit mir in's Grab". Sing a delicate *ritardando* at "ihr Blümlein alle, wovon so nass?" Hold "nass" and break it off as if your heart has stopped beating . . . Tears run down your cheeks (in your imagination). Tears moisten the dried flowers in your hand . . . But the green will never again return to their withered leaves, just as love will never again smile upon you . . . Sing with deep feeling: "Ach, Tränen machen nicht maiengrün, machen tote Liebe nicht wieder blüh'n . . ." Close this verse with a soft *ritardando*: "die Blümlein alle, die sie mir gab" . . . Lift out "sie" as if with an aching sigh . . . Your facial expression is somewhat more animated, a humble and touching joy pervades you as you sing: "Und wenn sie wandelt am Hügel vorbei und denkt im Herzen: der meint' es treu . . ." It makes you happy to think that when you are dead, she will realize how much you have loved her . . . Your dried flowers will bloom again in this happiness, they will grow again, as in the sunlight of spring and blossom from out of the grave, under whose green mound the truest and purest heart rests from its suffering . . . Sing with jubilance but at the same time with tenderness and warmth: "Dann Blümlein alle, heraus, heraus! Der Mai is kommen, der Winter ist aus . . ." Sing the repetitions of these phrases in exactly the same way—only end the song a little more broadly and emphasize "kommen" and "Winter" in the broad swing of the phrase.

In the postlude sink again into yourself—turn your thoughts to the faded flowers, those pitiful symbols of your brief and deceptive happiness.

DER MÜLLER UND DER BACH

But how can the miller lad fulfill his determination to die without confering with the brook, his only friend? So he stands upon its bank where his dragging steps have carried him and looks down into the depths of the brook as he communes with it . . . Sing almost without expression in a sombre monotony . . . Your soul is no longer really on earth. You have finished with life, the world seems dark around you and seems to have dissolved into a mystic distance . . . The moon, weeping, covers its face, in its shadow the lilies die, and the white angels, who in the evening float through the blue sky in golden clouds, do not want to see your pain and sing to you comforting songs through their burning tears of compassion, luring you to them . . . You tell all this in one tone as if passing away, you have already escaped from the earth . . . But the brook, the kind friend, is wise . . . For a long, long time it has been flowing through the world. It has seen much and learned much and it knows how transitory are the desires and pains of this earth, if one can only understand how to raise oneself above them . . . While the accompaniment breaks away from the dragging monotony of the first part of the song and begins to flow gaily, the brooklet speaks to the miller lad . . . It is as if it wanted to say: be quiet my boy . . . Your suffering will pass . . . Your loving heart will rise above this grief just as a swan soars out of the water into which it had plunged, as if it would never again return . . . So will your young heart arise again. And a new star will shine upon you and roses will bloom again from the withered and thorny branches and the angels who to-day are weeping above you, will come down to earth and you will greet them and will again be happy . . . Sing these phrases as if in play, with a light quality of voice. The brook is wise, the brook is cool and clear, the brook cannot realize the fatal wound within your warm heart . . . It only knows that it is the way of the world to be happy and to be sad, and he knows that everything, everything is transitory—pain as well as joy . . . Just as the brook chatters—charmingly, gaily, free from care, you should sing this song of the brook—coolly, clearly, playfully. But the words of nature which knows eternal resurrection, can find no way to this heart which is wounded unto death . . . Sing the last verse of this song with deep emotion. Put all the glow, all the warmth of your heart into the phrase—"Ach, Bächlein, liebes Bächlein, du meinst es so gut, ach, Bächlein, aber weisst du, wie Liebe tut?" Sing with infinite longing, with mystical desire, with great restraint, darkly, and as if you bend nearer and nearer to the brook, drawn with tenderness and kindness into its cool depths . . . Sing with half closed lips, almost fading away: "Ach, Bächlein, liebes Bächlein, so singe nur zu" . . . In your imagination you sink slowly, very slowly into the brook. Slowly, very slowly the clear blue waters close over you and you lie cradled in its depths freed of all earthly pain.

DES BACHES WIEGENLIED

Dying, passing, streaming away, you lie at the bottom of the brook . . . You feel the waves which at the edges of the brook splash and ripple their merry song, singing for you an eternal slumber song . . . Sing swaying softly, give the impression of being released, as with closed eyes you let your body sway almost imperceptibly with the rhythm of the music. Be one, in your thoughts, with the water, feel the blue infinity above you, feel this wonderful, gentle passing away . . . It is asking much of the singer, you will say, to make all this your own. Oh no: *Feeling is everything* . . . You have lived and suffered with the miller boy through an experience which for him—the world estranged, tender hearted dreamer—must have led to an end which was *final* . . . You have learned to love this figure, which you have awakened to life through your singing, your interpretation. You have suffered with him, you have lived through all his bitter tragedy and now you die with him. You feel now, how death is taking you into its arms, the cool kind arms, with which the brook, your friend, embraces you . . . Feel the sweet painlessness of death in this song—and you will find the right expression for this last song which is a comforting and wonderful requiem . . . Sing with a darkly colored voice but softly as if in a dream. There should be a great surge at "bis das Meer will trinken die Bächlein aus". There is a deep and phantastic joy in this surge of feeling: the ocean, the endless ocean which you have never seen, will drink the brook and with it will take you into itself, will roll you in its great waves from continent to continent, will make you one with the endless unapproachable distance.

I always sing only three verses, the first, third and fifth. If you want to sing them all, each one should be painted differently. But never forget that it is a dreamer, who is passing away, who sings. Never be rigid in your expression. Everything must be subdued, restrained, dreamlike . . . When in the third verse you sing of the hunting horn, it must be something very distant and unreal . . . Only the waves which enfold you are reality, they are the only reality . . . Sing the last verse more slowly, and let it be still slower toward the end but never drag in this song. Sing "Der Vollmond steigt, der Nebel weicht" with an expression of being withdrawn, very veiled, very mysterious, very unworldly. The ending—"Und der Himmel da oben, wie ist er so weit" should be trembling, silvery, absolutely ethereal. Soar away with this ending,—dissolving,—dying this sweet death which makes you one with beauty and with the blue of eternal distance until far, far away you merge with light itself.

DICHTERLIEBE

Heine   *Schumann*
I   *Im wunderschönen Monat Mai*

Be careful not to sing this song sentimentally. It is a young man who tells of his love, never forget this. What the young girl might perhaps express shyly and hesitantly, becomes enthusiasm and glowing passion when expressed by this enamoured poet.

Submerge yourself in the flowing poetry of the prelude which has the quality of flowering branches swaying in the breezes of spring. Begin *piano* but rapturously. Sing "Im wunderschönen Monat Mai" with an ecstatic expression,—feel the wonder and the beauty of spring, paint them in the word "wunderschönen". Your glance sweeps about you delightedly, as if you saw before you a garden filled with flowers.

Sing with a broad *crescendo* up to "die Liebe aufgegangen". This phrase is vocally very difficult. You can make the word "aufgegangen" easier by not making the consonants too distinct. This advice seems to me rather a sin against the Holy Ghost of expression . . . But it is better here to choose the lesser of two evils: better here (as an *exception*, please!) to be indistinct rather than to struggle vocally and give the impression that you cannot master the phrase from the technical standpoint . . . Sing the syllable "gen" in "aufgegangen" very broadly, making the "e" in "gen" sound like the "a" in "gang", that will also help you. Bring the dreaming delight of the first verse to a passionate exuberance in the second verse. Be careful to give each dotted and each sixteenth note its evact value. They take from the song all trace of sentimentality. And above all avoid any scooping or sliding.

II *Aus meinen Tränen spriessen*

The tears and sighs of which you sing here do not imply any grief. They are the sweet tears and trembling sighs of longing desire . . . So begin with an ethereal and silvery quality of voice. Notice the musical difference in the second and fourth phrases. In the second phrase the notes are delicately tied, whereas in the fourth phrase they are dotted. From this differentiation arises an absolutely enchanting tone painting. The flowers seem to be crowded close together—a garden full, meadows full of flowers—motionless in the radiant sunlight. The chorus of nightingales on the other hand is passionately animated and vibrates sweetly from out of the bushes.

The next phrase "und wenn du mich lieb hast, Kindchen" sing brightly, joyously, tenderly. It is almost as if you were speaking to a child. Accent "schenk" in "schenk' ich dir die Blumen all"—sing it with a whimsical expression. And sing the ending "und vor deinem Fenster soll klingen das Lied der Nachtigall" very *legato* and tenderly as if in a dream.

III *Die Rose, die Lilie, die Taube*

Above all things, this song should never be sung as if it were a virtuoso piece. The tempo is not excessively fast and it is not a situation which calls for a display of your long breath . . . I have even heard singers who were determined to rattle through this song on one breath and who were infinitely proud of this virtuoso accomplishment . . . The tempo should be gay not hasty. The quick flow of words is enchanting:

happiness overflows in the ecstatic and amorous phrases,—stammering confession, rapturous bliss . . . Don't sing in a straight line, sing in swinging phrases. Recite the poem in a rapid *tempo* noting which words are the high points as you recite them and you will then find the same high points in the musical phrase. Sing "sie selber, aller Liebe Wonne" very *legato*. Note the following *ritardando* which goes over into *a tempo* at "Taube". Breathe deeply before the final "die Eine". Sing it as if it were a sigh of delight.

IV *Wenn ich in deine Augen seh'*

The bright sun which has shone upon your love is clouded: you now begin to see your beloved with clearer eyes and in your inner being, you realize that she does not correspond to that ideal image which you have held in your heart . . . You are no longer free from suffering, for you are a victim of your love even though you know that your beloved is not worthy of it . . .

Begin this song from out of this inner realization. Begin with a sad smile, as if emerging from a dream. At "doch wenn ich küsse deinen Mund" you are overcome by passion. Sing it broadly, flowing, transported. The following phrases should be sung with a veiled *piano* as if under a spell of enchantment.

"Doch wenn du sprichst "ich liebe dich" comes like a warning. Certainly you know: it is not the truth. These are empty words. And your answer is bitter tears . . .

This song is very easy to build up if you clearly understand its logical construction: her look comforts,—her kiss heals,—her nearness is intoxicating,—but her oath of love is untrue and so brings a most painful awakening for you.

V *Ich will meine Seele tauchen*

Now you turn away from your grief and pain and seek peace in your loving thoughts. You search for words, for comparisons with which to express your love. No picture is beautiful enough, no word subtle enough, no comparison ethereal enough, to convey the exuberance of your devotion . . . This song should be pervaded with trembling emotion. Sing with a veiled *piano*, floating, unreal. Paint with the consonants in "Das Lied soll schauern und beben", lift out the *sch* and the *b*—"*sch*auern", "*b*eben" but do it without breaking the soft flow of the melody.

End the song with a broad surge at "den sie mir einst gegeben" and sing the triplet broadly and distinctly in "wunderbar süsser Stund". Sing

it with closed eyes and an expression of blissful rapture as you recall
the happiest moment in this experience of love.

VI *Im Rhein, im heiligen Strome*

In the first phrases paint the description of the lovely old city of
Cologne, with a broad line. Be careful not to force on the *e* and *f*. The
low position and the desire to sing with a magnificent breadth may be
dangerous for you. However it is not necessary to sing forcefully in
order to give strong *expression*: pronounce distinctly, lift out the principal word, sing with nobility—and you are more expressive than if you
sing loud tones which are forced.

At "Im Dom" your expression changes. Imagine that you have
often gone through the cathedral completely under the spell of the
consecrated solemnity which embraced you as you felt the presence of
God about you. And you are compelled again and again to stand before the lovely image of the madonna whose serene beauty stirs your
heart always anew . . . Sing with a soft *legato,* in a veiled *piano* as if
under a spell. Your eyes looking into the distance, are (in your
thoughts) uplifted to this picture. It is the most beautiful which you
have ever seen. From out of the confusion which has beset you, you
have looked up at it and it has seemed to shine upon you. Sing "in
meines Lebens Wildnis hat's freundlich hinein gestrahlt" like a prayer
of thanksgiving. It is like a miraculous image for you and you tell of
it with delight, as if it lived and were radiant within your heart: "es
schweben Blumen . . ." With astonishment you realize that this exalted face of the holy Virgin is like the beautiful face of your beloved.
Sing with a smiling melancholy: "die gleichen der Liebsten genau".
Hold this expression of tender melancholy until you feel the fateful
heavy *crescendo* in the postlude; this is your realization that while your
beloved may *outwardly* resemble the holy picture the likeness is only
superficial . . . With the heavy and increasingly sombre music, you
slowly bow your head as if to hide your griefstricken face, overwhelmed
by the depths of misery which the image of the holy Virgin, however
pure and beautiful, could not lift from your soul.

VII *Ich grolle nicht*

Now for the first time, you tell clearly of how deeply you are aware
of the true nature of your beloved. Make the situation clear to yourself, consider what has happened which has resulted in this song: there
must have been a disagreement between you. Hard words have been
used, confessions made, which have destroyed every bond that had remained between you. She is "forever lost" for you ("**ewig verlor'nes**

Lieb")—so you say and so you feel, there can be no question about it . . . But she, who has wounded you so deeply, so incurably, believes that with a sweet and friendly—"Don't be cross", she can make everything all right again. You look up, with a bitter smile, you reject her idea that you are only "cross". Sing "ich grolle nicht" broadly, with bitterness, with pride and austerity.

Change the quality of your voice which has been dark and flowing, at "Wie du auch strahlst in Diamantenpracht". Sing with a bright tone, disparagingly and ironically, as if you were saying: But don't think that I don't see through you! The splendour with which you surround yourself is all on the outside,—don't think that you can fool me, that you can make me forget what you really are! Sing broadly, with sorrowful accentuation—"das weiss ich längst".

I have always sung the second verse *piano*. Turning away from the beloved, still trembling from your outbreak of bitterness, you now speak more to yourself. For the first time you have told her clearly that you have seen through her, perhaps for the first time you have clearly admitted it to yourself . . . Now completely absorbed with yourself you repeat, trembling,—"Ich grolle nicht" . . . Beginning this verse with a restrained *piano* will also give a stronger effect in building up the dramatic climax of the song.

Sing "Ich sah dich ja im Traume" in a whispered *piano,* as one would whisper in telling a shocking secret . . . Build up the *crescendo* with grandeur until "die dir am Herzen frisst" . . . and be careful that "Herzen" isn't thrust out to the extent of losing its connection with the preceding words. Even this violent outburst must not overstep the limits of tonal beauty. Sing the following phrase—"ich sah, mein Lieb, wie sehr du elend bist," broadly, each syllable *sforzato*. These words, these tones are like the blows of a hammer which crushes to earth the glamorous picture of outward splendour . . . The repetition of "ich grolle nicht" should be strong, with deep emotion as if through tears.

VIII   *Und wüssten's die Blumen, die kleinen*

Sing with increased tempo as if driven by an inner unrest. Don't try to make something characteristically different of the flowers, the nightingales, the stars. The torment of your own heart is the important thing here. It runs through the whole song in one single flow of grief. At "sie alle können's nicht wissen" sing *pianissimo,* as if you said to yourself—whispering, explaining—"How could the world know how deeply I am wounded?"

In the next phrase: "Nur eine kennt meinen Schmerz" color your voice darkly and end with deep bitterness, with strong accentuation—in wild accusation, hurling out the last "zerrissen mir das Herz."

IX *Das ist ein Flöten und Geigen*

In this song, the wild tumult of the piano accompaniment is the
real melody, the voice being interwoven with it. Imagine that you stand
there rigid and austere in the turbulence of your thoughts, feelings,
fantasies . . . You are a defenceless victim: your mind is confused, your
strength paralyzed, you are a sacrifice to the sorcery of your imagination . . .

Sing with an expression of listening, as if under a spell. You stand
very rigid, very erect, feeling with every nerve the demonic wildness
which seems to swirl about you. Note the rhythm which is always repeated. Don't neglect this, it gives the song the strange savage austerity
which is necessary. Remain under the spell of your visions until the
end of the postlude. Listen to it as it dies away, as you would to a distant sound.

X *Hör' ich das Liedchen klingen*

From out of the confusion and gloom you find your way back to
the soft melancholy of memory. This song should be sung with soft
and flowing tones but without any sentimentality. At "es treibt mich
ein dunkles Sehnen hinauf zur Waldeshöh'," color your voice darkly.
Sing this with an impelling inner longing. Tie the two syllables of
"Sehnen" and also of "höh" in a strong curve dark and glowing.
Change the tone quality to the softest light silver quality at "dort löst
sich auf in Tränen . . ." End as if with tears. In the postlude the
dreamy mood which has enshrouded you like a consoling dream is
transformed into the bitter realization: but in reality, I am not released
and freed, I shall be destroyed by this love which consumes and an-
nihilates me.

XI *Ein Jüngling liebt ein Mädchen*

It is easy to explain psychologically, that a human being caught in
the frantic grief of his doomed passion may suddenly, with objectivity,
analyze and scorn this passion and bare it of its romantic aura. It is like
a sane moment in a confused mental state, like finding safety on an
island in the midst of a threatening ocean . . .

This escape from the love which threatens to engulf you demands
an entirely different kind of interpretation. This song must stand out
from the rest of the cycle in the same way as the objective self analysis
stands out from the wreath of poetry . . . I should like to say: sing this
song almost like a couplet—if it didn't sound too revolutionary, to say
such a thing about a song of Schumann. A sharply accentuated *par-*

lando lifts this song out from the others, sing it as if you were relating something quite objectively, as if you wanted to say: "What ridiculous things happen in life!" When you sing: "Der Jüngling ist übel d'ran," do it with a bitter smile of self scorn. At the end of the song you draw back into yourself: the mask falls, your apparently gay objectivity vanishes, grief again engulfs you.

Scorn flares again in the postlude but in the final chords there is the conclusion of your scorn of yourself and you return to tragedy, to sombre darkness, which gives the transition to the next song.

XII *Am leuchtenden Sommermorgen*

The sweetest of poetry follows this outbreak of realism . . . The flight into bitter laughter has failed, you are more than ever submerged in love and grief . . . Take up immediately with your whole body the melody of the accompaniment which has the fragile quality of falling dewdrops.

Sing very softly and ethereally. "Es flüstern und sprechen die Blumen" is whispered and "ich aber wandle stumm" should be broad and tender, as if with a muted violin tone.

From the whispered *piano* of "Es flüstern und sprechen die Blumen und schau'n mitleidig mich an" go over into a light, silvery, veiled *pianissimo*. It is the flowers who speak, so you must sing with an unearthly, floating quality: "Sei uns'rer Schwester nicht böse, du trauriger blasser Mann".

Remain under the spell of this enchanting music until the postlude has faded away.

XIII *Ich hab' im Traum geweinet*

Begin with quiet sadness. Your voice, your whole being emerges from sombre dreams. Sing the beginning of this song with restrained feeling, as if you were not yet entirely awakened to the reality of your grief. (Do not forget: you repeat the same sentence three times! You must *build up!*) The same mood, the same soft, sombre sadness lasts until the end of the first verse—"floss noch von der Wange herab."

Sing the second "Ich hab' im Traum geweinet" with mounting expression yet with restraint. "Mir träumt', du verliessest mich" is born of an inner shudder, from tormenting fear. The following: "Ich wachte auf" should have increased power, it has become reality, a painful awakening from the sombreness of dreams, to the sombreness of day . . . At "noch lange bitterlich" sing "*lange bitter*lich" with marked accentuation (the *l, b, tt* should be very distinct).

148

Now the accompaniment takes up your words and your facial expression shows your increased passion. With wide open eyes you listen to the piano melody which tells of the feeling in your heart . . .

Your last "Ich hab' im Traum geweinet" is to be sure *pianissimo* but it must nevertheless be filled with passion. Sing "mir träumte, du wärst mir noch gut" broadly and with grief. Now sing the end of the song driving on in broad swinging torturing bitterness, in an outburst of despair. Your last word—"Tränenflut" breaks off as if in a sob. Remain rigid with grief until the final chords of the postlude fade away.

XIV *Allnächtlich im Traume*

Again it is a dream which moves you. (Notice how after the one sudden outbreak of realistic self scorn in "Ein Jüngling liebt' ein Mädchen", you turned away from reality: flowers spoke to you, sombre dreams oppressed you—now again comes a dream which is kindly and comforting and brings you solace.) Sing the whole song as if you are breathless. You are excited, enchantment thrills you, it is as if you want to hold fast something which is passing by. Your heart beats, your whole being is in confusion, but your joy is delicate and unreal. Your voice must be tender, flowing, with an inner animation and full of subtle joy. "Und laut aufweinend stürz' ich mich zu deinen süssen Füssen" is an outburst of violent passion. Do not sing loudly, there is no *forte* tone in this whole song—but sing with strong accentuation, with grandeur and with fire.

Paint with your tones the delicate appearance of the beloved, for example: "schüttelst, schüttelst das blonde Köpfchen". Do not breathe after the second "schüttelst", but hold the tension, while giving a short break between the words. (This gives more than breathing, the impression that your heart stops beating.) The *crescendo* in the next phrase is only a slight one—you cannot speak of pearly tear drops in a *forte* tone . . .

Sing "du sagst mir heimlich ein leises Wort" with increased expression but always *piano*. The vision of the beloved seems to come nearer to you, nearer, more loving, more intimate . . . She offers you the wreath and you take it in your hands, but with a shock, you see that it is a cypress wreath plucked from those serene trees which grow in the cemetery. Sing "ich wache auf" heavily, then with a sudden *crescendo* "und der Strauss ist fort" and sing the last phrase: "und's Wort hab' ich vergessen" very quickly, as if thrust out in a hasty whisper.

XV *Aus alten Märchen*

Dreams and fairy tales seem the only refuge for you from the darkness of your day. After dreams which have shaken you, after dreams which have brought to you the lovely vision of your beloved, the gates of a wonderland, which is more than a dream, open before you: the land of fairy tales . . . Retreating into loneliness, you let your thoughts wander through the gay enchanted gardens of the old fairy tale, which you remember from the credulous days of your childhood . . .

Sing this song soaringly, in a lively *tempo,* with an expression of rapture. Your soul again has wings, as it used to have in that carefree time when passion had not yet darkened your life. Sing with inner joy, feeling yourself free since you have found the strength which has raised you above this ill fated love. Begin with a tone full of mystery and sing in a beautiful, soaring swing: "da singt es und da klingt es von einem Zauberland". Go back immediately to a *pianissimo* at "wo bunte Blumen blühen"—sing this very softly, with a silvery tone. At "und grüne Bäume singen uralte Melodei'n" color your voice more darkly—sing with a broad sweep. Feel the murmur of the forest, the swaying of the leafy branches in the summer breeze . . .

It seems strange that the melody at "und Nebelbilder steigen wohl aus der Erd' hervor" should seem so forceful, so strong and realistic. But in a fairy tale, the wonders are reality! The cloud images have nothing ghostly. They are dark and compact figures which dance their strange rounds before you. Will o' the wisps shining blue and red, flutter and shimmer about you—you are bewitched with astonishment and delight . . . Quicken the *tempo,* sing very distinctly, play with the consonants—especially let the r's roll in "im irren, wirren Kreis". Elated by its wild beauty, the fairy world seems to become more and more real to you. Yet suddenly the realization bursts upon you: But it is all only a dream . . . It is the enchanted world of your longing, the old forever unattainable fairy world which lies far beyond all seas, behind all mountains . . . Sing broadly with inner warmth, in a full flow of longing desire from "Ach, könnt' ich dorthin kommen" to "doch kommt die Morgensonne". A great, quiet sadness pervades you as you end the song. A sad smile plays about your mouth as you see disappearing before you, that which was nothing more than a mirage . . .

In the postlude, the dissolving fairy world seems to touch you yet again, like a pale shadow.

XVI *Die alten, bösen Lieder*

This final song is certainly more suited to a man than to a woman. If you, the woman singer, would make it credible, you must sing with great power of expression rather than force of tone.

Imagine the situation: you have now passed through every stage of delight, disillusionment, bitterness. You have sought oblivion in nature, in dreams, in fantasies, which have led you away from the world of reality. But ever again the old torturing love has gripped your heart, ever again it has enchained you, making you its helpless slave . . . Now you straighten up with the sudden decision to end this torment once and for all if you are not to be destroyed as its sacrifice. You must kill all that might have bloomed so wonderfully in your heart, if it had not been so cruelly shattered at the hands of your beloved . . . The songs which you have sung in joy and sorrow must be silenced, the dreams which have tormented and comforted you must vanish . . .

Begin the song very erect, with great energy, sing broadly and forcefully. (Note the exact value of each note. Every dot is a valuable support of expression!) In the delivery of this song you must understand how to combine triumph, bitterness, scorn and even a shadow of savage humor . . . You are now above pain, your fears are conquered, your sighs stilled. You have emptied your heart of all feelings which were tender and vulnerable. You have become master of yourself. The verses, the dreams, the tears have only made you miserable. Now you find bombastic words with which to hurl from you all that has brought you to the edge of destruction . . . Sing in this way to "gebürt ein grosses Grab."

In the next phrase it is as if you suddenly stand still, as if you suddenly interrupt the grand gesture with which you had, so to speak, conducted the dramatic structure of this scene. You whisper—and something akin to madness sounds through this whispered question—"Wisst ihr, warum der Sarg wohl so gross und schwer mag sein?" Slide the word "sein" up to the next phrase in a broad sweep: "Ich senkt' auch meine Liebe und meinen Schmerz hinein". Sing this broadly, painfully, beneath streaming tears. All your suffering, all your love, the whole blossoming world of your inner feeling pours out from you. Breathe before "hinein" with a great and exalted finality. You must give the impression—and you can only do so if you really feel it yourself—that the ocean is closing for eternity over your love. You have torn away from yourself and have buried all that you once felt. Now you are alone, engulfed in inner and outer emptiness.

In the postlude memory enfolds you. You listen to its melodies as to something long vanished . . . It can no longer give you pain because it is no longer a part of your being, it is only a sound from long ago, which brings a smile to your mute lips, a smile of soft melancholy, which can no longer wound you.

FRAUENLIEBE UND LEBEN

Chamisso   *Schumann*

One often hears Chamisso's poems for this cycle criticized as being old fashioned. Perhaps for those sophisticated ones who live one hundred per cent in the present, they are. But isn't this an indication of a lack of imagination? The rather sentimental maiden of this cycle may exaggerate her feelings, and her way of expressing them certainly is not "modern" but isn't love always a romantically exaggerated happiness or misery? Each period has its own peculiar expression. In this cycle try to forget the present and let yourself be free to enjoy the romantic sentimentality of a century which was far less matter of fact than our own . . .

You should begin the cycle with the kind of reverence and enchantment with which you might take from an old cabinet a rare piece of precious lace which had been the proud possession of your great grandmother. You would touch it very carefully and would be rather moved as you replaced it beside the little musical clock—another relic of a bygone day.

I am certainly a modern woman and I can't tolerate anything which is sentimental or "sweetish" and yet I say: Yes, to be sure, this cycle *is* old fashioned, but thank heaven that it is! One can never be an artist if one cannot place oneself convincingly in any atmosphere, however distant or foreign. So forget the present when you begin this cycle. Be a woman of the Biedermeier period, knowing that she loved and felt in the same way as the woman of to-day although she expressed herself differently.

I   *Seit ich ihn gesehen*

The dreamy chords of the first bar reveal immediately the way in which you must sing. Out of the great melody of love which floats from your heart, the restrained chords rise with a shy subtlety like trembling sighs. Begin as if with a deep sigh. Your voice should be soft, breathy, forlorn. At "seh' ich ihn allein" sing *ritardando* and give a soft accent to "ihn", no *crescendo*. Accentuate "heller" both times and exaggerate the "h". Your face which has been transfigured in ecstacy now becomes sad during the short interlude. You cannot quite understand the power of this magic spell which has possessed you. You cannot understand how even your dearest friends can seem so far away from you. Give your voice a darker color. Play with the consonants in "Schwestern" and accent "nicht be*gehr'* ich mehr." Sing *ritenuto* and be very careful not to slide or scoop at *"lieber* weinen still im *Kämmerlein."* Each syllable must be very distinct. Any scooping or sliding would make it much too sentimental. Be very careful to avoid this. The last —"glaub' ich blind zu sein" is an almost whispered *pianissimo.* Your face should be radiant with a soft enchantment until the end of the postlude.

II *Er, der Herrlichste von allen*

Now you are beginning to grow accustomed to this strange feeling of ecstacy which pervades you. You have no desire, you are contented in the knowledge of your own love, which it is impossible to share with anyone. Again and again you look with rapture at the image of your beloved which seems to be always before you and you find your greatest joy in raving about his virtues, his wonderful character and his great beauty. The absolute lack of passionate desire makes it possible for you to be completely happy in your love.

Begin this second song joyfully, radiantly, almost dizzy with delight. The first phrase is like a fanfare of victory. Sing with absolute accuracy in exact rhythm. Each time you emphasize another of your beloved's wonderful qualities make an ecstatic accent: *"Hol*de Lippen, *kla*res Auge." You feel: he is so far away, so far above you—like a star in the sky . . . You know that it would be futile to desire a star, futile to desire this starlike image of the one and only being whom you love... But you are sad that you are not more beautiful, more worthy of him . . . Sing the next phrase "So wie dort in blauer Tiefe" under the shadow of this thought and give an accent to "fern" (consonants!) with a certain hesitancy as if it gives you pain to say—"he is so far away". But in the interlude you find your way back to your inner contentment.

Sing "Wandle, wandle deine Bahnen" with nobility and in a warm flow. Bring out the lovely crescendo and *subito piano*: "deinen Schein, nur in Demut" and accent "Demut".

In the next phrase the *ritardando* at "selig nur und traurig sein" becomes *a tempo* but sing *piano*, softly, with restraint. You are overwhelmed, intoxicated, by your own humility. You long to sacrifice yourself, you long to feel small and insignificant and worthless at his feet . . . "Hoher Stern der Herrlichkeit" should be sung with ecstatic exuberance. Oh your love is boundless—you even enjoy talking about the happy woman whom he will take for his wife! But sing these phrases with inner restraint in spite of your willingness to sacrifice yourself, in spite of not really daring to imagine any happiness for yourself . . . "Darf beglücken deine Wahl" has a very discrete *crescendo*. Give the most restrained *pianissimo* possible to "und ich will die Hohe segnen". "Tausend mal" should have a warm *mezzoforte*. Accentuate "*wei*nen" (consonants!) "Selig, selig bin ich dann" has a *crescendo*— it is as if you are saying to yourself—"Oh yes, I shall be happy in his happiness . . ." Give a *subito piano* to "sollte mir das Herz auch brechen" almost with tears, and now you lay your sacrifice at his feet: "brich, o Herz, was liegt darin?" Sing this broadly, *forte*, with an almost religiously sacrificial quality.

The interlude brings you back to the ecstatic enthusiasm with which you began. But don't sing it with quite the same innocent joy: in the meantime you have lived in your imagination through *his* happiness and your renunciation. You have wanted to sacrifice your own heart, your own life, for him. There must now be a very subtle difference in the way in which you sing these phrases. Sing them fervently, with a delight which is almost on the verge of tears.

In the postlude your whole being should be transfigured by an overwhelming enchantment: feel the music streaming through your body, follow the musical line with your expression—but never overstep the limits which the style of Lieder singing imposes.

III *Ich kann's nicht fassen, nicht glauben*

This short breathless song should be sung as if you had just stopped running—you are so completely overwhelmed and stunned by your happiness that you have come running out of the house like a child . . . You are quite breathless, you can't be sure whether this was just a dream or an intoxicating reality! Begin the song as if *plunging* into it. Sing it passionately, almost wildly. The shock has been too overwhelming—you had never, never dreamed, even in your secret heart, that he could love you . . .

At "erhöht und beglückt" go over with a *ritardando* to a restrained *tempo*. Sing with a veiled *piano*: "Mir war's, er habe gesprochen". Sing this with an almost doubtful expression. You try to recall this incredible moment: yes, I *think* he said . . . And now you put your whole heart into the words "ich bin auf ewig dein". But immediately your doubt returns: "Mir war's, ich träume . . ." sing this with haste, accentuated—and sing the last "es kann ja nimmer so sein" broadly, almost in tears.

But no: it has been reality, it has not been only a dream. With this realization you throw your whole being into his life. Sing with the utmost warmth and abundance, broadly, *forte,* sing it as if you were standing in the warm summer sunshine, with the warm wind blowing through your hair, flowers all about you, your arms ecstatically outstretched: "O lass' im Traume mich sterben."

"In Tränen unendlicher Lust" is *adagio.* It has the enthusiasm of an almost religious fanaticism. The word "Lust" must give the transition to the next phrase, sing it *ff* ending it abruptly.

The repetition of the first phrases are now *piano,* whispered, breathy.

Don't neglect the *crescendo* at "hat ein Traum mich berückt" but it should be more a crescendo of expression than of force. Sing the music of the interlude with your thoughts—there can be no interruption in your expression, the *music* is *you—you* must express the *music.* Sing the last sentence with the softest of *pianissimos,* beneath tears of joy.

Hold the last tone letting it fade away gradually.

IV *Du Ring an meinem Finger*

This is a song of gaily animated happiness. Calm and contented in the realization of his love, you are almost childlike and as yet unawakened to passion. He loves you, how could you ask for anything more? Do you want complete surrender? Oh—you have surrendered your whole soul, your whole heart . . . Your senses are quiet. He, the hero of your dreams is yours forever. He shall determine your fate. You want only to follow his wish . . . That is the greatest happiness for which you could ask . . . He has given you the ring as his betrothed. This sign of bondage between you is your most precious possession. You caress it, you rejoice in its unaccustomed pressure upon your finger which seems like a caress.

Begin the song from out of this feeling of contentment. Your voice is softly floating, light and animated. You remember the time between childhood and adolescence—"ich fand allein mich, verloren im öden, unendlichen Raum . . ." At this time you had no idea of where you belonged. But then he came, opening the door of life and happiness for you. After "unendlichen Raum" sing "du" *ritenuto* and at "Ring an meinem Finger" *a tempo*. This must be done (very subtly!) in order to connect the phrases.

Don't misinterpret the words: "ihm angehören ganz, hin selber mich geben", there is neither passion nor desire here. The complete surrender of which you speak is the surrender of your soul. You have no idea of what will happen in marriage, you only know that you belong to him completely and that you will do whatever he asks of you... Sing with the deepest sincerity: "Verklärt mich in seinem Glanz". Sing it *ritardando* and then immediately *a tempo* at "Ring". (The word "du" is still ritardando. Remember the same phrase earlier in the song). Accent "Herze" and *feel* the happiness in the postlude.

V *Helft mir, ihr Schwestern*

The wedding day! You are surrounded by the friends of your childhood. A girl, for the last time, you are in your room under your father's roof. You are blissfully happy and excited but you cannot entirely overcome a virginal fear no matter how much you scold yourself for it . . .

Begin the song with great excitement. You talk to your friends in order to quiet your inner fear. You admit the strangeness of your beloved who with passionate impatience has always longed for the wedding day. You have never felt this driving impatience. You have been quiet and contented in the realization of being his betrothed. A strange and frightening experience seems to lie before you,—you ask your girlish friends to help you to overcome your silly fears . . . Sing "Helft mir, ihr Schwestern, helft mir verscheuchen eine törichte Bangigkeit", *piano,* whispering. Then freeing yourself from these disturbing thoughts you recall with delight the image of the man whose bride you will become today. You surrender yourself to him, in humility you bow your head . . . "All the flowers are for him, for my hero! Who am I?" This is the overflowing expression of your own complete surrender. But now attired in your bridal dress, you look about you and bid your friends good-bye. You are no longer one of them. Today you close a door upon the life you shared with them and open one upon a world to which they do not as yet belong. Womanhood will now separate you from these maidens . . . You have been like sisters. Now you say good-bye. This good-bye is like an interlude in the flow of the song as if while stepping forward to meet the bridegroom, your feet yet hesitate upon the threshold and you glance back once more into the faces of your friends. Sing "Aber euch Schwestern grüss' ich mit Wehmut" with emotion and then continue with pride and dignity: "Freudig scheidend aus eurer Schaar." Your farewell has been *ritardando* but start *a tempo* at "Freudig scheidend". Realize that you cannot change too suddenly from one emotion to another . . . Don't sing "Freudig scheidend" with a sudden plunge into radiance, sing it with happiness but there is still a last tear of your "good-bye" in it, a last trembling sigh . . . This is difficult to explain but try to imagine this scene: "Good bye my dear friends. I have loved you and will always love you but now I am no longer one of you . . . Oh I am happy to become the wife of my beloved. There is nothing I want more to be. I go to my marriage as if the doors of heaven were opening for me . . . Yet: Good-bye!" The tear of farewell mingles with the tear of happiness . . . You must feel this, in order to express it.

The postlude is the wedding march. In your imagination you are walking to the altar clad in your bridal gown. You stand erect, your face uplifted, radiant,—you look into the face of God who has blessed you with the wonder of love.

VI *Süsser Freund, du blickest*

You have changed. This must be very clear. The way in which you lean against the piano should be different, your body is relaxed, you are more experienced. You are a woman now who also experiences the ecstacy of love in a sensual way. You are awakened. You know the power of passion. You know desire and fulfillment. Your voice is more vibrant. It has lost the untouched whiteness of your girlhood. Your *piano* tones are velvety and glowing.

Take the first chords as if your husband, in whose arms you are lying, has just lifted your face to his. Your eyes in tears meet his puzzled and questioning gaze. You say to him: "Süsser Freund". Never during the rapturous period of your betrothal have you called him "süsser Freund"—this says so much, this tenderness, this caressing way of addressing him. In it is the maturity of your bondage. He is more than a lover now, he is your understanding friend, your companion for always. And he is "süss" because you share with him all the secret enchantment, all the sensual delights of being one. Sing "Süsser Freund" with a vibrant tone, give these two words all the glowing significance of which they are born.

Sing softly and with a lovely floating *piano*. The *crescendi* ("Lass' der feuchten Perlen" and "freudig hell erzittern") should be sung very discretely, almost unnoticeably. "Wie so bang' mein Bussen" should be sung with a breathy tone and then with sudden decision (very subtly) —"Komm' und birg dein Antliz". Sing "will in's Ohr dir flüstern" very gracefully and with a smile of secret joy.

The interlude is the confession of your sweet secret and his response overwhelmed with happiness.

Begin with a quiet dignity at "Weisst du nun . . .", don't quicken the tempo, sing very quietly, warmly, softly. "Du geliebter, geliebter Mann" is to be sung with passion and intensity (consonants!). The interlude (*tempo* more vivid) again expresses his delight. He wants to rise, to tell you how complete will be the happiness which you share, to say so many, many things . . . But you stop him, holding him tighter in your embrace. Sing "Bleib' an meinem Herzen" with a sudden start as if you hold him back. You sing *accelerando,* with glowing passion until "fester" (consonants!). The interlude leads you to dreams and a drowsy happiness.

With restrained tears of joy you speak of your child. Give "der Morgen" and "daraus dein Bildnis" a warm *crescendo.* The interlude is his glowing kiss and whispering beneath his caressing lips, you sigh —"Dein Bildnis". Hold this, letting it fade away.

VII   *An meinem Herzen, an meiner Brust*

Now you are a mother. Fate has brought you the fulfillment of human life and your happiness knows no bounds. This joyous song should be sung as if words are unimportant. Never mind what you say, never mind who listens to you. You look at the tiny infant in your arms and laugh and weep and talk and smile, all in one breath. Sing with warm sincerity "Nur die da säugt" and guide the *ritardando* over into the joyful outburst of motherly pride: "Nur eine Mutter". The phrase "o wie bedaur' ich doch den Mann" has a smiling humor. But your thoughts return immediately to your child and you talk rapidly to him with trembling joy.

The postlude is like a surging wave of joy. Feel its sweep, take it up with your body, your exultant face.

VIII   *Nun hast du mir den ersten Schmerz getan*

But life which has showered you with so many blessings now has dealt you a blow under which your happiness has crumbled away like ashes: your husband has died. Perhaps long years of contentment lie between this song and the last one. I always feel it this way. I always imagine that the children which you have borne, are now grown up and living their own lives, as is the fate of parents. You have been happy in the thought of growing old with the companionship of your husband. But God who has given you so much, has denied you this last blessing which life can bestow. Your loss has struck as lightning to the very center of your being.

You are changed. Softness and sweetness have left you. The one discord which struck you down has destroyed your life. The blow has been so sudden, bursting so unexpectedly upon your inner contentment that you realize your pain with fury, and challenge fate as if it were an enemy. Imagine that you kneel beside the deathbed of the one you loved, feeling: but why? Why had he to go, leaving me to this desper- ate loneliness? How could he do this to me? Injustice and senseless reproach often sound through the complaint of a pained heart.

Your voice is like a terrible outcry, harsh, lacking in any loveliness. There is a dark rebellion in it. You stand erect, as if you are paralyzed. Your eyes are wide with horror. At "Es blicket die Verlass'ne vor sich hin" consciousness returns to you, your eyes loose the frightening ex- pression of madness. Sing "Die Welt ist leer, ist leer" with what the French call—"voix blanche"—hold the first "leer" long enough to let it become a discord with the accompaniment.

Now you go over into a *piano* which is rigid and austere until "nicht lebend mehr". In this phrase a dark resignation pervades you. You sing *piano* with a softer and darker quality. Hold "Schleier" in the same way as you did "leer" but softly and give an accent to "fällt". Visualize the *finality* in this word "fällt": life in its fullness has ended for you, there is no longer any present or future, there is only the past . . . Sing very slowly, very distinctly and with a dark, velvety, veiled *pianissimo*: "Da hab' ich dich und mein verlor'nes Glück—du meine Welt." Give great emphasis (but very subtly) to these last words, especially "du meine Welt". You stand very quietly until the end of the long postlude. You are like a statue of mourning. An in- cident which I recall may help to make clear to you the impression which your attitude should give here: long ago a wonderful friend of mine died. He was buried near Vienna in a remote little graveyard surrounded by forests and mountains. He had loved this spot and want- ed to be buried there, far from the world. But he had been a great artist and hundreds of people came from Vienna to attend his funeral. His grave was high up on the slope of a hill. As we followed his flower laden coffin I watched his widow climbing behind the pall bearers. She was a fragile little woman but the terrible grief of losing her hus- band could not crush her. She walked upwards with an heroic erectness, a noble dignity, her face uplifted to the hill where stood the open grave. She seemed to have the grandeur of a Greek statue. This is the impres- sion which you must convey throughout the postlude, while the music tells of the past.

ENGLISH, ITALIAN, FRENCH,
RUSSIAN SONGS

SHE NEVER TOLD HER LOVE

Shakespeare   *Haydn*

At the beginning of the introduction your head is slightly bowed. During the introduction you slowly raise it. You are thinking—"but did he not know that I loved him? Oh no, I could not tell him! I went my way quietly (5th bar) and outwardly gay. But (7th bar) in my heart was my secret. And when his eyes rested questioningly upon me (10th bar) I smiled at him without giving any answer—oh no, he does not know of my love for him . . ."

And now you start to sing. Your expression is very soft. You sing the first sentence as if you were wondering at your inner strength. In the repetition there is a slight, soft *sforzato* at "never". The short note at "her" should be sung very gracefully and exactly. (Haydn's music is *pure* music, sing clearly and be more than ever careful to give each note its exact value.)

In "but let concealment" you sing in a subdued whisper—as if telling a secret. You must feel the shiver which comes over you at the thought that you, who are so openhearted, are forced to resort to concealment. This concealment tortures you. "Like a worm in the bud" it slowly destroys your beauty and feeds upon your youth . . . Sing this "feed on her damask cheek" with great tenderness. (You think—oh how beautiful I used to be—until this love within my heart began to consume my loveliness! Oh how he, my beloved, would have enjoyed the velvet smoothness of my cheek—kissing me, holding me in his arms—if only he had ever loved me!)

The interlude is like the song of a bird—like the song of love—of spring. Your soul listens to it—and then your thoughts turn away from this ray of sunlight—back to reality.

Your gaze is now fixed upon something far away. Sing with very clear and distinct diction—"She sat, like patience". Sing this with a deep wonder—as if you feel how wonderful it is to have accomplished so completely the concealment of your unhappy love. Make a little pause before "patience"—just a fraction of a second. The word "patience" should stand out—but not through tone value,—on the contrary sing no real *forte* throughout this whole song! "Patience" is *piano,* but it must have the greatest of significance. (I shall never forget how Helen Hayes said this word. It was the greatest impression of the performance, when I heard her in "Twelfth Night". She said it very spontaneously as if she were saying it for the first time, after the briefest pause in which she gave the impression of searching for the right word. Her great art made me shiver with delight!)

"On a monument" is *piantissimo* with long *coronas*. ("On" should be the shortest of the three *coronas*.) Your eyes gazing far away, are opened widely, your face is grave and has the expression of an almost sacred awe.

Now at "smiling, smiling at grief"—a sad smile lightens your face —and if you really understand the incredible beauty of this song, you will understand what I say:— your *lips* smile, but your eyes remain grave . . . Only by really *living* this song, will you be able to do what I mean. This music in its noble simplicity and purity is as beautiful as Shakespeare's words. If you feel both music and poem with your whole being, you will find this subtle expression between smile and secret tears. Give the word "grief" a soft *sforzato*. This is the only moment when you sing approaching a *forte*. But sing it with a warm, velvet quality. (Let the *r* roll—it gives importance to the word.)

The interlude is again like a song from a happier world. As if you think,—"Oh, how real and filled with bliss would be my smile, if only he might have loved me!"

The interlude begins with a full *forte* and fades away like a smiling sigh—and you repeat, smiling sadly,—"smiling, smiling at grief." The *coronas* should be long and very *piano*.

Sing each syllable very distinctly. There is a slight *ritardando* until the end. Your eyes retain their far away look—your lips—their sad smile, until the end of the postlude.

THE PLAGUE OF LOVE

Dr. Arne

You have said to yourself—"What is the matter with me?" I have changed. I am restless, I cannot think, I cannot work. Always before my inner eye is the one girl—always Celia. What is it? Can I be in love?"

These thoughts run through you, as you begin the song. Perhaps it is an answer to someone who has asked you all these questions. In any case imagine during the introduction, that there is a question. Then your face will have the right expression. Sing the first phrase—"Yes I'm in love" with a rather exaggerated little sigh—almost humorously, as if you say—"I know it is terrible to be such a victim of love . . .". "And Celia has undone me" should be sung with an almost helpless expression, but don't be at all tragic. It is a smiling surrender, a surrender which you thoroughly enjoy.

"And yet I swear" is *accelerando,* with a new and vivid expression. You say to yourself: "Why am I so in love with her? Why?" And you give yourself the answer, filled with astonishment: "I can't tell how the pleasing plague stole on me!" Give to "pleasing plague" an almost comic delight. "On me" should be a little slower—filled with happiness,—then quicken the *tempo* again in the repetition of the phrase. The second "The pleasing plague stole on me" should be very *"ritardando."* There should be a *corona* on "stole" and then sing "on me" quickly, with a piquant grace. The chord which follows these words is as if you wanted to say to the audience—"See???"

Then in the interlude you think—"But how is it that I fell in love? What is there about her which is so strangely attractive?" Give yourself the answer—"Her voice, her smile might give th' alarm". From here until the end, sing as you did in the first verse . . . Sing the final "stole on me" very gracefully, smiling, filled with delight. Hold the last tone —with an expression of questioning yourself and your audience.

PHILLIDA AND CORRIDON

Old English

Begin this song with a gay smile. "When you sing: "There I spy'd all alone" sing it as though you were telling a bit of gossip to a friend and sing "Phillida and Corydon" with a malicious smile, as if you said to someone else—"You see? I always told you so. They are lovers. Isn't it a scandal?" The whole song must be sung as if it is pure gossip.

"Much ado there was, God wot" seems very much an indication of gossiping. Sing it as if you were an old spinster whose morals are a bit shocked but who is just the same a little envious! You must change very quickly between *his* talking and *her* talking. You should sing this song very often for yourself so that it is absolutely familiar to you and you can make the quick changes without any effort. *He* is always very romantic, *she* is coy and finnicky. Sing quickly: "Corydon would kiss her then" and be very distinct when you sing: "She said maids would kiss no men".

The ending of this verse "Ne'er was loved so fair a youth" is slightly ironic—always smiling.

The last verse should be sung with much exaggeration, make a distinct *ritardando* at "was with kisses sweet concluded". Sing the ending with great haughtiness and superiority.

At the end laugh toward the audience. Always after a gay song give the audience the feeling that you enjoy it in the same way they do. Always be a part of the audience.

The original poem published from manuscript (author unknown) in Percy's Reliques of Ancient English Poetry. London. 1765. consists of seven verses. There are a number of musical settings which have used varying verses. I have used the edition of F. H. Potter in his Reliquary of English song. G. Schirmer, Inc. New York.

COME LET'S BE MERRY

Old English

This song should be sung as if it were a dance, very gay, carefree, jubilant. You must play with the audience—sing directly to it, let the audience, so to speak, take part in the singing and dancing which you are bringing to life. With the first chords you laugh toward the audience as if you were asking them to join you in your merry mood. Your body sways a little with the rhythm of the song (very discretely) and with the last chord of the introduction, you throw back your head and start singing as if you were calling to them all—"Come let's be merry!" Sing the first phrase and its repetition with increasing expression—in a gay *crescendo*. Sing with a playful expression—"for since the world's gone mad, mad, mad," and with a shrug of your shoulders—"Why alone should we be wise". In the next sentence at "and like dull fools" laugh at the audience as if you would say—"everyone who doesn't feel as I do is a fool". . . .

The piano interlude between the first and second verses is a dance. Your thoughts dance, your eyes dance with merriment, your body takes on the rhythm of the dance (with great discretion).

The second verse should be sung very smoothly. You must give your audience and yourself the delight of a quiet musical line. So just sing the second verse in a lovely floating tone. Take the phrase "shall be as gay"—very lightly, with a silvery quality. With the word "perplexed" you return to the humor with which you began the song. This word is the transition between the soft musical line and the dancing gaiety. Immediately take up the rhythm of the musical interlude. Look laughingly at the audience as if you were looking for someone among them with whom you could share your pleasure and joy.

Sing the last verse with a coquettish and almost naughty expression: "if you have leisure, follow pleasure . . ." sing this "follow pleasure" as if you were telling them a secret,—a rather naughty secret... (As a child might say to another child—"Come with me, I'll show you something, but don't tell anybody. It's a big secret!") The phrase— "For, as the fleeting moments fly" should be sung in a lovely broad tone. Then sing—"Time it will your youth decay" with a certain regret in your voice and in your expression, as if you were saying—"Ah, it is terrible, someday we shall all be old and cold . . . But I don't care now . . . I am young and happy and am going to enjoy life without thinking that someday all pleasure will be ended . . ."

The ending of the song—"Then try to live and enjoy while you may," should be sung as if you were saying to the audience—"See how right I am? Do as I advise you, be happy with me!" The words: "try to live and enjoy" should be sung in one breath. Sing with a lovely *forte* tone. Sing "while" with a gay *corona*—and with the last chord, end with your head thrown back gaily.

INVOCAZIONE DI ORFEO

Rinuccini   *Peri*

With the first chord of the introduction you must give the impression of being ecstatically happy. You want to embrace the whole world with the overflowing joy of your heart.

With the beginning of the musical introduction, think and feel the first rapturous call: "Gioite al canto mio!" If you really think and feel these words you will have the right facial expression and the right bearing. Begin radiantly and with a broad *forte*—but it must be a *forte* without any hardness—noble, inspired, elated. Feel this *forte* as if it comes from your own heart.

"Selve frondose" should be sung in a soft and exalted *mezzo voce,* one cannot sing harshly of something beautiful . . . A forest is serene, lovely, filled with the soft melody of the wind as it breathes through the swaying branches of the silent trees . . . So your voice melts from the first rapturous *forte* into a soft *mezzoforte.* This same quality continues through the first "Eco rimbombi dalle valli ascose,". The repetition of this phrase must be sung with a rapturous *pianissimo* as if in your imagination you hear the lovely and ethereal quality with which the echo brings back your own voice soaring through the air, yet a part of it. And now sing with an expression of quiet happiness. (Save, that you may build up!) Imagine singing to the accompaniment of a harp, imagine that you are Orpheus and have just found your Eurydice . . . Your body should convey the suggestion of walking with the rhythmic flow of the accompaniment.

"Risorto e il mio bel sol" is like a new beginning. The tempo is a little faster but do not sing too loudly. Always remember that one is not dependent upon volume of tone for expression.

At "Di raggiadorno" your eyes seem to see sunlight all about you. Don't fix your eyes upon anything definite. There is sunlight everywhere, not only above you.

"E coi begli occhi" should be sung with tenderness. The eyes of the sun, the eyes of Eurydice become *one* in your heart. "Onde fa scorno a Delo": Delos, the Greek island, with its shimmering white coast, seems as a shadow under the radiant eyes of the sun. (The radiant eyes of Eurydice you feel subconsciously.) Sing this smilingly, with the exaggeration of one in love.

With "Raddoppia fuoco all'alme e luce al giorno", return to the quiet rapture with which you sang "selve frondose" etc.

Now there is a slow *crescendo*, a preparation for the climax: "E fa servi d'amor". Don't sing the first "fa" with a too strong *forte*, if you do, you ruin the progressive effect and the construction of the aria, since you diminish the effect of the final climax if you sing too loudly here. (Save, prepare, build up!) Now give to the last sentence, to the repetition: "E fa servi d'amor la terra e il cielo", a broad, decisive and majestic *forte*. It is better to breathe before the last word but don't do it quickly and don't be unsure of yourself. Breathe with authority.

TU LO SAI

Torelli

This song is not a confession of love. Something terrible has come between you and your beloved. You have done something which has hurt her (or him). But whatever you have done, it did not touch your great devotion and love, which is more than everything to you. So you come to your beloved—confessing, asking forgiveness. There has been a long and painful conversation. But she has shown no pity for you. You have pleaded humbly, lovingly. But the face of your beloved has remained cold, her heart untouched, without understanding, without forgiving kindness.

Now you are at the end of your strength.

. .

This is the inner preparation for this song. Before the beginning of the musical introduction, you stand,—with your head slightly bowed, you may close your eyes for a moment. Concentrate! This very passionate song demands your whole being. So take your time, prepare yourself.

With the first chord you slowly raise your head. Your face mirrors your pain. Your eyes are sad and shadowed as if with tears. The *crescendo* of the introduction is the outburst of your desperation. An outburst without words . . . In the sudden *pianissimo* lies complete hopelessness—it is like a sigh of resignation,—as if you say to yourself—"Why do I try to tell her what I feel? I know it is in vain, all is in vain, all I have said and all I shall say." Out of this conviction devoid of any hope is sung the first sentence, subdued as if with tears. There is a slight *crescendo* before "crudel". Emphasize the consonants in "crudel", roll the *r* and make a slight pause before *d* as if you hesitate to say a scolding word. While you accuse her of being cruel, you at the same time ask her forgiveness for calling her cruel. The repetition of this sentence should be sung very quietly, with a lovely floating *legato*, almost without expression. (Sometimes the deepest grief can find no words. So this phrase must be quiet, empty, as if it would hurt if you should give it voice or soul.) The last word—"crudel" is the transition to the passionate plea, the last effort to touch the heart of your beloved. You can't suddenly jump into the *tempo agitato;* there must be a connection with the emptiness and exhaustion of your last phrase. This connection is the word "crudel". Now the tempo becomes faster. Feverishly, you pour out the bitterness of your thoughts and feelings. Sing the syncopated rhythm very distinctly. It gives dramatic energy to the phrase. Through the music should sound the restlessness of your beating heart. Your heartbeats should race with your words in a quickened and almost breathless tempo. "I want nothing from you, I want only that you should remember how I have always loved you. Then you may turn away from me". "Un infidel" should be sung *ritenuto*— as if you scarcely dare to say this word. But having said it, you repeat it (again *a tempo*) and with "sprezza" the *ritardando* has a very different meaning from the *ritardando* at "infidel". It is now as if you are bowed down by your pain and desperation. It is rather difficult to find the right moment to commence the *ppp* repetition of "tu lo sai". If you begin it too soon, you break the spell—if you start it too late you destroy the musical connection. Be careful here and study exactly when to come in.

Your eyes are closed, your face should look as if a hand from heaven had touched, it for you have now said everything which it is possible for you to say, you have given your heart, your soul, your life into the hands of your beloved, as if you gave yourself to God. Here even the word "crudel" has no bitterness, it is more like a caress—you say it unconsciously, softly and with the sweetest possible expression. The next repetition is a quiet musical line, *legato, piano.* Prepare slowly and carefully, the great *crescendo,* the terrible outbreak. As if slowly awaking from your heavenly trance you go over into a pathetic and almost threatening *fortissimo.* It is as if your whole being grows and grows, as if the whole tragedy has found at last the right expression. You are beyond tears, free of all restraint. You don't implore, you don't pray, you don't dream any more . . . You have done everything which is humanly possible to win back the heart of her whom you have loved so desperately. Now it is only your passion which speaks. The two *coronas* in "Quanto t'amai" are long and powerful. Notice now that there is again a *fortissimo* and a sudden *pianissimo.* (Remember the same effect in the introduction!) And here as in the introduction you feel—

"It is in vain—whatever I may say or do, it is in vain." But you are now exhausted. Perhaps this is not just the ending of a quarrel, of a misunderstanding. Perhaps it is the end of your *love*. Perhaps everything is now ended. Perhaps you will end your own life, perhaps you will go away, never to see again this being who has tortured you. All your bitterness is in the last: "lo sai, crudel!" There is a long *corona* at "sai" and make the short note in "crudel" very short and very dramatic.

Remember that you should never begin a song without first imagining the story which underlies it and that you should never end a song without considering the continuation of the story which goes beyond the ending of the song. In this aria you have brought to life a human tragedy. Feel as you end it, the overwhelming loneliness which lies before you.

LASCIATEMI MORIRE
LAMENTO DE ARIANNA

Monteverdi

There must be grandeur in the delivery of this lament. Do not drag it down to the level of mediocrity through sentimentality!

At the beginning your head is slightly bowed. Raise it slowly with the introductory chords. Sing the first "Lasciatemi morire" with restraint, like an inner prayer. Sing the second "Lasciatemi" mounting in an heroic pleading and then—withdrawn within yourself, with closed eyes, restrained, trembling—"morire". (I must always repeat, in order that there may be no misunderstanding, that the external means of expression—bowing and raising the head, closing the eyes, etc.—should arise from your own feeling. *Only what you really feel is convincing.* If you deliberately search for ways of expression, which instead of stemming from your own feeling, are the result of cold consideration, of calculation, you degrade the great task which, as a singer, is yours. Sincerity is always triumphant in life and real art is a pledge of purest truth. If I make suggestions of an apparently outward nature, you must understand that they are only intended as suggestions which I offer with the hope of awakening your own imagination and leading you away from the conventional tendency to "just sing" with feeling for the melody alone, into the sphere of singing as a living experience . . . Whether you close or open your eyes, raise or lower your head, is not essential. The important thing is that you bring to life both word and tone, infusing them with your own soul. If you make any gesture simply because you are told to, without yourself feeling the inner necessity for it, then that gesture is wrong for you. On the other hand if you

168

truly *feel,* you will find the expression suitable to your own personality
—in singing, facial expression, bearing . . .)

The whole middle part of this noble aria is one continuous mounting to the *fortissimo* "gran martire". Begin piano, with restraint: "E
che volete che mi conforte"—enunciate very clearly. There should also
be restraint in your bearing: stand as if shrinking into yourself, so that
you may straighten up with the slowly mounting *crescendo*: "In
cosi dura sorte, In cosi gran martire?" You now stand very erect. Your
eyes again close at the first "Lasciatemi morire"—sing this with a very
lightly colored voice, as if already remote from the world, ethereally,
in a softly welling *crescendo* and *decrescendo.* And now—at the end—
you pull yourself up yet again for the violent and pleading outburst:
"Lasciatemi." Each syllable is broad, accented, ejected with the greatest
energy. Imagine that you are looking into the face of the divinity,
which might give you release. This face is mute to your lament—now
your despair bursts from you and breaks in a great surge upon the stony
image of the divinity. Imagine that with the final word "morire" you
fall to your knees. Your wild demand becomes again a prayer, becomes
a tearful, trembling plea. Sing in a whisper as if through tears. Remain under the spell of the music, even after it has faded away in this
last sigh.

PLAISIRS D'AMOUR

Martini

This whole song is pervaded by a smiling resignation. For his own
consolation the disappointed lover has worked out a philosophic understanding of the changing and independent nature of love itself. He is
not even cross with the faithless Sylvie—how could he be? He knows
that she—like many changeable human beings—is a victim of her own
faithless nature. He understands, he forgives, he smiles . . . It seems
that this disappointment in love is not his first. One can't look philo-
sophically at the first sad experience of love. He seems to smile a little
at himself, that after so many disappointments, he could still have believed and hoped in spite of his own inner distrust. He takes this new
experience with a slight sigh of ironical self reproach: "fool that I am
again! Shall I never learn?"

The prelude begins with an *allegretto graziose.* You listen to the
gliding musical figures as if you hear in remembrance the gay laughter
of Sylvie. Then the *crescendo* is a slight sigh of resignation. Your facial
expression is quiet, you smile, your eyes have a far away look. Sing in
a soft *piano* with only a very tender *crescendo* at "amour". At "chagrin
d'amour" sing in a warm and dark *mezzoforte.* But the graceful and

almost elegant line of "vie" subdues the sad expression turning it into
one of smiling resignation. During the interlude the smile continues.

Now start with a slightly quickened tempo—"J'ai tout quitté."
Your eyes should reflect a feeling almost of scorn for your own weakness and "elle me quitte" is mixed with bitterness and understanding
and forgiveness.

The interlude is a transition from a subdued expression of bitterness to an openly scornful smile,—as if you say to yourself: "see—I
have always known it. How foolish to have illusions still, when I know
reality."

You repeat now "Plaisir d'amour" with irony. Don't turn it into
tragedy! It must not loose the character of being superior in an understanding way about your own disappointment. Bring a faint shadow
of sentimentality into the last *ritardando* at "vie" and close with a beautiful *pianissimo.*

During the interlude, think—"oh what lovely things she used to
say to me! Blessed time, when I believed in her! But alas, I soon
learned!"

Now sing with a slightly exaggerated tenderness, in a quickened
tempo, with a broad *crescendo* and as much dramatic expression as is
possible within the framework of this little song. But one must feel
that you *intentionally* sing dramatically and with exaggerated expression. At "me répétait Sylvie" return to a subdued tone. This sentence
should be sung *mezzoforte* as if in a parenthesis. Now change *immediately*: "L'eau coule encore" is *subito pianissimo* and *ritardando.* Your
smile is sad, you try in vain to look at your unfortunate love affair with
ironical superiority. Under the shadow of reminiscence, sadness falls
like a veil over your face,—and your smile is filled with disappointment
and inner pain. This expression is the transition to the last "Plaisir
d'amour".

Continuing this rather sad mood through the interlude, you start
to sing with deep expression in a warm *crescendo* and *decrescendo* up to
"moment". There is a *sforzato* on each syllable of "Chagrin d'amour".
Do this as if you were supporting yourself, as if you must pull yourself
together to find your way back to your philosophical irony.

The last "la vie" is *piano* and *ritardando.* Your smile returns and
should not leave your face until the end.

LA FLÛTE DE PAN

Louys   *Debussy*

You are a very young girl, hardly more than a child. In any case
though a child in years there buds within you the first suggestion, the
first shy flow of unrealized emotion . . . And he, the man whom, with
your childish enthusiasm, you adore, finds such pleasure in this half
child, that he gladly talks with you and teaches you and has discovered
with delight your love for music . . . Now he will teach you to play the
little songs which you have often sung for him with your sweet voice,
for he has given you a flute, a most enchanting little rosewood flute.
You should begin to convey this even in the *prelude*: feel the playful
guing present and how overjoyed you were with it . . . Sing with a
lightly colored, childlike voice, very sweetly and with a restrained
and delicate music, think of the day when he brought you this intri-
tempo: "Pour le jour des Hyacinthies, il m'a donné une syrinx faite de
roseaux bien taillés, unis avec la blanche cire qui est douce à mes lèvres
comme le miel." Sing "comme le miel" with great restraint and an expression of greediness as if you felt the sweet taste of honey upon your
lips, making these words very childlike and charming . . . Sing *a tempo*: "Il m'apprend à jouer, assise sur ses genoux,—mais je suis un peu
tremblante . . ." At this recollection a shiver of delight runs through
you . . . It was sweet and wonderful to sit upon his knees, just like a
nice child,—but it makes you tremble to be so near him . . . He played
for you upon the little rosewood flute—so softly that you could scarcely hear him . . . Or was it the violent beating of your heart which
drowned the sweet music? Sing with a soft shyness: "Il en joue après
moi, si doucement que je l'entends à peine . . ." You would have so
gladly thanked him, so gladly have spoken a loving word to him but
you couldn't think what to say. And he was quiet too. What could you
say to one another? You were near to each other—wasn't that enough?
Sing gently, with great devotion, as if lost in remembrance: "Nous
n'avons rien à nous dire, tant nous sommes près l'un de l'autre" . . .
But your heart would answer his music, you bent toward him and meet-
ing you, he drank from your lips the silent words which became one
with his upon the rosewood of the flute . . . Sing with restraint but with
a soft animation, trembling sweetly: "Mais nos chansons veulent se ré-
pondre, et tour à tour nos bouches s'unissent sur la flûte". Make a *ritardando* at "bouches" spinning it out with an expression of longing, with
great devotion, very sweetly and warmly. In the short interlude it is as
if you straighten up from out of his arms which have gently embraced
you. You try to be again the nice child, in confusion you look around

you and in your imagination you slide from off his knee . . . Sing with a light voice quality and with changed expression, very alert as if with a sudden start: "Il est tard; voici le chant des grenouilles vertes, qui commence avec la nuit." In the interlude escaping from your friend you want to go away, but remain standing still as if in a kind of enchantment, listening to the song of the frogs coming from the meadows. You turn toward him and say with a roguish coquetry: "Ma mère ne croira jamais que je suis restée si longtemps à chercher ma ceinture perdue . . ." This should be sung whimsically, half laughing. Hold an expression of smiling consideration until the end of the postlude.

COLLOQUE SENTIMENTAL

Verlaine *Debussy*

This whole song is overshadowed by an atmosphere of uncanniness and the cold of death. The fearful emptiness of an old frozen and abandoned park on a bleak and desolate winter day grips the heart as with the hands of death. The lifeless branches of the skeleton-like trees are shrouded in a heavy fog. You see gliding through the fog, two figures, two disembodied ghosts, over whom, perhaps, when they were young and vividly alive, the green trees of this old park had once arched, very, very long ago, when the park still flourished and was green and filled with bloom, and when the ruined statues still shone out from amidst the dark concealing shrubbery in all their pure beauty,—when the old stone benches now falling to pieces were still inviting for rest and for a stolen hour of love . . .

With the beginning of the prelude feel the icy stillness, the lifeless gruesome desolation of the abandoned park. Stand rigidly, as if under a spell,—your glance sweeps into the distance in breathless concentration—as if you see the two uncanny figures passing by . . . Begin to sing without expression. Syllable after syllable falls from your lips which scarcely seem to move: "Dans le vieux parc solitaire et glacé Deux formes ont tout à l'heure passé." Sing with horror and bated breath: "Leurs yeux sont morts et leurs lèvres sont molles"—sing "molles" as if with an inner shudder. Become slower in *tempo* (it was from the beginning *molto lento*) and sing still more softly: "Et l'on entend à peine leurs paroles". Sing a little more animatedly and very distinctly but with the utmost *pianissimo*: "Dans le vieux parc solitaire et glacé" and with "Deux spectres ont évoqué le passé" make a broad *ritardando* emphasizing each word in a half *parlando*.

Now you listen to the strange conversation between the two ghosts. The figure which had once been the woman is still bound to the earth by the shadow of her longing, her melancholy memories. The music surges with a strange confusing sweetness, breaking in upon the icy and drab desolation of the fog like a flickering light. Feel this music within you as if with a deep sigh. Your head which has been bowed is raised slowly and gently, you smile, as if from a memory wafted to you from afar, (for *you* are now the spirit of this woman who is remembering and yearning . . .)—Sing "Te souvient-il de notre extase ancienne?" very softly but with a sentimental exuberance, in a veiled *pianissimo*, making it transcendent and unreal, with a passion which has lost every vestige of earthliness.

The answer of the other ghost comes as if from another sphere. He is far removed from any earthly bondage for he no longer remembers and all that was earthly has fallen from him. His soaring through this old abandoned park is only something accidental and unsought for . . . His voice must sound as if it comes from out of the grave. Color your voice very darkly, giving it a hollow quality, sing as if emerging from a stupor, half unconscious, and very *piano*, veiled, each syllable heavily accentuated, with great restraint: "Pourquoi voulez-vous donc qu'il m'en souvienne?" There is again a surge of the sweetest music, again memory sweeps over *you*, the spirit of the *woman*: "Ton coeur bat-il toujours à mon seul nom? Toujours vois-tu mon âme en rêve?" You must realize that these two figures although they are together, floating side by side through the park, actually are soaring through different spheres . . . Question and answer meet, so to speak, in the air—there is a question, there is an answer, but neither spirit really knows anything of the other's presence. For this reason the woman does not react to the rejection (if one may use here such a worldly expression) but continues to live only in her own world of blissful memories, while the spirit of the man feels the question only as a kind of disturbance which he dismisses with subconscious resistance . . . So sing this question—"Ton coeur bat-il toujours à mon seul nom" etc. with the same enthusiastic sentimentality as the previous one. His answer is a quiet, expressionless —"non". But she loses herself completely in the loveliest memories— kisses, which she had exchanged during secret impassioned nights with her beloved, who, once loved above all else, now invisibly and unknow ingly goes his own way, at her side—kisses, which both once enjoyed and which she has been unable to forget. With overflowing joy, you sing: "Ah! les beaux jours de bonheur indicible, où nous joignions nos bouches!" The great longing of the floating figure beside him awakens a vestige of his lost memory . . . It is like a momentary pause in the peaceful gliding, like a faint touch upon his brow, like a moment of emerging from the oblivion of sleep . . . So you sing, half *parlando*, with an amazement in which there is no earthly trace: "C'est possible . . ." It is as if the vast emptiness has now touched you, the woman, as if the vast and icy desolation has pressed in upon you . . .

You tremble . . . Your voice quivers. If you were human, it would
be tears which make you tremble—when you sing, slowly, and drawn
out as with a deep sigh: "Qu'il était bleu, le ciel, et grand l'espoir!"
And from out of an infinite coolness, an inconceivable emptiness, the
answer comes—dark and restrained, slowly and sharply accentuated:
"L'espoir a fui, vaincu, vers le ciel noir." The ever resurgent questions
of the woman with their vivid flow of memories have pressed in upon
him like shadows . . . Now he buries them with all the earthly cumber-
someness from out of which he floated so very long ago . . . Like an
icy hand the burden of his disillusionments is placed upon the passionate questioning of the woman: it is the last word which he says, a word
of hopelessness . . . You see the two spirits floating away, lost in the
density of the fog, both speaking their own words, neither with any realization of the other, the one filled with senseless desire, the other
merely drifting away . . .

The night now hears their words . . . *You are the night*—stand
quietly listening to them, looking after them, without expression, without life . . .

LA CHEVELURE

Louys   *Debussy*

To do justice to this song, you must sing it without restraint. A
young singer once said to me that it was impossible to sing any song
so realistically, that it made her feel ashamed—as if she were "undres-
sing in public" if she surrendered her whole being to the glowing sen-
suality of these verses and music. In my opinion this attitude is a very
false one. It is much better not to sing this song at all, if one has
prudish inhibitions, or if one thinks: the song in itself is beautiful and
effective, I sing it beautifully and it will have just as much effect as if
I do "too much" with it . . . No: this song is a surrender. Sing it with
complete devotion, you must be the woman who is so passionately in
love, who in this secret hour tells her closest friend the intimate mys-
teries of her love . . .

Begin very slowly, as if emerging from the rapture of sweet dreams.
Don't sing "Il m'a dit" with the lugubrious and heavily emphasized
importance with which I have sometimes heard it sung. No, sing it
lightly with a soft quality and without any sentimentality. The slow
tempo might mislead one into singing this phrase with a melancholy
which is entirely out of place. Consider this carefully and imagine how
you would say it if you were confiding a delightful secret to your friend
—smilingly, intimately, with a light and silvery quality.

Now you repeat the words of your beloved—do this with all the passion which had trembled in his voice when he himself spoke to you . . . The tempo quickens—don't drag this song! Sing with restraint, in a veiled *piano*: "cette nuit j'ai rêvé". There should be an expression of dreamy reminiscence and a quiet flow in the phrases: "J'avais ta chevelure autour de mon cou. J'avais tes cheveux comme un collier noir autour de ma nuque" and then make a glowing *crescendo* at "et sur ma poitrine". Sing this with an inner trembling, impulsively and passionately. Then again return to a quieter *tempo* and *piano* in a lovely warm timbre at: "Je les caressais, et c'étaient les miens" with deep emotion, radiant with love. Build up in the following phrases, rising from a voluptuously spun out *piano* to the passionate outburst: "et nous étions liés pour toujours ainsi", (at "toujours" begin the *crescendo*) "par la même chevelure la bouche sur la bouche." This should be sung impulsively with an inner violence. (Note the very accentuated notes at "sur la"). Cut off the word "bouche" sharply in a strong, resounding *forte*—and sing *subito piano* and in a quieter *tempo*: "ainsi que deux lauriers n'ont souvent qu'une racine". Sing this with a certain wistfulness, filled with glowing passion but with restraint.

The next phrases have the same mounting climax as before (at "et nous étions liés): begin *pianissimo* making a gradual *crescendo* until, with quickened *tempo,* pressing and impetuous, you close with a broad *fortissimo*—as if intoxicated and overwhelmed: "Et peu à peu, il m'a semblé, tant nos membres étaient confondus, que je devenais toi-même ou que tu entrais en moi comme mon songe". Hold the *fermate* of the accompaniment with your eyes closed, your head thrown back in a gesture of complete surrender. With the change of key you pull yourself out of this spell of passionate reminiscence and are again the young woman who is *telling* all this . . . Color your voice lightly, singing in a slow *tempo,* as if dreaming, with a smile of enchantment: "quand il eut achevé il mit doucement ses mains sur mes épaules." Each word should be sung with a delicate emphasis, experience again your exitement at his touch upon your shoulders, rejoice in this memory. Now sing still more slowly, with great restraint, in a veiled *pianissimo*: "et il me regarda d'un regard si tendre, que je baissai les yeux avec un frisson". Accent "regarda" and "tendre" with great tenderness. Let the last phrase "que je baissai les yeux avec un frisson" die away with the utmost *pianissimo,* singing "avec un frisson" half *parlando.* Feel the shiver which runs through you again, making you hold your breath as his glance melts into yours. . . .

FANTOCHES

Verlaine   *Debussy*

With the beginning of the prelude you look smilingly and attentively into the distance. You seem to be searching uncertainly as if you
see indistinct figures scurrying by with the capricious notes of the accompaniment. Begin laughingly and as if, at the moment when you
begin to sing, you recognize the figures in the dark. The "la la la" is
to be sung laughingly, you are very much amused. Sing with a mocking
dignity: "Cependant l'excellent docteur Bolonais cuielle avec lenteur
Des simples" and with an artificial and comically hollow voice—(always with great amusement!)—"parmi l'herbe brune". Here your expression changes: you see his charming daughter, sing with a smile of
delight, with a roguish piquancy: "Lors sa fille, piquant minois, sous
la charmille, en tapinois Se glisse demi nue", sing this very coquettishly and note the upward slide from "se" to "glisse" and the *staccati*.
Sing this "la la la" seductively, coquettishly, with flashing eyes, as if
imitating the girl who is so very conscious of her charm . . . Sing "en
quête De son beau pirate espagnol" with great mystery and with an expression of audacity. One must see before one the fiery Spaniard who
awaits the pretty girl with burning impatience . . . It will help you to
give the right effect if you sing the consonants in "pirate espagnol" very
sharply and roll the *r*.

With "Dont un amoureux rossignol Clame la détresse à tuctête"
change the quality of your voice, this should be sung with the enthusiasm and sentimentality of one in love. Sing vicaciously but in a soft
flow with a lovely swinging *crescendo* to "tuctête". This last word
should be sung very *pianissimo* and should fade away with the greatest
delicacy but give a light *staccato* ending to the last syllable.

In the rapid scurrying of the interlude, you seem to listen to the distance with smiling amusement. Sing the first "la la" with a mockingly
rapturous expression as if you are quite amused by this secret little adventure of the doctor's pretty daughter . . . Sing the last "la la" like a
very sentimental sigh which dies away. But keep your smile—nothing
in this graceful and playful song should ever be taken seriously.

LE MANOIR DE ROSAMONDE

de Bonnieres   *Duparc*

Something akin to madness rages through this song. Pursuing one
goal, following one feverish desire, your whole life has been a frantic
pursuit. Somewhere—far off in the distance—must exist the mansion

where Rosamonde lives and reigns as its lovely queen. You have only seen her fleetingly. Perhaps as a young knight, you saw her in all her queenly glamour, surrounded by her followers. And perhaps as you bowed before her, you looked up into the dazzling blue of her eyes. Like a bolt of lightning her glance flashed into your heart. The smile with which she greeted you was a burning torch—setting alight the fire of your passion. You saw from her eyes that you pleased her. But she went away—fading like a mirage into the blue horizon. Ever since then her smile has haunted you. You know nothing of her. You know only her name—Rosamonde. Did you hear someone calling her—or is it only the name your dreams have given her? You do not know . . . Because you cannot find her, your life seems worthless . . . Your burning passion has become a kind of obsession. You must find her, you must find her home, her far away home where she merged with the blue horizon.

And so you leave your home and begin your endless quest for Rosa-monde. Your life has become nothing but this mad pursuit. Possessed and driven by passionate desire, you race on through the world, seek-ing—a phantom. You know that in the end this wild chase will only destroy you, but you are lost. It is your fate to be destroyed. Like the victim of an avalanche, you rush into the abyss of your destruction.

Sometimes the voices of your friends seek to hold you back. Some-times loving hands try to restrain you. Sometimes others ask desper-ately—"Where are you going? Let me join you!" It is all in vain. You must be alone. One, possessed as you are, may have no friends.

Before beginning this song, imagine the terrible loneliness, the des-pair, the mad resolution of this man. Imagine that someone has come to you asking insistently—"why do you destroy yourself?"—someone who tries to hold you back.

For a moment you rein in your savage black horse. It halts, trem-bling. It pants and foams . . . And you hurl your answer into the face of your questioning friend: "This love has bitten me like a mad dog." Sing this with accentuation and with a wild and terrifying expression. End "vorace" and "mordu" abruptly, very short and hard.

The interlude is an expression of your mad impatience. Laughing wildly you answer the question which you have seen in your friend's eyes,—"But how can I follow you?" Your answer is savage—"Follow the traces of my blood. That is the trail to follow." Sing with increas-ingly threatening wildness and *crescendo* to: "Si la course ne te haras-se." This last sentence is full of scorn and of the dark and sombre triumph of one who knows that no one would ever dare to share your wild life, with all its dreadful deeds . . .

The interlude is the transition from scorn to deep pain. A kind of exhaustion sweeps over you. You feel weak, as you suddenly realize the futility of your mad pursuit and know that it will be forever in vain . . . You see before you your lonely and tragic end. You know that it will soon be upon you. Sing slowly and *piano*—"En passant par où j'ai passé—" (In the accompaniment is a brief suggestion of your horse's wild hoof beats.) You sing the next broken words as if overcome with pain, breathing heavily. Make a desperate *crescendo* at "J'ai parcouru ce triste monde," while the accompaniment says—"upward, onward, always madly forward . . ." With the *forte* chord it is as if you see before you the commanding figure of death . . . Your end, your surrender, and the realization in dying that everything has been senseless and futile. You never reached your goal. You must die without ever again seeing Rosamonde. The blue horizon has consumed her image. The mansion where she reigns, the blue mansion of your dreams and your desire, has been only an illusion. Fate has been unwilling that you should die upon the threshold of this mansion,—no, you may only die in lonely and senseless destruction . . .

At the end of the song, you fade away, like a ghost, into emptiness.

L'INVITATION AU VOYAGE

Baudelaire   *Duparc*

A bewitching half light pervades this entire song—playful dreaming . . . longing without desire, without pain . . . imagination searching for beauty . . . an eagerness to give happiness, without asking anything in return . . . a dream such as one might dream on a lovely summer day, when the sun is warm and veiled in mist and you lie stretched out upon a flowering meadow beside your beloved—contented, relaxed in revery . . .

The music begins with a delicate weaving, like billowing veils of mist, warmed by the sun, light and silvery . . . Begin to sing as if emerging from a lovely dream—sing with a quality of remoteness, softly and devotedly. The words and tones: "Mon enfant, ma soeur," radiate the deep contentment which pervades you . . . At this moment you are so free from any desire, so completely free of passion, that you can say: "my sister" . . . Sing with a soft swing, with a delicate *crescendo* and *decrescendo,* rising and falling like a gentle wave: "Songe à la douceur D'aller là-bas vivre ensemble, Aimer à loisir, Aimer et mourir au pays qui te resemble!" Sing these last words with great tenderness. Become a little more animated at "Les soleils mouillés De ces ciels brouillés" and a little restrained at "pour mon esprit" going on with tender delight: "ont les charmes Si mystérieux De tes traîtres yeux". Emphasize the *r* in "traîtres", there should be a suggestion of slumbering passion in the way you caress these words . . . Sing "Brillant à travers leurs larmes" *diminuendo*—so that you can sing "larmes" in the sweetest *pianis-simo*. The accompaniment now emerges from its weaving rhythm and becomes soaring, silvery chords, as if white alabaster columns enclose a quiet house flooded with sunshine . . . The house in which you would like to live with her, the sister, the child, the beloved: the house of your dreams—far, far away, bathed in radiance . . . Sing with quiet delight: "Là, tout n'est qu'ordre et beauté, Luxe, calme et volupté." . . . (The word "ordre" is so enchantingly French . . . Nothing shall interfere with love . . . Everything must be smooth, no anxiety, nothing to think about . . . Only delightful concentration . . .) Now in your imagination, you straighten up a little and with a smile look down upon the river which seems to sleep so peacefully in the half light, as it flows past the soft meadow in which you rest with your beloved . . . The accompaniment again weaves about you, but you rouse yourself from the lulling rhythm of the rocking melody—you watch the ships which lie dreami-ly in the harbor, sails reefed, resting and expectant . . . You yourself feel within you the unrest of adventure . . . In your imagination you see them setting sail in the morning—toward the distance, which lies mysterious and alluring beneath the blue hills, through which the river winds . . . Sing with a little more animation: "Vois sur ces canaux Dor-mir ces vaisseaux Dont l'humeur est vagabonde"—in this moment your heart is "vagabonde"—you would love to go with them, out into space . . . A bold desire swings through your voice—the never ending longing of an adventure-loving imagination . . . Sing with mounting passion—"C'est pour assouvir Ton moindre désir Qu'ils viennent du bout du monde". Sing this broadly, floatingly, devotedly, with the warmth of exuberant feeling. Within you glows the ever recurrent ecstacy of the lover: to give everything to the beloved one—everything, the moon, the stars, the whole world . . . And now you feel the beauty of the earth unfolding before you—you feel how the sun will pour its flood of gold about you, enveloping you and her, embracing you and her and the whole world in gold and red and the fading lavender of its twilight . . . There where it goes down, there in the shimmering dis-tance, lies the gold and red and lavender—the land of dreams . . . And you repeat, ecstatically, lost in dream and painless longing: "Là, tout n'est qu'ordre et beauté, Luxe, calme et volupté!" Remain withdrawn until the end of the song.

AU PAYS OÙ SE FAIT LA GUERRE

Gautier   *Duparc*

This song is an intense dramatic scene. I can see the situation in all its pictorial detail: the lovely house set deep within its garden, the broad steps flooded with moonlight leading up to the terrace—the wide opened door through which the warm summer wind blows, playing with the lace curtains,—the beautiful young woman wandering restlessly back and forth,— with her pale face and burning eyes . . .

You are this woman. You have been very lonely since your beloved was sent to war. Daily, hourly, you await his return. And even if it is only for a short time,—you feel: he will come, he will be there in your arms, just as in that lovely time which has passed and now seems only a dream—when there was peace . . .

The music of the prelude is like a military march. In your imagination you seem to hear the soldiers marching in the distance—far away, and among them is your gallant young beloved . . . Wherever you may be this melody pursues and torments you . . . It has become a part of you, yourself, so you take up with your voice this music which runs mechanically through your subconsciousness. Sing the beginning *piano* as if lost in thought, simply, as if telling a story: "Au pays où se fait la guerre mon bel ami s'en est allé —" and moved by your grief sing with a slightly quickened tempo: "il semble à mon coeur désolé Qu'il ne reste que moi sur terre". Sing this "reste que moi" with a welling *crescendo* and *decrescendo*. (In your inner loneliness you think of neither family nor friends. Nothing matters to you, no one seems close to you, since he who is the essence of your life has had to leave you.) Now sing with trembling restraint: "En partant" and breathe (or at least make a distinct pause) after "partant" and sing tenderly, remembering with pain: "au baiser d'adieu, Il m'a pris mon âme à ma bouche . . ." Sing this *crescendo* with a great swing. It is as if the memory of your parting kiss has abruptly dragged you back to the cruel emptiness of reality. With the *forte* chord of the accompaniment change the quality of your voice: sing dramatically in a sudden outburst: "Qui le tient si longtemps, Mon Dieu?" With restless agitation, pressing, *piano,* restrained: "Voilà le soleil qui se couche, Et moi toute seule en ma tour J'attends encore son retour." (You want to say—another day has gone by, another day without him. And yet I wait and wait . . .) Make a great *ritardando* and *diminuendo* at "son retour". Again the martial melody runs through the interlude. You listen to it as if you listen to your own thoughts—and toward the end of the interlude your glance sweeps very slowly upward as if you hear from the edge of the roof, the cooing of doves, of which you speak in the next phrase. Sing with a little more animation, tenderly, with a lovely yearning contemplation: "Les pigeons sur le toit roucoulent amoureusement Avec un son triste et charmant." Now your glance is lowered and sweeps into the distance: "Les eaux sous les grands saules coulent". Again your timbre changes: from the delicate, dreaming, light quality with which you told of the doves and the surging waters, you go over into a trembling restraint, singing darkly and vibrantly: "Je me sens tout près de pleurer,

Mon coeur comme un lys plein s'épanche, Et je n'ose plus espérer". Sing "n'ose" *ritenuto,* with the utmost *pianissimo*—and sing *a tempo,* restlessly and as if confused: "Voici briller la lune blanche, Et moi toute seule en ma tour J'attends encore" and falling as if with a deep sigh: "son retour". In a long pause the emptiness seems to close in around you. With the accompaniment (*plus vite*) you straighten up as if startled. You have heard steps—and immediately there is the mad hope: it is he! Sing very realistically as if in a whispered outcry— "Quelqu'un" and with bated breath you listen to the accompaniment in the next measure. With a wildly beating heart, storming on in a passionate *crescendo,* sing: "monte à grands pas la rampe . . . Serait—ce lui, mon doux amant?" But it is not he, it is the young servant and your face mirrors your deep disappointment. Relentlessly a bit of the military march runs through your head . . . Sing softly and with resignation: "Ce n'est pas lui, mais seulement mon petit page avec ma lampe . . ." But flowering from this instant of expectation, of hope, your heart greets the distant beloved in a warmly flowing melody, which like a shimmering song in itself rises from out the distraction of this musical scene: "Vents du soir, volez, Dites-lui Qu'il est ma pensée et mon rêve, Toute ma joie et mon ennui", sing this beginning softly with much swing and make a *crescendo* to a *fortissimo* of glowing passion. In the following phrases the voice remains *fortissimo* but it now has a changed quality, it has lost its warmth, this is a very dramatic outburst and should be harsh and powerful. With horror you see the sun rising after the restless and sleepless night. You see a new day approaching—a new day without your beloved, a day which will bring you nothing but emptiness and desperate, futile waiting . . .

Sing with the force of despair: "Voici que l'aurore se lève, Et moi toute seule en ma tour J'attends encore son retour". At "j'attends encore" begin a *decrescendo* but it is not one which fades into a soft *piano,* it is one which breaks down in tears. Sing "son retour" long drawn out, weeping. Remain standing with closed eyes until the end of the postlude.

APRÈS UN RÊVE

Bussine   *Fauré*

Begin this song as if still in a dream. It is tremendously important that each phrase be sung with a swing, with a soft rise and fall. There is no straight line, everything is floating unreality. The *fortes* are soft and warm, never heroic, never dramatic. This applies to the whole song. Begin with a delicate ecstasy, in a sustained and soft flow: "Dans un sommeil que charmait ton image Je rêvais le bonheur ardent mirage"—and now sing with a very slight acceleration and with great expression, the enraptured description: "Tes yeux étaient plus doux, ta voix pure et sonore". You must paint the picture of your beloved with an inner enthusiasm which radiates through both words and tones. The phrase "Tu rayonnais comme un ciel éclaré par l'aurore" is carried ecstatically upward in a softly mounting *forte*. Sing broadly and with a glowing *crescendo,* going over warmly and gently into the *forte* at "tu m'appellais—et je quittais la terre". This phrase is the climax of the blissful dream: she calls you to her—you raised yourself toward her . . . Sing with rapturous devotion—"pour m'enfuir avec toi vers la lumière"— it is as if you again float away with her into the light in the memory of this heavenly dream. The following phrases are silvery, very bright, very ethereal—in your imagination you float with her through a sphere which is far above this world . . . You and she—you are transfigured by the strange light in which you have arisen . . Sing with a subtle ecstacy: "Les cieux pour nous entr'ouvraient leurs nues, splendeurs inconnues, lueurs divines entrevues"—sing all this as if remote from the earth, intoxicated by unreality. *Immediately* change your expression at "Hélas! Hélas, triste réveil des songes". Note carefully the very abrupt change here: it is an absolutely new thought, an awakening, which in its suddenness plunges you from your dream into reality . . . Change your facial expression as well as your voice quality: from the blissfulness of your dream you awaken to the loneliness of the cruel day . . . The first "Hélas" is the only really painful outcry in the song. At "songe" memory already weaves again about you. Already like a veiled net, unreality enshrouds you, taking away the pain of awakening, returning you to new dreams . . . Sing softly, filled with longing—"je t'appelle, o nuit, rends-moi tes mensonges . . ." You know: Night is yours—night with its dreams so far removed from this world . . . You await her, the comfortress—night . . . Sing the final phrases with a gentle swing: "Reviens, reviens radieuse, Reviens, o nuit mystérieuse!" Again sing this as in a dream, very remote from all reality. Your waking is unimportant, is a disturbance, is for you *Unreality*: your dream is *life* and happiness . . . You live for this dream . . .

RENCONTRE

Grandmougin   *Fauré*

The sadness of which you, the poet, tell here, is not a deep sadness of your soul. It is rather the sadness of your imagination. In this song you play with your solitude, with your loneliness. You are playing with sad thoughts,—creating a woman of your phantasy. You saw a woman passing by. As you looked at one another a new world opened before you—the world from which the poem flows. Inspiration is the name of this woman, not love . . .

You must understand the charm of the French character, the fluttering wings of phantasy which soar vibrantly over the surface of feeling. But remember that this does not necessarily mean a rapid tempo. Hastiness in this song will destroy the silvery flow of the musical line instead of giving it the character which it should have.

At the beginning of the song your face should have a dreamy expression. Sing the first sentence with the slight exaggeration which gives the French song its flavor—an exaggeration without depth, even without strength. Fauré says *"dolce"* at the beginning—sing *dolce* and with elegance.

"O dis-moi" is a new idea—begin it with the suggestion of a sigh. It is best to breathe quickly after "dis-moi" so that you can sing "Serais-tu la femme inespérée". Make a lovely *ritardando* at "rêve ideal poursuivi vainement?" Musically this line should have the quality of surf— but it should be soft. Return to a light elegance in the next sentence: "O passante aux doux yeux" and make the same surflike *crescendo* and *ritardando* at "au poète isolé". The following phrase must be sung with a great sweep. After "natal" breathe audibly and sing "sur un coeur d'exilé" rapturously. (Here you realize that all the loneliness, the life in exile is absolutely voluntary and much relished. You have *chosen* this life—far away from the crowd.)

The whole song now becomes a play of words, a play of subtle enchantment. The sunset, the immensity of the ocean, the beauty of the evening—everything seems made just for you and for this woman whom you feel to be the fulfillment of all your dreams. Make a lovely *crescendo* and *ritardando* (again like surf) at "à ta belle âme est cher". Sing "Une mystérieuse" as if you are telling of a secret and wonderful miracle . . . In "Et mon âme frémit" roll the *r* in "frémit". By painting this word with its consonants and vowels you should be able to make the shiver of delight which you feel, convincing. (When you sing "te chérit" be careful that the *i* is not too pinched. Think of mixing it with an *a* sound.) Sing this phrase with great expression and make it a real climax, not only in voice but also in *expression*. It is as if you said—You are dear to my heart even if I do not know you. I know that you were made for me and I for you. I don't need to really know you. You live in my imagination and my dreams. All my life you have been mine because you and I are one.

NELL

de Lisle   *Fauré*

While the tempo of this song is rapid, you should be careful not to sing too fast. Temperament and lightness of expression are very often confused with impetuous restlessness... Just as one can sing passionately in a slow tempo, so one can bring the lightness so characteristic of the French and that certain "esprit" of French elegance in a tempo which will make possible quick changes and permits of the enchanting half lights which make singing really colorful . . . I have heard this song sung in a quick almost hurried tempo and have enjoyed its enchanting lightness. I myself however would sing it differently, with lightness certainly but with much more nuance. The French have an especial feeling for dramatic effect, they have the fragrance of exalted exaggeration,—the delicate sigh of dreaming delight. But if you rush through a song it is very difficult to bring out all these charming nuances which lift it above the flow of a "melody without words". So I try to mix the French deftness in song with the joy of dramatic construction.

Begin *piano* and give a lovely and expressive *crescendo* to "ô Juin". You should realize that in this song you speak continually of two different things—what is *outside yourself*—the rays of the sun, flowers, springtime, moonlight, foliage—everything in nature. But this on the other hand inspires you to take it all into your own being. It gives you always the cue for *your own ecstacy.* So this song should be sung surgingly, going back and forth in your expression. This is very easy to do if you understand what I mean. For instance—"mon coeur à ta rose est pareil".—That is *you.* But "Sous le mol abri" is again *nature.* This reference to nature brings you back to yourself—"o mon coeur, sa plainte amoureuse." The doves are sighing—but it is—"ô *mon coeur*" like the language of your own heart.

"Que ta perle" is again *nature.* But "Mais combien plus douce" is again *you.* Give a strong accent to "chère amour, ô Nell". You sing her name here, her beloved name and you sing it with delight.

Be careful of the vowel "i" in "fleurisse"—mix it with an "a"—and sing it with much passion and abandon. Breathe after "plus", but I mean a breath of expression—audibly. Sing the *subito pianissimo* with an expression of intoxication and hold this expression until the end.

L'HEURE EXQUISE

Verlaine   *Hahn*

This whole song is a feast of subtlest *piano* tones. There is not a *mezzoforte* tone to be found, everything falls within the enchanting half light of feeling, in the expression of which the French are such unsurpassed masters. Sing throughout the song with a gently rocking rhythm. For heaven's sake sing no straight phrases!!!

In the prelude feel with your whole being the soft undulating flow of the meadows and the woods in the gentle evening breeze. Who does not love this hour between day and evening, when the moon is still pale in the heavens—and far away is the last rosy sheen of the setting sun, amidst the deep blue of the evening firmament . . . This is the hour in which all colors become deeper and clearer, this is the hour in which as one looks off into the distance one may have dreams which vanish with the broad light of day . . . Sing with a soft expression as if painting the landscape with loving words . . . "O bien aimée!" is like a sigh of delight. Draw it out, letting it fade away completely in sweetest longing . . . Become a little more animated at "L'etang reflête, profond miroir" and let there be a feeling of mystery in "ou le vent pleure". Feel about you the warm wind which touches you like a caressing hand. You are overcome with longing—and you call (*pianissimo!*) "Rêvons!" You do not want to be alone in this hour of enchantment. With your longing you call your beloved to you—that she may share your dreams, and feel with you your warm delight. Sing "C'est l'heure" like a whisper, with closed eyes, lost in the magic of this hour . . . You say: "this is the hour which we must not experience apart, this is the blessed hour of purest, sweetest beauty . . ."

At "Un vaste et tendre Apaisement" become still slower, sing this phrase very softly and floatingly. Feel the mounting quality of the interlude. Your deep inhalation before the last phrase is like a sigh and now you sing very slowly and with great clarity and silver purity of tone: "C'est l'heure exquise". Do not slide here, sing clear tones, don't ruin this song through sentimentality. Make an imperceptible *crescendo* at "exquise" but then immediately make a *decrescendo* and sing the ending completely fading away. Hold the expression of inner blissful withdrawal during the postlude.

PAYSAGE

Theuriet   *Hahn*

This song is called "Landscape" but the landscape which you describe is only the frame for your experience, your feeling, for dream

and reality ... In both words and music is seduction, persuasion, longing ... Imagine that you are speaking to a woman who once refused
your plea to follow you and that you are now again seeking to lure her
to a quiet place where you may enjoy together beauty and love. You
speak with secret urgency, with repressed passion. Throughout the song
the accompaniment rises and falls like the play of waves. Take up this
quality in the prelude: see before you the lovely spot which you are trying to describe ... Begin with a restrained expression as if you want
to tell a secret—a lovely exciting secret ... (Hahn indicates: *"très
intime"*) Sing in a quiet flow up to: "de la terre Bretonne"—then the
memory of this place overpowers you, the hope that you may once be
there with your beloved, regret that she had not been there to experience with you your surrender to the quiet beauty of nature ... Sing
as if with an outburst but always with a delicate restraint, without any
realism: "Où j'aurais tant aimé, pendant les jours d'automne, Chère, à
vous emmener!" Sing the word "Chère" like a caress, very softly with
a breathy quality. In "à vous emmener" must sound all the longing with
which you speak to her ... Now you become a little more animated,
sing as if in quiet description until—"Une source dont l'eau claire a le
reflet vert De vos yeux de sirène" ... Here again your passionate desire colors your description ... Sing "sirène" almost between your teeth.
Perhaps you have often told her that she has the beauty of a siren. Now
you say it in a half tone as you look with delight into her upturned
face ... Let the words float away, making a slight pause before you
sing further—again with the quality of quiet description: "La mésange,
au matin, sous la feuille jaunie" sing this with your head slightly raised,
as if you saw the lovely bird before you. And sing *crescendo* with passionate fire but with restraint: "viendrait chanter pour nous". Now you
have thrown aside your restraint and given yourself up completely to
your glowing desire: sing broadly, with great power and passion: "Et
la mer, nuit et jour, Viendrait accompagner nos caresses d'amour". Sing
"nuit et jours" with an expression of extravagant expansiveness—"Oh
we would love one another day and night—and day and night the song
of the sea would resound for us ..." End glowingly and aggressively
with a broad *fortissimo*: "De sa basse infinie." The triumph of the
man who has succeeded in making his beloved his own, must sound
through this final phrase. For one must have no doubt that she will
follow him. (I hope so!)

D'UNE PRISON

Verlaine   *Hahn*

The everlasting and barren monotony of your life in prison has
brought an apathetic uniformity even to your dreams: your longing to

be free no longer breaks out in violent impatience as it might have at first,—time with a relentless quietude has forced your heart to slumber in lifeless resignation . . . Now you are able to look contemplatively through the little window which frames the world for you. A bird flying by, a fluttering leaf—everything is an event for you—the scant bit of heaven is all you know of dream and desire and adventure . . .

The emptiness of your imprisoned life is reflected in the uniform melody of the accompaniment. With the very beginning of the prelude take up the mood of the song: your head is slightly raised, your gaze directed sadly into the distance. In your imagination you see the infinite blue of the summer sky through the narrow frame of the prison window . . . Begin very quietly, with half voice, without any emotion, with the quietness of resigned contemplation: "Le ciel est par-dessus le toit, si bleu, si calme". . . Sing very evenly, your voice must be absolutely quiet without a trace of *vibrato*. Enunciate distinctly. At "Un arbre, par-dessus le toit berce sa palme" give "arbre" a light accent of longing: this tree swaying in the warm summer breeze is forest and field for you—its branch against the blue of the heavens is the concentration of all the beauty of a world which you yourself have destroyed . . .

Now you hear—carried by the wind, the sound of a distant bell. With an expression of listening (but absolutely quietly and with the greatest discretion) sing "La cloche dans le ciel qu'on voit, doucement tinte". Color your voice more darkly in this phrase: there is bitterness within you, as you hear this voice, this call coming from the distant church whose protection you have forfeited. The time in which you knelt with purity and devotion before altars is long past for you—and the churchbell is only a sad intimation of the innocence which you have lost . . . Sing the next phrase *diminuendo*. Hahn has indicated *"diminuendo encore si possible"* so sing with the utmost *pianissimo,* in a yearning *ritardando*: "Un oiseau sur l'arbre qu'on voit, chante sa plainte". Imagine what it might mean to one imprisoned to hear the song of a bird: a song born of a lust for life, of the blissful summertime . . . Perhaps you will see this free, lovely creature flying past your barred window, merging with the azure of the heavens . . . So sing this phrase with an exquisite melancholy in a voice vibrant with feeling. The delicate shock which the song of the bird has given you is the cause of the outburst of despair in the next phrase. So "Un oiseau sur l'arbre qu'on voit, chante sa plainte" must be sung with restraint but at the same time with deep emotion. Now sing the next phrase with repressed violence: you turn away from your diminished outer world back to your own misery, which through your guilt, you have created for yourself. But the strength for a real outburst can only develop slowly within your heart, which has become so powerless through sombre resignation . . . So sing: "Mon Dieu, mon Dieu! La vie est là simple et tranquille", as if with a heavy sigh. The fact that there exists beyond your walls, a life which flows with simplicity, in contemplative quiet, seems incomprehensible. Sing this with a shuddering amazement, distinctly accentuated, giving your voice a quality of harshness. The next phrase should be sung with a breathy quality, *pianissimo,* almost in a whisper: "Cette paisible rumeur là vient de la ville". . . Oh—over there is the town with its bustling life, which I abused. People live there in freedom, loving, laughing, working, going their way in the peaceful life of everyday!

Heavily the accompaniment emerges from the monotony of its dragging melody—heavily it rolls upwards and your voice falls like a cry upon the piano chord, in a broad *forte:* "Qu'as-tu fait, o toi que voilà pleurant sans cesse, Dis! qu'as-tu fait, toi que voilà, de ta jeunesse?" Let this outburst of complaint break in upon the breathtaking restraint of the song with a quality of grandeur. Sing with a piercingly dramatic quality, with very distinct accentuation, through tears of despair. One must have the impression that with the last wild words of complaint—"qu'as-tu fait, toi que voilà, de ta jeunesse?" you break down. Sing the words "de ta jeunesse" *ritardando, diminuendo:* your strength collapses under tears, you have forgotten how to complain, how to rage against yourself. You could only arouse yourself for this one brief outcry, now you are exhausted and sink back lost in the resignation which has slowly destroyed your will to live . . .

Sing as if through quietly flowing tears, with audible breath, as if only half conscious: "Le ciel est par-dessus le toit si bleu, si calme". . . At this moment you no longer see the heavens, you are blinded by your tears, your eyes are closed . . . You see only the heaven of your dreams, blue, broad, unending . . . Remain standing as if withdrawn until the end of the postlude.

*NUR WER DIE SEHNSUCHT KENNT
(NONE BUT THE LONELY HEART)

Goethe   *Tschaikovsky*

This song suffers from being sentimentalized. It is so often heard over the radio, from records and from popular orchestras, that it has become almost a folk song. It very much needs to be infused with a new vitality . . . It should be saved from the sentimental dragging of tempo, which deprives it of the ardent passion which is the essence of this music . . .

At the very beginning immerse yourself in the deep melancholy of the prelude. Feel the first words of this noble poem singing from

---

*Although this song has become popular in America in the English translation, I have used the German words in my explanation since the original text is German.

out the accompaniment and you will find the right expression in face and bearing . . .

Begin with great feeling and color your voice very darkly. Try to give the melody the deep velvet quality of a wonderful cello, rising and falling in a soft *crescendo* and *decrescendo*. Sing as if from the very depths of your soul: "Nur wer die Sehnsucht kennt, weiss, was ich leide! Allein und abgetrennt von aller Freude." This sentence is incomplete being interrupted by the accompaniment, but don't give the impression that it is interrupted: hold the tension between the phrases through the expression of your face and your bearing. Hold it fast with bated breath as explained in the introduction. Glide, so to speak, from the music of the interlude over into the continuing phrase: "Seh' ich an's Firmament nach jener Seite." This should be sung *crescendo* with mounting excitement. Your glance is directed into the distance. The tempo should be somewhat quickened and you should sing with driving force. Go over into a broader tempo as if with a heavy sigh at —"Ach! der mich liebt und kennt, ist in der Weite." Accent "kennt" with a delicate expression of pain . . . You are alone, among strangers. No one really understands you. There has only been one being who has understood you. That was he, who is now far away . . . Sing "in der Weite" dying away, completely lost in your anquish. You pull yourself together—but it is only to strengthen yourself for the outburst of complaint and despair: "Nur wer die Sehnsucht kennt, weiss, was ich leide!" Now sing with a continuously mounting *crescendo* up to the wild outbreak of despair: "Allein und abgetrennt von aller Freude" Your strength seems to leave you . . . In your imagination you break down and swaying, steady yourself upon the edge of the window, through which you look, filled with longing, into the endless, emptiness of the night . . . Sing now very, very slowly, as if with ebbing strength, half fainting: "Es schwindelt mir, es brennt mein Eingeweide". Accent the consonants very sharply in "brennt". Sing as if suppressing physical pain. End the song with a sigh—as if dissolving in tears: "Nur wer die Sehnsucht kennt, weiss was ich leide . . ." Let this fade away completely as if you bury your head in your arms, weeping—alone and desolate—without relief or hope.

OVER THE STEPPE

Pleshtcheieff   *Gretchaninoff*

English version by
Deems Taylor and Kurt Schindler

The beginning of this song is pervaded by the dark melancholy of the vast and lonely Russian plains. Your face should have a sombre expression, your gaze seeks to penetrate the unending darkness, which like the wings of night, spreads threateningly and with uncanniness over the immensity of the lonely steppe.

Sing evenly and floatingly, with a darkly colored voice, almost without expression. The emptiness which is around you, the greyness of the darkened sky, are best expressed through a *lack of expression*. Sing without any sentimentality—tone by tone should stand like black and leafless tree trunks, cold and impersonal.

At "Hardly I know"—you change completely. The second part of the song begins here. It is absolutely different from the first part. Here your face becomes alive, your eyes shine, you smile, you throw your whole being into a delight which has awakened in you through the vision of your beloved. "Visions of thee" should be sung with utter abandon, with a warm glowing *fortissimo*. The *tempo* quickens. Breathe after "Comes now the song" so that you can sing "nightingale" and the next sentence in one breath. Sing "melting away like a sigh" very smoothly and with a sweet *piano* quality. Look around you as if you are enchanted at "Flowers are nodding" and look up as you enjoy in your imagination, all the brilliant stars in the sky above you. Don't make a *decrescendo*. Spin out the last tone ("sky") clearly and jubilantly. Your head is raised, your face retains an expression of enchanted delight until the very end of the song.

AH TWINE NO BLOSSOMS

Rathaus   *Glière*

English version by
Deems Taylor

You had fled into a solitude which has brought you peace. Turning away from pain and harsh disillusionment, you have saved yourself, in a world in which there should be nothing which could remind you of him whom you had left when you realized his worthlessness... But after a long time of separation he again crossed your path . . . His smile broke in upon your hard won peace—this smile in which you can no longer believe, from which you had fled . . . Now he has again brought unrest into your life . . .

From out this feeling begin the song.

The syncopated music of the prelude expresses your inner unrest— show this in your facial expression: look into the distance with an expression of wanting to defend yourself, and begin to sing—"Ah twine no blossoms fair and fragrant To weave anew my crown of woe," with deep feeling. It is as if you sing turning away from him . . .

Your whole bearing must be one of rejection, your shadowed glance seems to penetrate through him, to condemn the man before you . . .

Sing in a quiet *legato*: "The flame of all my dreaming flickered And died in darkness long ago". This should be sung with a very dark quality, mounting to the word "darkness" and then falling in resignation. But he, whom you address, does not turn away . . . Certain of his power over you, he persists in this smile,—his glance consumes you . . . A deep bitterness pervades you and you sing in disdainful rejection: "Ah, come no more to smile upon me . . . That limpid smile so long forgot." And now the whole ardour of the old half buried love, which has so tormented you in the past, overwhelms you: "My heart's desire, my own beloved . . ." Sing this with great feeling, with deep and heartfelt emotion. You say these words without realizing it, against your will they escape from you, against your will you speak to him with the true feeling of your wounded heart . . . But suddenly your deep emotion gives way to an outburst of scorn . . . You want to save yourself from the old unhappy spell, which threatens to engulf you anew. You seek refuge in scorn and contempt. And with bitter triumph you hurl into his face the words which you would so often make him believe: "Dost thou not hear? I love thee not . . ." Sing these two phrases with almost brutal power—each syllable should be thrust out with sharp accentuation.

In the interlude desperation again overpowers you,—it is as if your heart reels under the smile which will rob you of your peace and of your reason—as always and forever . . . Sing with trembling restraint —*piano,* with sharp accentuation—"Oh, wake no more the fire that sleepeth; From passion's bondage set me free." Unwillingly you now confess that you are still enchained by your passion—that all your peace, your bitter scorn, your contempt is only a pose. That you reel under the power of this consuming love, helpless, without any defence . . . And now in wild complaint there breaks from you all the misery of your shattered life: "Wasted my soul with bitter longing". Sing this *rubato,* lifting out each syllable with fiery impulsiveness and end as if with a sobbing cry—"What now remains to give to thee?" Though he has destroyed you, you yet fear his disillusionment, in finding you so miserable, for how can he, who goes through life so lightly and so confidently, understand that others can be destroyed by a love, which means for him only play . . . Hold an expression of deep grief until the end.

IN THE SILENCE OF THE NIGHT

Fet   *Rachmaninoff*

English version by
Geo. Harris Jr. and Deems Taylor

In my opinion this song is generally sung too slowly. This is of course a matter of personal conception—but I see developing from the delicate beginning and mounting in the warm *crescendo* of the prelude, an ecstatic and impulsive passion. The accompaniment begins with a mystic *piano pianissimo* and from the texture of tone arises the vision of the beloved. Your glance is directed into the distance where you seem to see the vision. You react to the first *forte* tone of the prelude—suddenly looking up as if you see the figure of your beloved before you, rising from the misty distance.

Begin with a sigh of excitement: the "oh" should not sound like a lovely and melodiously produced vowel . . . It should be a trembling sigh welling from deep within you. Sing romantically and with ecstacy: "Oh—in the silent night I see your vision nearing," and now with delight you describe the beauty of your beloved: "With your caressing voice, your artful smile, smile endearing." Sing with great tenderness: "Your hair that I was wont to stroke —your hair in flowing strands of black;" you loved this beautiful black hair, you remember how often you have caressed it . . . But the past in spite of all the bliss of love was certainly not completely free of conflict for you. Sing with an expression of wildness: "How oft I bid you go" but immediately change and sing with almost a touch of humor in complete understanding of your own weakness: "how oft I called you back". This last phrase is *crescendo* (mounting from *mezzoforte*) to a warmly flowing *forte.* Sing with animation and restrained passion: "The phrases of the past anew I try to fashion" and with a slow *crescendo*: "I whisper and recall the words that voiced our passion" up to the forceful outburst—"Wild and despairing, I summon past delight". Now become broader with increasing power, so that the phrase: "With your beloved name I wake the silent night" mounts to the climax of the song, with wild passion. Sing the repetition with sharp emphasis, each syllable accented and in an unbroken *fortissimo,* as if torn from a flood of passionate desire. Sing the next: "I wake the silent night" *diminuendo,* as if in a reaction from the wild outburst, trembling and with restraint.

The past in which you were happy with your beloved, even if misunderstandings did often threaten you with separation, now closes about the person, the image of the beloved, as with impenetrable walls.

Only at night does the separating distance seem to vanish and the vision of the beloved and longed for being emerge before you,—floating mysteriously about you in the phantastic darkness . . . In the end of the song convey this feeling of mystic delight: sing with restraint, with a veiled *piano*, very repressed and ecstatic until the very end. Hold the last tone—"night", letting it fade away completely and remain withdrawn and blissful until the last chord dies away.

A CATALOGUE OF
SELECTED DOVER BOOKS
IN ALL FIELDS OF INTEREST

A CATALOGUE OF SELECTED DOVER
BOOKS IN ALL FIELDS OF INTEREST

CELESTIAL OBJECTS FOR COMMON TELESCOPES, T. W. Webb. The most used book in amateur astronomy: inestimable aid for locating and identifying nearly 4,000 celestial objects. Edited, updated by Margaret W. Mayall. 77 illustrations. Total of 645pp. 5⅜ x 8½.
20917-2, 20918-0 Pa., Two-vol. set $10.00

HISTORICAL STUDIES IN THE LANGUAGE OF CHEMISTRY, M. P. Crosland. The important part language has played in the development of chemistry from the symbolism of alchemy to the adoption of systematic nomenclature in 1892. ". . . wholeheartedly recommended,"—Science. 15 illustrations. 416pp. of text. 5⅝ x 8¼.
63702-6 Pa. $7.50

BURNHAM'S CELESTIAL HANDBOOK, Robert Burnham, Jr. Thorough, readable guide to the stars beyond our solar system. Exhaustive treatment, fully illustrated. Breakdown is alphabetical by constellation: Andromeda to Cetus in Vol. 1; Chamaeleon to Orion in Vol. 2; and Pavo to Vulpecula in Vol. 3. Hundreds of illustrations. Total of about 2000pp. 6⅛ x 9¼.
23567-X, 23568-8, 23673-0 Pa., Three-vol. set $32.85

THEORY OF WING SECTIONS: INCLUDING A SUMMARY OF AIR-FOIL DATA, Ira H. Abbott and A. E. von Doenhoff. Concise compilation of subatomic aerodynamic characteristics of modern NASA wing sections, plus description of theory. 350pp. of tables. 693pp. 5⅜ x 8½.
60586-8 Pa. $9.95

DE RE METALLICA, Georgius Agricola. Translated by Herbert C. Hoover and Lou H. Hoover. The famous Hoover translation of greatest treatise on technological chemistry, engineering, geology, mining of early modern times (1556). All 289 original woodcuts. 638pp. 6¾ x 11.
60006-8 Clothbd. $19.95

THE ORIGIN OF CONTINENTS AND OCEANS, Alfred Wegener. One of the most influential, most controversial books in science, the classic statement for continental drift. Full 1966 translation of Wegener's final (1929) version. 64 illustrations. 246pp. 5⅜ x 8½.(EBE)61708-4 Pa. $5.00

THE PRINCIPLES OF PSYCHOLOGY, William James. Famous long course complete, unabridged. Stream of thought, time perception, memory, experimental methods; great work decades ahead of its time. Still valid, useful; read in many classes. 94 figures. Total of 1391pp. 5⅜ x 8½.
20381-6, 20382-4 Pa., Two-vol. set $19.90

YUCATAN BEFORE AND AFTER THE CONQUEST, Diego de Landa. First English translation of basic book in Maya studies, the only significant account of Yucatan written in the early post-Conquest era. Translated by distinguished Maya scholar William Gates. Appendices, introduction, 4 maps and over 120 illustrations added by translator. 162pp. 5⅜ x 8½. 23622-6 Pa. $3.50

THE MALAY ARCHIPELAGO, Alfred R. Wallace. Spirited travel account by one of founders of modern biology. Touches on zoology, botany, ethnography, geography, and geology. 62 illustrations, maps. 515pp. 5⅜ x 8½. 20187-2 Pa. $6.95

THE DISCOVERY OF THE TOMB OF TUTANKHAMEN, Howard Carter, A. C. Mace. Accompany Carter in the thrill of discovery, as ruined passage suddenly reveals unique, untouched, fabulously rich tomb. Fascinating account, with 106 illustrations. New introduction by J. M. White. Total of 382pp. 5⅜ x 8½. (Available in U.S. only) 23500-9 Pa. $5.50

THE WORLD'S GREATEST SPEECHES, edited by Lewis Copeland and Lawrence W. Lamm. Vast collection of 278 speeches from Greeks up to present. Powerful and effective models; unique look at history. Revised to 1970. Indices. 842pp. 5⅜ x 8½. 20468-5 Pa. $9.95

THE 100 GREATEST ADVERTISEMENTS, Julian Watkins. The priceless ingredient; His master's voice; 99 44/100% pure; over 100 others. How they were written, their impact, etc. Remarkable record. 130 illustrations. 233pp. 7⅞ x 10 3/5. 20540-1 Pa. $6.95

CRUICKSHANK PRINTS FOR HAND COLORING, George Cruickshank. 18 illustrations, one side of a page, on fine-quality paper suitable for watercolors. Caricatures of people in society (c. 1820) full of trenchant wit. Very large format. 32pp. 11 x 16. 23684-6 Pa. $6.00

THIRTY-TWO COLOR POSTCARDS OF TWENTIETH-CENTURY AMERICAN ART, Whitney Museum of American Art. Reproduced in full color in postcard form are 31 art works and one shot of the museum. Calder, Hopper, Rauschenberg, others. Detachable. 16pp. 8¼ x 11. 23629-3 Pa. $3.50

MUSIC OF THE SPHERES: THE MATERIAL UNIVERSE FROM ATOM TO QUASAR SIMPLY EXPLAINED, Guy Murchie. Planets, stars, geology, atoms, radiation, relativity, quantum theory, light, antimatter, similar topics. 319 figures. 664pp. 5⅜ x 8½. 21809-0, 21810-4 Pa., Two-vol. set $11.00

EINSTEIN'S THEORY OF RELATIVITY, Max Born. Finest semi-technical account; covers Einstein, Lorentz, Minkowski, and others, with much detail, much explanation of ideas and math not readily available elsewhere on this level. For student, non-specialist. 376pp. 5⅜ x 8½. 60769-0 Pa. $5.00

THE SENSE OF BEAUTY, George Santayana. Masterfully written discussion of nature of beauty, materials of beauty, form, expression; art, literature, social sciences all involved. 168pp. 5⅜ x 8½.   20238-0 Pa. $3.50

ON THE IMPROVEMENT OF THE UNDERSTANDING, Benedict Spinoza. Also contains *Ethics, Correspondence,* all in excellent R. Elwes translation. Basic works on entry to philosophy, pantheism, exchange of ideas with great contemporaries. 402pp. 5⅜ x 8½.   20250-X Pa. $5.95

THE TRAGIC SENSE OF LIFE, Miguel de Unamuno. Acknowledged masterpiece of existential literature, one of most important books of 20th century. Introduction by Madariaga. 367pp. 5⅜ x 8½.
                                                                  20257-7 Pa. $6.00

THE GUIDE FOR THE PERPLEXED, Moses Maimonides. Great classic of medieval Judaism attempts to reconcile revealed religion (Pentateuch, commentaries) with Aristotelian philosophy. Important historically, still relevant in problems. Unabridged Friedlander translation. Total of 473pp. 5⅜ x 8½.   20351-4 Pa. $6.95

THE I CHING (THE BOOK OF CHANGES), translated by James Legge. Complete translation of basic text plus appendices by Confucius, and Chinese commentary of most penetrating divination manual ever prepared. Indispensable to study of early Oriental civilizations, to modern inquiring reader. 448pp. 5⅜ x 8½.   21062-6 Pa. $6.00

THE EGYPTIAN BOOK OF THE DEAD, E. A. Wallis Budge. Complete reproduction of Ani's papyrus, finest ever found. Full hieroglyphic text, interlinear transliteration, word for word translation, smooth translation. Basic work, for Egyptology, for modern study of psychic matters. Total of 533pp. 6½ x 9¼. (USCO)   21866-X Pa. $8.50

THE GODS OF THE EGYPTIANS, E. A. Wallis Budge. Never excelled for richness, fullness: all gods, goddesses, demons, mythical figures of Ancient Egypt; their legends, rites, incarnations, variations, powers, etc. Many hieroglyphic texts cited. Over 225 illustrations, plus 6 color plates. Total of 988pp. 6⅛ x 9¼. (EBE)
                                             22055-9, 22056-7 Pa., Two-vol. set $20.00

THE STANDARD BOOK OF QUILT MAKING AND COLLECTING, Marguerite Ickis. Full information, full-sized patterns for making 46 traditional quilts, also 150 other patterns. Quilted cloths, lame, satin quilts, etc. 483 illustrations. 273pp. 6⅞ x 9⅝.   20582-7 Pa. $5.95

CORAL GARDENS AND THEIR MAGIC, Bronsilaw Malinowski. Classic study of the methods of tilling the soil and of agricultural rites in the Trobriand Islands of Melanesia. Author is one of the most important figures in the field of modern social anthropology. 143 illustrations. Indexes. Total of 911pp. of text. 5⅝ x 8¼. (Available in U.S. only)
                                                                  23597-1 Pa. $12.95

THE PHILOSOPHY OF HISTORY, Georg W. Hegel. Great classic of Western thought develops concept that history is not chance but a rational process, the evolution of freedom. 457pp. 5⅜ x 8½.　20112-0 Pa. $6.50

LANGUAGE, TRUTH AND LOGIC, Alfred J. Ayer. Famous, clear introduction to Vienna, Cambridge schools of Logical Positivism. Role of philosophy, elimination of metaphysics, nature of analysis, etc. 160pp. 5⅜ x 8½. (USCO)　20010-8 Pa. $2.75

A PREFACE TO LOGIC, Morris R. Cohen. Great City College teacher in renowned, easily followed exposition of formal logic, probability, values, logic and world order and similar topics; no previous background needed. 209pp. 5⅜ x 8½.　23517-3 Pa. $4.95

REASON AND NATURE, Morris R. Cohen. Brilliant analysis of reason and its multitudinous ramifications by charismatic teacher. Interdisciplinary, synthesizing work widely praised when it first appeared in 1931. Second (1953) edition. Indexes. 496pp. 5⅜ x 8½.　23633-1 Pa. $7.50

AN ESSAY CONCERNING HUMAN UNDERSTANDING, John Locke. The only complete edition of enormously important classic, with authoritative editorial material by A. C. Fraser. Total of 1176pp. 5⅜ x 8½.
20530-4, 20531-2 Pa., Two-vol. set $17.90

HANDBOOK OF MATHEMATICAL FUNCTIONS WITH FORMULAS, GRAPHS, AND MATHEMATICAL TABLES, edited by Milton Abramowitz and Irene A. Stegun. Vast compendium: 29 sets of tables, some to as high as 20 places. 1,046pp. 8 x 10½.　61272-4 Pa. **$19.95**

MATHEMATICS FOR THE PHYSICAL SCIENCES, Herbert S. Wilf. Highly acclaimed work offers clear presentations of vector spaces and matrices, orthogonal functions, roots of polynomial equations, conformal mapping, calculus of variations, etc. Knowledge of theory of functions of real and complex variables is assumed. Exercises and solutions. Index. 284pp. 5⅝ x 8¼.　63635-6 Pa. $5.00

THE PRINCIPLE OF RELATIVITY, Albert Einstein et al. Eleven most important original papers on special and general theories. Seven by Einstein, two by Lorentz, one each by Minkowski and Weyl. All translated, unabridged. 216pp. 5⅜ x 8½.　60081-5 Pa. $3.50

THERMODYNAMICS, Enrico Fermi. A classic of modern science. Clear, organized treatment of systems, first and second laws, entropy, thermodynamic potentials, gaseous reactions, dilute solutions, entropy constant. No math beyond calculus required. Problems. 160pp. 5⅜ x 8½.
60361-X Pa. $4.00

ELEMENTARY MECHANICS OF FLUIDS, Hunter Rouse. Classic undergraduate text widely considered to be far better than many later books. Ranges from fluid velocity and acceleration to role of compressibility in fluid motion. Numerous examples, questions, problems. 224 illustrations. 376pp. 5⅝ x 8¼.　63699-2 Pa. $7.00

THE AMERICAN SENATOR, Anthony Trollope. Little known, long un-available Trollope novel on a grand scale. Here are humorous comment on American vs. English culture, and stunning portrayal of a heroine/villainess. Superb evocation of Victorian village life. 561pp. 5⅜ x 8½.
23801-6 Pa. **$7.95**

WAS IT MURDER? James Hilton. The author of *Lost Horizon* and *Good-bye, Mr. Chips* wrote one detective novel (under a pen-name) which was quickly forgotten and virtually lost, even at the height of Hilton's fame. This edition brings it back—a finely crafted public school puzzle resplendent with Hilton's stylish atmosphere. A thoroughly English thriller by the creator of Shangri-la. 252pp. 5⅜ x 8. (Available in U.S. only)
23774-5 Pa. **$3.00**

CENTRAL PARK: A PHOTOGRAPHIC GUIDE, Victor Laredo and Henry Hope Reed. 121 superb photographs show dramatic views of Central Park: Bethesda Fountain, Cleopatra's Needle, Sheep Meadow, the Blockhouse, plus people engaged in many park activities: ice skating, bike riding, etc. Captions by former Curator of Central Park, Henry Hope Reed, provide historical view, changes, etc. Also photos of N.Y. landmarks on park's periphery. 96pp. 8½ x 11. 23750-8 Pa. **$4.95**

NANTUCKET IN THE NINETEENTH CENTURY, Clay Lancaster. 180 rare photographs, stereographs, maps, drawings and floor plans recreate unique American island society. Authentic scenes of shipwreck, light-houses, streets, homes are arranged in geographic sequence to provide walking-tour guide to old Nantucket existing today. Introduction, captions. 160pp. 8⅞ x 11¾. 23747-8 Pa. **$7.95**

STONE AND MAN: A PHOTOGRAPHIC EXPLORATION, Andreas Feininger. 106 photographs by *Life* photographer Feininger portray man's deep passion for stone through the ages. Stonehenge-like megaliths, forti-fied towns, sculpted marble and crumbling tenements show textures, beau-ties, fascination. 128pp. 9¼ x 10¾. 23756-7 Pa. **$6.95**

CIRCLES, A MATHEMATICAL VIEW, D. Pedoe. Fundamental aspects of college geometry, non-Euclidean geometry, and other branches of mathe-matics: representing circle by point. Poincare model, isoperimetric prop-erty, etc. Stimulating recreational reading. 66 figures. 96pp. 5⅝ x 8¼.
63698-4 Pa. **$3.50**

THE DISCOVERY OF NEPTUNE, Morton Grosser. Dramatic scientific history of the investigations leading up to the actual discovery of the eighth planet of our solar system. Lucid, well-researched book by well-known historian of science. 172pp. 5⅜ x 8½. 23726-5 Pa. **$3.95**

THE DEVIL'S DICTIONARY. Ambrose Bierce. Barbed, bitter, brilliant witticisms in the form of a dictionary. Best, most ferocious satire America has produced. 145pp. 5⅜ x 8½. 20487-1 Pa. **$2.50**

CATALOGUE OF DOVER BOOKS

THE ART OF THE CINEMATOGRAPHER, Leonard Maltin. Survey of American cinematography history and anecdotal interviews with 5 masters—Arthur Miller, Hal Mohr, Hal Rosson, Lucien Ballard, and Conrad Hall. Very large selection of behind-the-scenes production photos. 105 photographs. Filmographies. Index. Originally *Behind the Camera*. 144pp. 8¼ x 11.   23686-2 Pa. $5.00

THE COMPLETE NONSENSE OF EDWARD LEAR, Edward Lear. All nonsense limericks, zany alphabets, Owl and Pussycat, songs, nonsense botany, etc., illustrated by Lear. Total of 321pp. 5⅜ x 8½. (Available in U.S. only)   20167-8 Pa. $4.50

INGENIOUS MATHEMATICAL PROBLEMS AND METHODS, Louis A. Graham. Sophisticated material from Graham *Dial*, applied and pure; stresses solution methods. Logic, number theory, networks, inversions, etc. 237pp. 5⅜ x 8½.   20545-2 Pa. $4.95

BEST MATHEMATICAL PUZZLES OF SAM LOYD, edited by Martin Gardner. Bizarre, original, whimsical puzzles by America's greatest puzzler. From fabulously rare *Cyclopedia*, including famous 14-15 puzzles, the Horse of a Different Color, 115 more. Elementary math. 150 illustrations. 167pp. 5⅜ x 8½.   20498-7 Pa. $3.50

THE BASIS OF COMBINATION IN CHESS, J. du Mont. Easy-to-follow, instructive book on elements of combination play, with chapters on each piece and every powerful combination team—two knights, bishop and knight, rook and bishop, etc. 250 diagrams. 218pp. 5⅜ x 8½. (Available in U.S. only)   23644-7 Pa. $4.50

MODERN CHESS STRATEGY, Ludek Pachman. The use of the queen, the active king, exchanges, pawn play, the center, weak squares, etc. Section on rook alone worth price of the book. Stress on the moderns. Often considered the most important book on strategy. 314pp. 5⅜ x 8½.   20290-9 Pa. $5.00

LASKER'S MANUAL OF CHESS, Dr. Emanuel Lasker. Great world champion offers very thorough coverage of all aspects of chess. Combinations, position play, openings, end game, aesthetics of chess, philosophy of struggle, much more. Filled with analyzed games. 390pp. 5⅜ x 8½.   20640-8 Pa. $5.95

500 MASTER GAMES OF CHESS, S. Tartakower, J. du Mont. Vast collection of great chess games from 1798-1938, with much material nowhere else readily available. Fully annotated, arranged by opening for easier study. 664pp. 5⅜ x 8½.   23208-5 Pa. $8.50

A GUIDE TO CHESS ENDINGS, Dr. Max Euwe, David Hooper. One of the finest modern works on chess endings. Thorough analysis of the most frequently encountered endings by former world champion. 331 examples, each with diagram. 248pp. 5⅜ x 8½.   23332-4 Pa. $3.95

THE COMPLETE BOOK OF DOLL MAKING AND COLLECTING, Catherine Christopher. Instructions, patterns for dozens of dolls, from rag doll on up to elaborate, historically accurate figures. Mould faces, sew clothing, make doll houses, etc. Also collecting information. Many illustrations. 288pp. 6 x 9. 22066-4 Pa. $4.95

THE DAGUERREOTYPE IN AMERICA, Beaumont Newhall. Wonderful portraits, 1850's townscapes, landscapes; full text plus 104 photographs. The basic book. Enlarged 1976 edition. 272pp. 8¼ x 11¼. 23322-7 Pa. $7.95

CRAFTSMAN HOMES, Gustav Stickley. 296 architectural drawings, floor plans, and photographs illustrate 40 different kinds of "Mission-style" homes from The Craftsman (1901-16), voice of American style of simplicity and organic harmony. Thorough coverage of Craftsman idea in text and picture, now collector's item. 224pp. 8⅛ x 11. 23791-5 Pa. $6.50

PEWTER-WORKING: INSTRUCTIONS AND PROJECTS, Burl N. Osborn. & Gordon O. Wilber. Introduction to pewter-working for amateur craftsman. History and characteristics of pewter; tools, materials, step-by-step instructions. Photos, line drawings, diagrams. Total of 160pp. 7⅞ x 10¾. 23786-9 Pa. $4.50

THE GREAT CHICAGO FIRE, edited by David Lowe. 10 dramatic, eye-witness accounts of the 1871 disaster, including one of the aftermath and rebuilding, plus 70 contemporary photographs and illustrations of the ruins—courthouse, Palmer House, Great Central Depot, etc. Introduction by David Lowe. 87pp. 8¼ x 11. 23771-0 Pa. $4.95

SILHOUETTES: A PICTORIAL ARCHIVE OF VARIED ILLUSTRA-TIONS, edited by Carol Belanger Grafton. Over 600 silhouettes from the 18th to 20th centuries include profiles and full figures of men and women, children, birds and animals, groups and scenes, nature, ships, an alphabet. Dozens of uses for commercial artists and craftspeople. 144pp. 8⅜ x 11¼. 23781-8 Pa. $4.50

ANIMALS: 1,419 COPYRIGHT-FREE ILLUSTRATIONS OF MAM-MALS, BIRDS, FISH, INSECTS, ETC., edited by Jim Harter. Clear wood engravings present, in extremely lifelike poses, over 1,000 species of animals. One of the most extensive copyright-free pictorial sourcebooks of its kind. Captions. Index. 284pp. 9 x 12. 23766-4 Pa. $8.95

INDIAN DESIGNS FROM ANCIENT ECUADOR, Frederick W. Shaffer. 282 original designs by pre-Columbian Indians of Ecuador (500-1500 A.D.). Designs include people, mammals, birds, reptiles, fish, plants, heads, geometric designs. Use as is or alter for advertising, textiles, leathercraft, etc. Introduction. 95pp. 8¾ x 11¼. 23764-8 Pa. $4.95

SZIGETI ON THE VIOLIN, Joseph Szigeti. Genial, loosely structured tour by premier violinist, featuring a pleasant mixture of reminiscenes, insights into great music and musicians, innumerable tips for practicing violinists. 385 musical passages. 256pp. 5⅝ x 8¼. 23763-X Pa. $5.00

TONE POEMS, SERIES II: TILL EULENSPIEGELS LUSTIGE STREICHE, ALSO SPRACH ZARATHUSTRA, AND EIN HELDEN-LEBEN, Richard Strauss. Three important orchestral works, including very popular *Till Eulenspiegel's Marry Pranks*, reproduced in full score from original editions. Study score. 315pp. 9⅜ x 12¼. (Available in U.S. only)
23755-9 Pa. $9.95

TONE POEMS, SERIES I: DON JUAN, TOD UND VERKLARUNG AND DON QUIXOTE, Richard Strauss. Three of the most often performed and recorded works in entire orchestral repertoire, reproduced in full score from original editions. Study score. 286pp. 9⅜ x 12¼. (Available in U.S. only)
23754-0 Pa. $9.95

11 LATE STRING QUARTETS, Franz Joseph Haydn. The form which Haydn defined and "brought to perfection." (*Grove's*). 11 string quartets in complete score, his last and his best. The first in a projected series of the complete Haydn string quartets. Reliable modern Eulenberg edition, otherwise difficult to obtain. 320pp. 8⅜ x 11¼. (Available in U.S. only)
23753-2 Pa. $8.95

FOURTH, FIFTH AND SIXTH SYMPHONIES IN FULL SCORE, Peter Ilyitch Tchaikovsky. Complete orchestral scores of Symphony No. 4 in F Minor, Op. 36; Symphony No. 5 in E Minor, Op. 64; Symphony No. 6 in B Minor, "Pathetique," Op. 74. Bretikopf & Hartel eds. Study score. 480pp. 9⅜ x 12¼. 23861-X Pa. $12.95

THE MARRIAGE OF FIGARO: COMPLETE SCORE, Wolfgang A. Mozart. Finest comic opera ever written. Full score, not to be confused with piano renderings. Peters edition. Study score. 448pp. 9⅜ x 12¼. (Available in U.S. only)
23751-6 Pa. $13.95

"IMAGE" ON THE ART AND EVOLUTION OF THE FILM, edited by Marshall Deutelbaum. Pioneering book brings together for first time 38 groundbreaking articles on early silent films from *Image* and 263 illustrations newly shot from rare prints in the collection of the International Museum of Photography. A landmark work. Index. 256pp. 8¼ x 11.
23777-X Pa. $8.95

AROUND-THE-WORLD COOKY BOOK, Lois Lintner Sumption and Marguerite Lintner Ashbrook. 373 cooky and frosting recipes from 28 countries (America, Austria, China, Russia, Italy, etc.) include Viennese kisses, rice wafers, London strips, lady fingers, hony, sugar spice, maple cookies, etc. Clear instructions. All tested. 38 drawings. 182pp. 5⅜ x 8.
23802-4 Pa. $2.75

THE ART NOUVEAU STYLE, edited by Roberta Waddell. 579 rare photographs, not available elsewhere, of works in jewelry, metalwork, glass, ceramics, textiles, architecture and furniture by 175 artists—Mucha, Seguy, Lalique, Tiffany, Gaudin, Hohlwein, Saarinen, and many others. 288pp. 8⅜ x 11¼. 23515-7 Pa. $8.95

THE CURVES OF LIFE, Theodore A. Cook. Examination of shells, leaves, horns, human body, art, etc., in *"the* classic reference on how the golden ratio applies to spirals and helices in nature . . . . "—Martin Gardner. 426 illustrations. Total of 512pp. 5⅜ x 8½.   23701-X Pa. **$6.95**

AN ILLUSTRATED FLORA OF THE NORTHERN UNITED STATES AND CANADA, Nathaniel L. Britton, Addison Brown. Encyclopedic work covers 4666 species, ferns on up. Everything. Full botanical information, illustration for each. This earlier edition is preferred by many to more recent revisions. 1913 edition. Over 4000 illustrations, total of 2087pp. 6⅛ x 9¼.   22642-5, 22643-3, 22644-1 Pa., Three-vol. set **$28.50**

MANUAL OF THE GRASSES OF THE UNITED STATES, A. S. Hitchcock, U.S. Dept. of Agriculture. The basic study of American grasses, both indigenous and escapes, cultivated and wild. Over 1400 species. Full descriptions, information. Over 1100 maps, illustrations. Total of 1051pp. 5⅜ x 8½.   22717-0, 22718-9 Pa., Two-vol. set **$17.00**

THE CACTACEAE,, Nathaniel L. Britton, John N. Rose. Exhaustive, definitive. Every cactus in the world. Full botanical descriptions. Thorough statement of nomenclatures, habitat, detailed finding keys. The one book needed by every cactus enthusiast. Over 1275 illustrations. Total of 1080pp. 8 x 10¼.   21191-6, 21192-4 Clothbd., Two-vol. set $50.00

AMERICAN MEDICINAL PLANTS, Charles F. Millspaugh. Full descriptions, 180 plants covered: history; physical description; methods of preparation with all chemical constituents extracted; all claimed curative or adverse effects. 180 full-page plates. Classification table. 804pp. 6½ x 9¼.
23034-1 Pa. **$13.95**

A MODERN HERBAL, Margaret Grieve. Much the fullest, most exact, most useful compilation of herbal material. Gigantic alphabetical encyclopedia, from aconite to zedoary, gives botanical information, medical properties, folklore, economic uses, and much else. Indispensable to serious reader. 161 illustrations. 888pp. 6½ x 9¼. (Available in U.S. only)
22798-7, 22799-5 Pa., Two-vol. set **$15.00**

THE HERBAL or GENERAL HISTORY OF PLANTS, John Gerard. The 1633 edition revised and enlarged by Thomas Johnson. Containing almost 2850 plant descriptions and 2705 superb illustrations, Gerard's *Herbal* is a monumental work, the book all modern English herbals are derived from, the one herbal every serious enthusiast should have in its entirety. Original editions are worth perhaps $750. 1678pp. 8½ x 12¼.
23147-X Clothbd. **$75.00**

MANUAL OF THE TREES OF NORTH AMERICA, Charles S. Sargent. The basic survey of every native tree and tree-like shrub, 717 species in all. Extremely full descriptions, information on habitat, growth, locales, economics, etc. Necessary to every serious tree lover. Over 100 finding keys. 783 illustrations. Total of 986pp. 5⅜ x 8½.
20277-1, 20278-X Pa., Two-vol. set **$12.00**

GREAT NEWS PHOTOS AND THE STORIES BEHIND THEM, John Faber. Dramatic volume of 140 great news photos, 1855 through 1976, and revealing stories behind them, with both historical and technical information. Hindenburg disaster, shooting of Oswald, nomination of Jimmy Carter, etc. 160pp. 8¼ x 11. 23667-6 Pa. $6.00

CRUICKSHANK'S PHOTOGRAPHS OF BIRDS OF AMERICA, Allan D. Cruickshank. Great ornithologist, photographer presents 177 closeups, groupings, panoramas, flightings, etc., of about 150 different birds. Expanded Wings in the Wilderness. Introduction by Helen G. Cruickshank. 191pp. 8¼ x 11. 23497-5 Pa. $7.95

AMERICAN WILDLIFE AND PLANTS, A. C. Martin, et al. Describes food habits of more than 1000 species of mammals, birds, fish. Special treatment of important food plants. Over 300 illustrations. 500pp. 5⅜ x 8½. 20793-5 Pa. $6.50

THE PEOPLE CALLED SHAKERS, Edward D. Andrews. Lifetime of research, definitive study of Shakers: origins, beliefs, practices, dances, social organization, furniture and crafts, impact on 19th-century USA, present heritage. Indispensable to student of American history, collector. 33 illustrations. 351pp. 5⅜ x 8½. 21081-2 Pa. $5.50

OLD NEW YORK IN EARLY PHOTOGRAPHS, Mary Black. New York City as it was in 1853-1901, through 196 wonderful photographs from N.-Y. Historical Society. Great Blizzard, Lincoln's funeral procession, great buildings. 228pp. 9 x 12. 22907-6 Pa. $9.95

MR. LINCOLN'S CAMERA MAN: MATHEW BRADY, Roy Meredith. Over 300 Brady photos reproduced directly from original negatives, photos. Jackson, Webster, Grant, Lee, Carnegie, Barnum; Lincoln; Battle Smoke, Death of Rebel Sniper, Atlanta Just After Capture. Lively commentary. 368pp. 8⅜ x 11¼. 23021-X Pa. $11.95

TRAVELS OF WILLIAM BARTRAM, William Bartram. From 1773-8, Bartram explored Northern Florida, Georgia, Carolinas, and reported on wild life, plants, Indians, early settlers. Basic account for period, entertaining reading. Edited by Mark Van Doren. 13 illustrations. 141pp. 5⅜ x 8½. 20013-2 Pa. $6.00

THE GENTLEMAN AND CABINET MAKER'S DIRECTOR, Thomas Chippendale. Full reprint, 1762 style book, most influential of all time; chairs, tables, sofas, mirrors, cabinets, etc. 200 plates, plus 24 photographs of surviving pieces. 249pp. 9⅞ x 12¾. 21601-2 Pa. $8.95

AMERICAN CARRIAGES, SLEIGHS, SULKIES AND CARTS, edited by Don H. Berkebile. 168 Victorian illustrations from catalogues, trade journals, fully captioned. Useful for artists. Author is Assoc. Curator, Div. of Transportation of Smithsonian Institution. 168pp. 8½ x 9½. 23328-6 Pa. $6.50

SECOND PIATIGORSKY CUP, edited by Isaac Kashdan. One of the greatest tournament books ever produced in the English language. All 90 games of the 1966 tournament, annotated by players, most annotated by both players. Features Petrosian, Spassky, Fischer, Larsen, six others. 228pp. 5⅜ x 8½.   23572-6 Pa. $3.50

ENCYCLOPEDIA OF CARD TRICKS, revised and edited by Jean Hugard. How to perform over 600 card tricks, devised by the world's greatest magicians: impromptus, spelling tricks, key cards, using special packs, much, much more. Additional chapter on card technique. 66 illustrations. 402pp. 5⅜ x 8½. (Available in U.S. only)   21252-1 Pa. **$5.95**

MAGIC: STAGE ILLUSIONS, SPECIAL EFFECTS AND TRICK PHO-TOGRAPHY, Albert A. Hopkins, Henry R. Evans. One of the great classics; fullest, most authorative explanation of vanishing lady, levitations, scores of other great stage effects. Also small magic, automata, stunts. 446 illustrations. 556pp. 5⅜ x 8½.   23344-8 Pa. $6.95

THE SECRETS OF HOUDINI, J. C. Cannell. Classic study of Houdini's incredible magic, exposing closely-kept professional secrets and revealing, in general terms, the whole art of stage magic. 67 illustrations. 279pp. 5⅜ x 8½.   22913-0 Pa. **$5.95**

HOFFMANN'S MODERN MAGIC, Professor Hoffmann. One of the best, and best-known, magicians' manuals of the past century. Hundreds of tricks from card tricks and simple sleight of hand to elaborate illusions involving construction of complicated machinery. 332 illustrations. 563pp. 5⅜ x 8½.   23623-4 Pa. $6.95

THOMAS NAST'S CHRISTMAS DRAWINGS, Thomas Nast. Almost all Christmas drawings by creator of image of Santa Claus as we know it, and one of America's foremost illustrators and political cartoonists. 66 illustrations. 3 illustrations in color on covers. 96pp. 8⅜ x 11¼.
                                                        23660-9 Pa. $3.50

FRENCH COUNTRY COOKING FOR AMERICANS, Louis Diat. 500 easy-to-make, authentic provincial recipes compiled by former head chef at New York's Fitz-Carlton Hotel: onion soup, lamb stew, potato pie, more. 309pp. 5⅜ x 8½.   23665-X Pa. $3.95

SAUCES, FRENCH AND FAMOUS, Louis Diat. Complete book gives over 200 specific recipes: bechamel, Bordelaise, hollandaise, Cumberland, apricot, etc. Author was one of this century's finest chefs, originator of vichyssoise and many other dishes. Index. 156pp. 5⅜ x 8.
                                                        23663-3 Pa. **$2.95**

TOLL HOUSE TRIED AND TRUE RECIPES, Ruth Graves Wakefield. Authentic recipes from the famous Mass. restaurant: popovers, veal and ham loaf, Toll House baked beans, chocolate cake crumb pudding, much more. Many helpful hints. Nearly 700 recipes. Index. 376pp. 5⅜ x 8½.
                                                        23560-2 Pa. **$4.95**

ILLUSTRATED GUIDE TO SHAKER FURNITURE, Robert Meader. Director, Shaker Museum, Old Chatham, presents up-to-date coverage of all furniture and appurtenances, with much on local styles not available elsewhere. 235 photos. 146pp. 9 x 12. 22819-3 Pa. $6.95

COOKING WITH BEER, Carole Fahy. Beer has as superb an effect on food as wine, and at fraction of cost. Over 250 recipes for appetizers, soups, main dishes, desserts, breads, etc. Index. 144pp. 5⅜ x 8½. (Available in U.S. only) 23661-7 Pa. $3.00

STEWS AND RAGOUTS, Kay Shaw Nelson. This international cookbook offers wide range of 108 recipes perfect for everyday, special occasions, meals-in-themselves, main dishes. Economical, nutritious, easy-to-prepare: goulash, Irish stew, boeuf bourguignon, etc. Index. 134pp. 5⅜ x 8½. 23662-5 Pa. $3.95

DELICIOUS MAIN COURSE DISHES, Marian Tracy. Main courses are the most important part of any meal. These 200 nutritious, economical recipes from around the world make every meal a delight. "I . . . have found it so useful in my own household,"—N.Y. Times. Index. 219pp. 5⅜ x 8½. 23664-1 Pa. $3.95

FIVE ACRES AND INDEPENDENCE, Maurice G. Kains. Great back-to-the-land classic explains basics of self-sufficient farming: economics, plants, crops, animals, orchards, soils, land selection, host of other necessary things. Do not confuse with skimpy faddist literature; Kains was one of America's greatest agriculturalists. 95 illustrations. 397pp. 5⅜ x 8½. 20974-1 Pa. $4.95

A PRACTICAL GUIDE FOR THE BEGINNING FARMER, Herbert Jacobs. Basic, extremely useful first book for anyone thinking about moving to the country and starting a farm. Simpler than Kains, with greater emphasis on country living in general. 246pp. 5⅜ x 8½. 23675-7 Pa. $3.95

PAPERMAKING, Dard Hunter. Definitive book on the subject by the foremost authority in the field. Chapters dealing with every aspect of history of craft in every part of the world. Over 320 illustrations. 2nd, revised and enlarged (1947) edition. 672pp. 5⅜ x 8½. 23619-6 Pa. $8.95

THE ART DECO STYLE, edited by Theodore Menten. Furniture, jewelry, metalwork, ceramics, fabrics, lighting fixtures, interior decors, exteriors, graphics from pure French sources. Best sampling around. Over 400 photographs. 183pp. 8⅜ x 11¼. 22824-X Pa. $6.95

ACKERMANN'S COSTUME PLATES, Rudolph Ackermann. Selection of 96 plates from the Repository of Arts, best published source of costume for English fashion during the early 19th century. 12 plates also in color. Captions, glossary and introduction by editor Stella Blum. Total of 120pp. 8⅜ x 11¼. 23690-0 Pa. $5.00

THE ANATOMY OF THE HORSE, George Stubbs. Often considered the great masterpiece of animal anatomy. Full reproduction of 1766 edition, plus prospectus; original text and modernized text. 36 plates. Introduction by Eleanor Garvey. 121pp. 11 x 14¾. 23402-9 Pa. $8.95

BRIDGMAN'S LIFE DRAWING, George B. Bridgman. More than 500 illustrative drawings and text teach you to abstract the body into its major masses, use light and shade, proportion; as well as specific areas of anatomy, of which Bridgman is master. 192pp. 6½ x 9¼. (Available in U.S. only) 22710-3 Pa. $4.50

ART NOUVEAU DESIGNS IN COLOR, Alphonse Mucha, Maurice Verneuil, Georges Auriol. Full-color reproduction of *Combinaisons ornementales* (c. 1900) by Art Nouveau masters. Floral, animal, geometric, interlacings, swashes—borders, frames, spots—all incredibly beautiful. 60 plates, hundreds of designs. 9⅜ x 8-1/16. 22885-1 Pa. $4.50

FULL-COLOR FLORAL DESIGNS IN THE ART NOUVEAU STYLE, E. A. Seguy. 166 motifs, on 40 plates, from *Les fleurs et leurs applications decoratives* (1902): borders, circular designs, repeats, allovers, "spots." All in authentic Art Nouveau colors. 48pp. 9⅜ x 12¼. 23439-8 Pa. $6.00

A DIDEROT PICTORIAL ENCYCLOPEDIA OF TRADES AND IN-DUSTRY, edited by Charles C. Gillispie. 485 most interesting plates from the great French Encyclopedia of the 18th century show hundreds of working figures, artifacts, process, land and cityscapes; glassmaking, paper-making, metal extraction, construction, weaving, making furniture, clothing, wigs, dozens of other activities. Plates fully explained. 920pp. 9 x 12. 22284-5, 22285-3 Clothbd., Two-vol. set $50.00

HANDBOOK OF EARLY ADVERTISING ART, Clarence P. Hornung. Largest collection of copyright-free early and antique advertising art ever compiled. Over 6,000 illustrations, from Franklin's time to the 1890's for special effects, novelty. Valuable source, almost inexhaustible.
Pictorial Volume. Agriculture, the zodiac, animals, autos, birds, Christmas, fire engines, flowers, trees, musical instruments, ships, games and sports, much more. Arranged by subject matter and use. 237 plates. 288pp. 9 x 12. 20122-8 Clothbd. $15.95

Typographical Volume. Roman and Gothic faces ranging from 10 point to 300 point, "Barnum," German and Old English faces, script, logotypes, scrolls and flourishes, 1115 ornamental initials, 67 complete alphabets, more. 310 plates. 320pp. 9 x 12. 20123-6 Clothbd. $16.95

CALLIGRAPHY (CALLIGRAPHIA LATINA), J. G. Schwandner. High point of 18th-century ornamental calligraphy. Very ornate initials, scrolls, borders, cherubs, birds, lettered examples. 172pp. 9 x 13. 20475-8 Pa. $7.95

GEOMETRY, RELATIVITY AND THE FOURTH DIMENSION, Rudolf Rucker. Exposition of fourth dimension, means of visualization, concepts of relativity as Flatland characters continue adventures. Popular, easily followed yet accurate, profound. 141 illustrations. 133pp. 5⅜ x 8½.
23400-2 Pa. $2.75

THE ORIGIN OF LIFE, A. I. Oparin. Modern classic in biochemistry, the first rigorous examination of possible evolution of life from nitrocarbon compounds. Non-technical, easily followed. Total of 295pp. 5⅜ x 8½.
60213-3 Pa. $5.95

PLANETS, STARS AND GALAXIES, A. E. Fanning. Comprehensive introductory survey: the sun, solar system, stars, galaxies, universe, cosmology; quasars, radio stars, etc. 24pp. of photographs. 189pp. 5⅜ x 8½. (Available in U.S. only)
21680-2 Pa. $3.75

THE THIRTEEN BOOKS OF EUCLID'S ELEMENTS, translated with introduction and commentary by Sir Thomas L. Heath. Definitive edition. Textual and linguistic notes, mathematical analysis, 2500 years of critical commentary. Do not confuse with abridged school editions. Total of 1414pp. 5⅜ x 8½.
60088-2, 60089-0, 60090-4 Pa., Three-vol. set $19.50

Prices subject to change without notice.

Available at your book dealer or write for free catalogue to Dept. GI, Dover Publications, Inc., 31 East 2nd St. Mineola., N.Y. 11501. Dover publishes more than 175 books each year on science, elementary and advanced mathematics, biology, music, art, literary history, social sciences and other areas.